Rethinking Miles Davis

Rethinking Miles Davis

Edited by

ROGER FAGGE

NICOLAS PILLAI

TIM WALL

OXFORD
UNIVERSITY PRESS

OXFORD
UNIVERSITY PRESS

Oxford University Press is a department of the University of Oxford. It furthers the University's objective of excellence in research, scholarship, and education by publishing worldwide. Oxford is a registered trade mark of Oxford University Press in the UK and in certain other countries.

Published in the United States of America by Oxford University Press
198 Madison Avenue, New York, NY 10016, United States of America.

CIP data is on file at the Library of Congress

ISBN 9780190085803 (pbk.)
ISBN 9780190085797 (hbk.)

DOI: 10.1093/9780190085834.001.0001

Paperback printed by Marquis Book Printing, Canada
Hardback printed by Bridgeport National Bindery, Inc., United States of America

The manufacturer's authorized representative in the EU for product safety is Oxford University Press España S.A. of Parque Empresarial San Fernando de Henares, Avenida de Castilla, 2 – 28830 Madrid (www.oup.es/en or product.safety@oup.com). OUP España S.A. also acts as importer into Spain of products made by the manufacturer.

MIX
Paper | Supporting responsible forestry
FSC® C103567

Contents

Contributors

Pedro Cravinho is Senior Research Fellow in Jazz Studies and Ethnomusicology, Royal Birmingham Conservatoire, Birmingham City University. https://orcid.org/0000-0002-4961-7955.

William Ellis is a professional photographer and freelance researcher.

Roger Fagge is Associate Professor in the Department of History, University of Warwick. https://orcid.org/0009-0005-0250-3220.

Will L. Finch is a freelance researcher. https://orcid.org/0009-0001-2552-3612.

Bobbie-Jane Gardner is Lecturer in Composition, Royal Birmingham Conservatoire, Birmingham City University. https://orcid.org/0000-0003-2702-518X

Nicholas Gebhardt is Professor of Jazz and Popular Music Studies, Royal Birmingham Conservatoire, Birmingham City University. https://orcid.org/0000-0002-0864-0534.

Nicolas Pillai is Assistant Professor of Creative and Critical Practice at University College Dublin. https://orcid.org/0000-0001-9851-6782.

Tim Wall is Professor of Radio and Popular Music Studies, Birmingham City University. https://orcid.org/0000-0003-4619-7665.

Tony Whyton is Professor of Jazz Studies, Royal Birmingham Conservatoire, Birmingham City University. https://orcid.org/0000-0002-6745-9911.

Introduction

Roger Fagge, Nicolas Pillai and Tim Wall

Rethinking Miles Davis sits within a broader series of books taking new approaches to understanding seminal music makers who have been major contributors to a canon of great works. This is the first book in OUP's 'Rethinking' series to focus on a musician/composer outside the Western canon. It is not surprising that, in looking to expand the series, the jazz trumpeter Miles Davis (1926–1991) was an obvious candidate. For many, Davis' recordings represent a high point in jazz expression; the music's classical form. In popular culture, one Davis recording reigns supreme and signals the standard approach to understanding Davis' place in jazz. Richard Williams' words exemplify this point: "Before *Kind of Blue* there had been slow jazz, mournful jazz, romantic jazz, astringent jazz. But there had never been anything that so carefully and single-mindedly cultivated an atmosphere of reflection and introspection, to such a degree that the mood itself became an art object. *Kind of Blue* seems to have taken place in a sealed environment, with all its individual sensibilities pointing inwards" (2009, 2–3). Williams expresses something of the sense that *Kind of Blue* and, by extension, Davis' best work more generally is transcendent. However, in constructing this narrative, it also points to the potential for solipsism in jazz criticism and scholarship. We propose that jazz scholarship has itself often been too sealed in its own environment, with all its individual sensibilities pointing inward. Perhaps too often its main purpose is simply to prove the greatness of the music preferred by the authors. The very notion that jazz needs to be understood through its genius creators and their canonical recorded works has underpinned jazz studies for a century. Beginning in the 1990s, though, what has been termed the new jazz studies has resulted in jazz scholarship that aims to interrogate this kind of monotheism. This book is indebted to these strands of thought. Following these new jazz scholars, we aim to explore the music, history and cultural impact of Miles Davis through various

Roger Fagge, Nicolas Pillai and Tim Wall, *Introduction* In: *Rethinking Miles Davis*. Edited by: Roger Fagge, Nicolas Pillai, and Tim Wall, Oxford University Press. DOI: 10.1093/9780190085834.001.0001

interdisciplinary approaches and to unsettle accepted notions of 'genius'. In this book we hope to question forms of biographical narrative and so to interrogate common understandings of where value lies in the Davis chronology.

We pose these questions:

> What is the construct 'Miles Davis' in the 21st century?
> How it can be productively be rethought for a wider and deeper understanding?

We have approached 'rethinking' as an active verb; this is not a book called 'Miles Davis Rethought'. Too often in jazz studies claims to 'rethink' jazz history, its greats, or its canon have simply reinforced that hierarchy. We start with a dual recognition that jazz studies has a lot to learn from other disciplines and that new approaches developed in the study of jazz have a lot to offer the study of music making and culture more generally. As will be apparent in the chapters that follow, the studies collected here owe a particular debt to the ways that historical scholars have constructed histories of labour and society, that media researchers have understood processes of recording and marketing and that cultural academics have generated meanings. In this collection, the authors seek to rethink the discipline by asking fundamental questions about how jazz studies tells its own story.

This is also not a biography of an individual music maker. Indeed, one of our precepts has been that this widely used approach to exploring the work of jazz musicians needs interrogating. That is quite a bold position in approaching Davis and jazz given the dominance of this approach in exploring the individual artist and their creative works. While recognising the value of existing biographies of Davis in establishing core information about his life and activities, this volume does not present a comprehensive or cohesive vision of Miles Davis.

Rethinking Jazz

This is not the first attempt at a rethink within jazz studies. Certainly, Krin Gabbard's 1995 invitation to 'rethink history' as a section of his edited *Jazz Among the Discourses*, collected earlier key articles on the quality of ideological and definitions of jazz and oral histories and the use of recordings in jazz history (see, for instance, Gendron 1993; Mackey 1992; Rasula 1995). Much of this foundational work underpins approaches in the chapters of this book. Gabbard's introduction positions 'rethinking' in relation to canon formation, and as we have already noted, this speaks powerfully to this project to generate new insights beyond the settled dominant stories about a great musician. Although it is probably Rasula's idea of "the seductive menace" of records in jazz history that has been most influential, many of these chapters return to records. This time the rethink positions records as culturally meaningful texts, not just landmarks in a single jazz career. However, the importance of critical context and the ideologies of jazz from Gendron, and attention to representational wording from Mackey, is apparent in many of the chapters.

Alyn Shipton starts off his *New History of Jazz* (2001) with an introduction inviting us to rethink jazz history. His caution about being restricted by the mythology of jazz is apposite here. Only a few jazz musicians achieve the status of mythical beings, and Davis would be in that number. But jazz itself, as a music and a culture, is consistently mythologised. And by myth, of course, we mean those stories that tell of origins and involve supernatural beings. So, in studying Davis, the authors do not seek some empirical truth to juxtapose against the hyperbole or romanticism but seek to understand how the mythical stories play out across a range of media and what they construct and for whose benefit. Certainly locating jazz in its commercialised context was important to Shipton. It serves to complicate narratives produced by Panassié (1934, 1943, 1944, 1946) about early jazz just as much as it does in rethinking the enormous biographic body of work on Davis and his long career from a 21st-century perspective.

Both Gabbard's and Shipton's publications also sit within the new jazz studies, with approaches more firmly rooted in a broad academic but interdisciplinary scholarship than in the journalistic and aficionado biographic studies of the past. These latter approaches can certainly be found in mediated histories of jazz, and very notably in those that include Davis. George Lipsitz's (2004) critique of Ken Burns' PBS television series *Jazz*, and its key ideas of modernity, America and artistic genius, is also apposite here. Lipsitz argues that these ideas restrict our understanding of jazz's time frame, place and agents. Certainly Davis is one of the dominant personalities of the three Burns episodes that cover the period 1945 to 2001, and a key spin-off compilation CD offers itself up as the *Ken Burns Jazz Collection: The Definitive Miles Davis*. For Lipsitz, *Jazz*'s positioning of individual musicians as heroic artists, alienated from mainstream American culture, obscures the social relations of jazz, including gender relations, and ignores the cultural practices that afford creative production. We see this volume as part of a long-overdue attempt to rectify that obfuscation. We certainly follow Tucker (1998), who, in reviewing Gabbard's book, suggests that these new approaches should draw on interdisciplinary debates with roots in wider popular music studies in which traditional musicology is not at the fore. It is certainly true that the chapters in *Rethinking Miles Davis* emphasise the former and not the latter. Such approaches have much to offer a wider attempt at rethinking music makers represented by the OUP series in which this book sits.

It is also worth making a point about the geographic positionality of the authors. While attempts at rethinking jazz have been prominent in the US—and O'Meally et al. (2004) offer a collective statement of US perspectives on new jazz studies—this book emerges from an increasing globalisation of both jazz studies and jazz as our object of study. We follow Bruce Johnson's premise that "jazz was not 'invented' and then exported: it was invented in the process of being disseminated" (2019, n.p.). Davis was an American musician, widely known across the world. While we have deliberately sought to ensure a breadth of ideas and disciplines are covered in its chapters, the book clearly represents the application of approaches primarily developed in Europe of a musician overwhelmingly mythologised as American. Of course, cultural distance can result in misunderstanding and misinterpretation of another nation's art, heritage and traditions. However, our aim has been to offer insights less invested in the mythologised modernist America and the musical genius that Davis is taken to represent, and to be more interpretative of those myths, their benefits and their beneficiaries.

This 'rethinking' of Miles Davis, then, comes out of a very specific context, which includes the *Jazz Research Journal*, the Rhythm Changes international conferences and key work in the Jazz Research Cluster at Birmingham City University in the UK. All three editors have close connections to the centre, and five of the other authors do as well.

The leadership of Nicholas Gebhardt and Tony Whyton also needs highlighting. Both as contributors to this book and as leaders of BCU's Jazz Research Cluster, they have also edited two key collections of essays which have defined the approach taken in this book. Whyton (2011) sets out to explore jazz through the politics of the popular, representations, scenes and mediation, while the contributions to Gebhardt et al. (2019) frame such studies in terms of historical perspectives, method, issues, collectivity, discourse and debates. Such frames have guided the editorial decisions and contributions to this book. While these two collections draw on contributions from across the world, it is noteworthy that the leadership of these strands of jazz study is European.

Rethinking from the Late Miles

Rethinking Miles Davis emerges from an attempt to use Davis' 1980s recordings as a way to problematise the tendency to canonise and mythologise the records he produced in the 1950s and 1960s. There is clearly an opportunity to reframe understandings of Davis through a reconsideration of 'lateness' in more biographical and critic-driven studies. This ambition has its origins in discussions that resulted from the conference Miles Davis and John Coltrane at 90: Prospect and Retrospect, held at the University of Surrey in 2016. The co-editors presented a joint panel titled 'Late Miles', which aimed to reframe and interrogate his 1980s output. We noted at the time that we were the only scholars at the conference presenting on this later work; indeed, the 1980s oeuvre was hardly mentioned in other papers. It was also clear that for a majority of the presentations at later conferences, the demythologisation propounded by the new jazz studies had not penetrated the dismissive attitude of many jazz critics to Davis' experiments of the 1980s.

Of course, Western art music scholarship has produced significant studies on the topic of 'lateness'. In a famed essay on the late Beethoven, Theodor Adorno noted that understanding a musical work as 'late'—a term with its own connotations of death—can tempt listeners to bring biography to bear on appreciation: "In this way, late works are relegated to the outer reaches of art, in the vicinity of document. In fact, studies of the very late Beethoven seldom fail to make reference to biography and fate. It is as if, confronted with the dignity of human death, the theory of art were to divest itself of its rights and abdicate in favour of reality" (2002, 564). By warning us of "the psychological interpretation" (566) which reads every late work as a foreshadowing of mortality, Adorno gives us a starting point for a reconsideration of Davis. We might begin by challenging the sense of discrete periods in Davis' career, defined by acoustic or electronic instruments, by suits or dashiki. A more granular attention to moments reveals considerable slippage between these supposed demarcations, inspiring many of the authors in this book. As Adorno suggests, such an approach unpicks the mythic and the subjective: "The only way to arrive at a revision of the [dominant] view of late style would be by means of the technical analysis of the works under consideration. This would have to be oriented, first of all, toward a particularity that is studiously ignored by the popular view: the role of conventions" (565). Adorno reminds us to look outside the interior, the intimations of Promethean subjectivity that underlie traditional conceptions of genius. Beethoven's stylistic accomplishment was shaped by musical convention and by his reaction to it. So too our authors have thought through how external factors (the music industry, sociopolitics, technological and aesthetic mediation) contribute to those works we understand make up 'Miles Davis'.

As Joseph Straus (2008) has argued, there are no encompassing definitions of aesthetic features of late musical style or even agreement as to when 'lateness' begins in a composer's work, other than through proximity to death. Where Straus does find overlap is in the notion of 'disability style': "To the extent that composers find new ways of writing their nonnormative bodies or inscribing their disabilities in their music, late style may be less about anticipating death than living with a disability, less about the future hypothetical than the present reality" (2008, 6). This chimes well with the work of George McKay, who has argued that "jazz is a form of music founded on disability; it is a form of music sounded on disability; it is a socio-cultural practice made by and making space for disability" (2019, 183). As authors such as Fagge, Finch and Pillai have observed in this volume, one important context for the production of Davis' late work was his aging body. As a digression, one may note the extent to which disability has been suppressed in jazz writing versus its foregrounding in many televisual and filmic representations. In Ken Russell's BBC Monitor film *Delius: Song of Summer*, we are shown how Frederick Delius' ability to compose music was severely compromised by blindness and quadriparesis. Similarly, Bertrand Tavernier's *Round Midnight* defines the final years of fictional musician Dale Turner through his depression and alcoholism; it is a particular coup that Turner is played by real-life saxophonist Dexter Gordon, who was similarly afflicted. In each film, the declining artist becomes dependent on a male amanuensis figure (played, respectively, by Christopher Gable and François Cluzet), and this pattern is repeated in Rolf de Heer's *Dingo*, as discussed by Finch in this book.

For Edward Said, late style offered the possibility of redefinition, a kind of defiant retreat. This conceptualisation is useful when we think of how Davis' late work was often dismissed out of hand rather than seen as set of decisions and deliberate strategies: "Lateness . . . is a kind of self-imposed exile from what is generally acceptable, coming after it, and surviving beyond it. . . .

There is therefore an inherent tension in late style that abjures mere bourgeois aging and that insists on the increasing sense of apartness and exile and anachronism, which late style expresses and, more important, uses to formally sustain itself" (Said 2006, 16–17). Many of the chapters in this book proceed from this point: that Davis' late style is indeed a self-conscious and deliberate artistic position rather than a diminishment of talent or surrender to commercial forces. There is of course the temptation then to valorise and over-claim for these late works. This book may well be criticised for its lack of attention to the landmarks of Davis' early life. However, central to our rethinking has been a suspicion of the narrative models that structure life writing. Biography has been central to the storifying of jazz, and especially so for the stories of the life of Miles Davis. For a music that places the performing musician, and the improvisational skills of the performing musician, at the heart of the value of the music, jazz biography seeks to explain personal motivations as narrative forces for understanding the music. It is a very worthy attempt to get at the agency that musicians have within jazz to be themselves. Yet too often the details of the individual's life are stated but never explored; that this thing happened in their life is enough. Better still if it is a barrier to their ultimate triumph. Tom Perchard (2007, 120) has neatly expressed the limitation of biographies where "written lives were often held to be synonymous with historical exposition". He summarises the critiques of others about the construction of "life-course" writing of "great men", the challenges of writing about personal development thorough non-literary culture, like music, and the tendency to use existing stories which allow the "neatness of this apparent narrative fit to become a radical streamlining" of the events of a life (123). For Michel Foucault, these are characteristics of total history which, in the words of Madan Sarup, "inserts events into grand explanatory systems and linear processes, celebrates great moments and individuals and seeks to document a point of origin" (1993, 53).

Starting with the later life of Miles Davis as a route into rethinking his whole career also reverses the narrative of that career, starting with its meaningful end, encourages us to ask different questions and think about telling different stories and the way they are told. This is a common theme in the chapters from Gebhardt, Wall and Fagge. Of course, biography is valuable because it puts the creative musician at the heart of the making of jazz, but it also can restrict us from exploring this with other forms of narrative and senses of meaningfulness. Central to this is a way of exploring Davis' agency. Specifically, we ask a core question Scott DeVeaux posed about

Coleman Hawkins and the birth of bebop in the late 1940s and early 1950s. Paraphrasing DeVeaux (1997, 45), we ask what it meant for a young African American man to pursue the career of professional jazz musician in the later decades of the 20th century. In particular, what did it mean for him to be progressive? It is, nevertheless, perfectly possible to romanticise and overdetermine late style. One thinks of Eric Rohmer, writing in the film journal *Cahiers du cinéma*, "The history of art offers no example, as far as I know, of an authentic genius who has gone through a period of true decline at the end of his career; this should encourage us rather to detect, beneath what seems to be clumsy or bald, the traces of that desire for simplicity that characterises the 'last manner' of painters such as Titian, Rembrandt, Matisse, or Bonnard, composers such as Beethoven or Stravinsky" (quoted in Bazin 2008). Rohmer's hypothesis is flawed by his insistence on the exceptionalism of genius, a trait which characterises much jazz writing, and the cliché that late work is distinguished by common traits of simplicity. One detects here a tendency to position late style as an apotheosis. As Chris Dingle has argued, "The notion of late style too often relies on the conceit of posterity that an artist's output has reached its final possible manifestation when he or she dies" (2020, 134). Dingle even encourages speculation about what a career would have been like if death had not occurred. In the era of AI, such finality seems absurd. Indeed, as many chapters in this book attest, the power of Davis' work lies in its ongoing capacity for recontextualisation. Fagge writes of the posthumous legacy of *Doo-Bop*, while Pillai and Whyton both engage with how the artists and the music are remembered. Liam Maloney (2022) has even gone as far as imagining a collaborative Miles album of jazz–hip-hop fusion built upon Afrofuturism.

The Contributions

The final form of the book, like any, has been the long process of development and writing for the authors at the same time that we face other demands in our professional and personal lives. We are conscious that the final collection does not reflect the breadth of authorial background that we hoped and that we are too similar to the dominant group of authors who usually produce books like this. Nevertheless, we hope that many of the perspectives articulated will contribute to the change that we need to see in broadening jazz studies into a more inclusive community. Hopefully the processes of rethinking we promote can operate at the level of who gets to speak, as well as the subjects we get to address.

In the opening chapter, Tony Whyton tackles one of the more difficult aspects of a musician who is constructed as a mythologised hero but whose personal conduct in relation to women has rightly been condemned. In 'Miles Behind: Jazz Studies, Masculinity, and #MeToo', Whyton takes a pressing contemporary frame to deal with an aspect of Davis' career that often feels awkward for many to address. He explicitly deals with the posthumous representation of Davis and the complex way he has come to stand for beliefs in and about music and culture, using this to address us as jazz academics about "our own behaviour and attitudes as scholars, musicians, fans, and educators". For Whyton it is in the mediated stories of jazz stars like Davis that the masculine myths are the strongest, and his chapter explores a number of examples in filmic and written form. In the latter he takes critical issue with a sweep of biographies of Davis, exploring in some detail how they construct Davis' masculinity and how his male violence is represented in recent films. Most powerfully, Whyton calls on work by Michael Flood (2019) to challenge us to take three practical actions on an issue which should be far less difficult than it is within the academy. There can be no better way to open a book on rethinking Davis' career and no better agenda to set for the whole book.

Roger Fagge's chapter, '"Just Kickin' That Doo-Bop Sound": Miles Davis, Jazz and Hip-Hop', engages with questions around Davis' place within popular music more generally, especially in the context of his last studio commercial record releases. This emphasis exemplifies the general approach of the book, locating a rethink of Davis' career at its end. Davis' embrace of hip-hop and its production—already controversial within a number of contexts around popular music in the 1980s and 1990s—became a source of critical concern as Davis released a series of recordings with younger musicians in these decades. *Doo-Bop*, released posthumously in 1992, was, in the conventional sense, Davis' final album, and Fagge contextualises its place within similar recordings released by other stars of popular music. Following a detailed exploration of the context in which the recording came into being, Fagge explores the cultural meanings of its critical reception, as well as the cultural context in which the criticism was framed and understood. Finally, he offers up some reflections on the place of *Doo-Bop* in jazz and hip-hop, expanding the frame of reference for evaluating Davis' recorded catalogue. It nicely sets up the two chapters which follow.

These two linked chapters from Tim Wall pivot around Davis' 1986 Warner Bros. Records' commercial release, *Tutu*. They both utilise an idea of maps of meaning to investigate the way Davis understood his musical ambitions during this period of his career and the longer place he occupied within the popular music-recording industry. They turn on their head conventional approaches to understanding how musicians make decisions about their professional and musical direction. The first, 'Locating *Tutu*', explores the album's place in the meanings of mid-1980s popular music. Jazz studies, limited by its state of solipsism, usually locates individual recordings in a diachronic sense of the music's development rather than its synchronic place in a wider sphere of music culture. Wall starts by setting out the dominant ways in which *Tutu* has been framed in relation to the music and those who created it, before examining how Davis' record relates to three defining areas of 1980s music practice in 'electric pop', smooth jazz and the musical output of the trumpeter's collaborator Marcus Miller. The chapter ends with a speculative discussion about the ways these musical resources performed change, articulating Davis' sense of agency and identity as a progressive black American male musician.

'Miles on a Second Major: Miles Davis' Career from Columbia to Warner Bros. Records', reimagines diachronic jazz studies to map the elements of professional decision-making which are usually treated in synchronic isolation in most biographic readings of Davis. It seeks to answer a question often posed in biographies of the trumpeter but never convincingly answered: Why did Davis move from Columbia to Warner Bros. Records in 1985? Wall sets out the historical specificities of the Columbia and Warner record companies, and their semantic place in the wider music culture, to explore what Warner meant to Davis in 1985 and what Columbia meant earlier in his career. This approach challenges us to go beyond seeing record companies as instrumental functionaries that record and release commercial records, to explain rather than simply name them, especially as they would be understood by a veteran jazz musician determined to ensure he was understood as contemporary and relevant. The chapter's three-part analysis starts with the standard biographical stories, then details the meaningfulness of Davis' career to changes at Columbia and its contrast to Warner Bros. up to 1985, and finally applying the same approach to understanding Davis' relationship to Warner through to the trumpeter's death in 1991.

Will Finch's chapter takes as its central subject Davis' first and only extended acting role on film, in the Franco-Australian film directed by Rolf de

Heer and written by Marc Rosenberg, *Dingo* (1991). Returning to frames of late career innovations, Finch writes, *Dingo* represents "a significant example of the artist's later commitment to diverse creative collaborations that transgressed the boundaries of different media and fields of cultural production. The film demonstrated his appetite for ventures within the mainstream and his careful negotiation of white-dominated culture industries". 'Resurrecting Miles in *Dingo* (1991): Michel Legrand, Billy Cross and Miles Davis' explores the parallels between Davis' own career and that of the fictional character he plays in the film. Finch links this to Davis' other contribution to the film, his musical performances in the soundtrack co-created by the French composer and pianist Michel Legrand. In doing so Finch explores a multilayered sense of collaborative agency which more traditional positioning of Davis often fails to capture.

These questions of the visual and aural representation on Davis on film, TV and video are continued in Nicolas Pillai's chapter, 'Fashioning Miles Davis: Dressing and Undressing Television Stardom'. Pillai extends our sense of Davis' visual performativity into his sartorial image and the way the meanings of clothes work with jazz, and their mythical role in jazz in audiovisual media. The chapter echoes and extends the points about representation made by both Whyton and Finch, especially around Davis' sense of agency in his later career. Starting with some observations on the use of Davis' image on a T-shirt in a fictional world, Pillai takes us into the way Davis talked about expensive clothes as status symbols, and the way those he selected to wear on stage in photoshoots and on film, TV and video related to his sense of himself as a contemporary black American man. In doing so, he returns to Whyton's theme of sexualised male power, reframing the 1980s criticism of Davis in the "overdetermined heterosexuality of Crouch and Marsalis as forms of moral panic", and so recasts the specificities of late Miles in a radically different manner.

William Ellis' visual essay of photographic portraits offers a rethink of the visual representation of Davis' commercial recordings in the record cover, but locating them in the cultural lives of a series of musicians for whom Davis' records are personal and powerfully meaningful. Ellis' portraits are supported by excerpts of an interview with his photographic subject about why they chose a particular Davis record as the 'One LP'. The subjects include Terence Blanchard, David Liebman, Marcus Miller, Mike Stern, Tomasz Stanko and Norma Winstone. These portraits are part of a larger photographic endeavour of the same name undertaken by Ellis, which itself forms part of a wider research collaboration with Tim Wall. The 'One LP' project has built up a body of portraits with supporting interviews in which musicians and cultural workers are invited to select one commercial recording that is personally meaningful. The portraits are often taken in places of the subject's own choosing or spaces in which they work. Ellis is particularly interested in developing a dialogue with his subjects about the way they relate to Davis' recordings, and the results offer a fascinating and often unheard insight into the meaningfulness of the music of Davis in their own lives and careers. The collaboration with Wall, with whom Ellis wrote the chapter's introduction, is built around wider considerations of how the portrait is conventionally used in music photography and how it could be reimagined as an expression of ideas from media and cultural studies.

'Orchestrating Miles: Collaborations with Gil Evans, George Avakian, Marcus Miller and Tommy LiPuma', a jointly authored chapter by Bobbie-Jane Gardner and Tim Wall, deals with the widely noted collaborative nature of music making. Using the idea of orchestrating as a musical and cultural practice, Gardner and Wall examine two vital musical and two important professional collaborations, which marked out Davis' career as a leading jazz musician. While the trumpeter's work with orchestrator Gil Evans has been subject to detailed biographic and musicological study, his seemingly identical relationship with multi-instrumentalist and producer Marcus Miller is too often dismissed as the over-domination of an improvising genius by a pop-record producer. In a similar vein, Davis' professional relationships with record bosses George Avakian at Columbia and Tommy LiPuma at Warner are too often seen in terms of the amount of creative freedom or control the executives exercised. Gardner and Wall return to themes of musician agency that have run through this book, to frame them in new contexts around collaboration, orchestration and the black aesthetic. The chapter is the product of a long-running discussion of the roles of collaboration and orchestration in African American popular music, defined by their very different academic fields: Gardener as a practicing contemporary composer-orchestrator and practice-based researcher and Wall with a background in popular music media and cultural studies. Rather than seeking a definitive answer, their method in constructing this chapter has been to capture something of the open-ended nature of their discussions and the ways we can learn from each other as an invitation for others to extend this work in other ways.

Pedro Cravinho's 'Encounter, Surprise and Acceptance: Revisiting Miles Davis On and Off Stage in Portugal' is an exemplar for dealing with Davis' career outside the American context. Building on a detailed analysis of the Portuguese press coverage of Davis' three visits to Portugal in the latter two decades of the trumpeter's career, the study is particularly informative about the European context of jazz performance because Davis' first visit was at a point when the country was controlled by the dictatorship of the far-right Estado Novo (New State) regime. As one of Europe's last formal colonial empires, Portugal was under extensive international pressure to decolonise, and Cravinho explores the way Davis made a political stand at a festival which acted as a showcase for international contemporary jazz but became an important moment for the expression of anticolonial attitudes. In 1991, Davis returned to the country, which now embraced democracy and was a member of the European Union, and where the trumpeter was received as a pop star. This changing relationship between culture, national politics and music performance, especially in contexts beyond the US, is too often neglected in studies of international jazz stars like Davis.

The collection ends with an open and investigative chapter which, we hope, sets the way the book will be read and interpreted. In 'It's Never Too Late: Miles Davis and Modernism', Nicholas Gebhardt explores the power of stories in and about jazz "to establish jazz as the privileged medium of aesthetic individualism'. Gebhardt focuses on Davis' 'late period' live performance of 'My Man's Gone Now', which was released on the 'comeback' record *We Want Miles* (1981), as a way of exploring jazz's contribution to American modernism. Among other themes, Gebhardt proposes "that the ability to say something in jazz is inseparable from the fact of finding one's voice and, in the process, learning how to use it". In many ways, this proposition defines a thread that runs through the whole book: that meaning, and the musician's sense of agency, are central to any rethink of jazz, especially to rethinking the music's heroes, such as Davis. For Gebhardt, this is about "the assertion of a musical identity that was derived explicitly from as well as evaluated according to the depth of their engagement with the expressive resources of African American musical traditions". In the later part of Davis' career, this is an act of "re-voicing the past".

We hope that the individual chapters and the book as a whole will act as our re-voicing the past that is Miles Davis.

References

Adorno, Theodor. 1937. 'Late style in Beethoven'. Collected in Adorno, Theodor. In *Essays on Music*, edited by Richard Leppert. 2002. University of California Press.

Bazin, André. 2008. 'De la politique des auteurs'. In *Auteurs and Authorship: A Film Reader*, edited by Barry Keith Grant, 19–28. Wiley-Blackwell.

DeVeaux, Scott. 1997. *The Birth of Bebop: A Social and Musical History*. University of California Press.

Dingle, Christopher. 2020. 'Éclairs sur l'Au-Delà . . . . Messiaen's Career After His Final Work'. In *Le grand âge et ses oeuvres ultimes*, edited by Diane H. Bodart and Jean Gribenski. Presses Universitaires de Rennes.

Flood, Michael, 2019. 'Men and# MeToo: Mapping Men's Responses to Anti-violence Advocacy'. In *# MeToo and the Politics of Social Change*, 285–300. Springer International Publishing.

Gabbard, Krin. 1995. *Jazz Among the Discourses*. Duke University Press.

Gebhardt, Nicholas, Nichole Rustin-Paschal and Tony Whyton, eds. 2019. *The Routledge Companion to Jazz Studies*. Routledge.

Gendron, Bernard. 1993. 'Moldy Figs and Modernists: Jazz at War (1942–1946)'. *Discourse* 15 (3): 130–157. http://www.jstor.org/stable/41389289.

Johnson, Bruce. 2019. *Jazz Diaspora: New Approaches to Music and Globalisation*. Routledge.

Lipsitz, George. 2004. 'Songs of the Unsung: The Darby Hicks History of Jazz'. In *Uptown Conversation: The New Jazz Studies*, edited by Robert G. O'Meally, Brent Hayes Edwards and Farah Jasmine Griffin. Columbia University Press.

Mackey, Nathaniel. 1992. 'Other: From Noun to Verb'. *Representations* (39): 51–70.

Maloney, Liam. 2022. 'Hip Bop: The Imaginary Collaborations of Miles Davis'. *Jazz Research Journal* 15 (1–2): 87–106.

McKay, George. 2019. 'Jazz and Disability'. In *The Routledge Companion To Jazz Studies*, edited by Nicholas Gebhardt, Nichole Rustin-Paschal, and Tony Whyton. Routledge.

O'Meally, Robert G., Brent Hayes Edwards and Farah Jasmine Griffin, eds. 2004. *Uptown Conversation: The New Jazz Studies*. Columbia University Press.

Panassié, Hugues. 1934. *Le Jazz Hot*. Corrêa.

Panassié, Hugues. 1943. *La musique de Jazz et le Swing*. Corrêa.

Panassié, Hugues. 1944. *Les rois du jazz, notes biographiques et critiques sur les principaux musiciens de jazz*. 2nd ed. 2 vols. Grasset.

Panassié, Hugues. 1946. *La véritable musique de jazz*. 12th ed. R. Laffont.

Perchard, Tom. 2007. 'Writing Jazz Biography: Race, Research and Narrative Representation'. *Popular Music History* 2 (2): 119–145.

Rasula, Jed. 1995. 'The Media of Memory: The Seductive Menace of Records in Jazz History'. In *Jazz Among the Discourses*, edited by Krin Gabbard. Duke University Press.

Said, Edward W. 2006. *On Late Style: Music and Literature Against the Grain*. Pantheon.

Sarup, Madan. 1993. *An Introductory Guide to Post-Structuralism and Post-Modernism*. Harvester Wheatsheaf.

Shipton, Alyn. 2001. *A New History of Jazz*. Continuum.

Straus, Joseph. 2008. 'Disability and "late style" in Music'. *Journal of Musicology*, 25 (1): 3–45.

Tucker, Mark. 1998. 'Review: Musicology and the New Jazz Studies'. *Journal of the American Musicological Society* 51 (1): 131–148. https://www.jstor.org/stable/831899.

Whyton, Tony. 2011. *Jazz*. Ashgate.

Williams, Richard. 2009. *The Blue Moment: Miles Davis's* Kind of Blue *and the Remaking of Modern Music*. Faber and Faber.

1
Miles Behind
Jazz Studies, Masculinity and #MeToo

Tony Whyton

Warning: The following chapter focuses on the work of a misogynist and serial abuser of women. Any pleasure derived from the study of Miles Davis should be considered in direct relation to these acts. When listening to Miles Davis, we should think critically about our values and the world around us. Despite calls to separate music from the people who produce it, it is important to remember that there is no such thing as 'the music itself'.

> Masculinity is implicated directly in men's perception of rape and sexual harassment, but also in men's widespread inaction or complicity in the face of men's violence against women. At the same time #MeToo has prompted valuable public scrutiny of the narrow and dangerous ideals of masculinity which inform men's violence towards women. (Flood 2019, 285)

Introduction

Miles. That one word embodies a legacy of musical innovation and change. In the years since his death, and even within his own lifetime, Miles Davis became larger than life, and his musical output went on to have a profound impact on music history. And yet music can only partially account for Davis' enduring legacy and ongoing value for people today. When we talk about Miles Davis, therefore, we cannot avoid the trappings of jazz myth-making and the role our values, tastes, needs and desires play in this. In what ways do jazz musicians inspire us? How do they sometimes encourage an obsessive following of writers, musicians, record collectors and enthusiasts, and

Tony Whyton, *Miles Behind* In: *Rethinking Miles Davis*. Edited by: Roger Fagge, Nicolas Pillai, and Tim Wall, Oxford University Press. © Oxford University Press 2026. DOI: 10.1093/9780190085834.003.0001

why do they continue to generate a wealth of artistic tributes today, from musical homages to experimental poetry, fashion and film? Considering the impact Miles Davis continues to have on people, I began to think about the posthumous representation of artists and how they come to stand for certain beliefs about music and culture, how they inform the ways of talking and thinking about jazz, of narrating and understanding the past, and how new meanings accrue following death. This reflection also made me think about the nature of jazz studies, the relationship between controversial jazz icons and our own behaviour and attitudes as scholars, musicians, fans and educators. When we continue to revere and celebrate artists such as Miles Davis, our tributes comment as much on our own tastes and desires as they do on the artists themselves—they comment on who we are, who we align ourselves with, and they can be an expression of lifestyle choices or who we want to be. Related to this, Scott DeVeaux describes the process of meaning-making and narrative construction that occurs when dealing with historical writings and posthumous representations of artists: "[C]ultural memory begins with death: the death of the creator. The search for meaning is left to the survivors. It is up to us to decide how to tell the story, how best to represent the struggle and achievement of artists whose lives belong to the past but whose music continues to live in the present" (1997, 450). When we narrate the past and tell the stories of others, therefore, we cannot help but reflect on issues of taste and bias, what we consider meaningful, what aspects of history are considered valuable, worth preserving, and what should be ignored or left out. Within this context, discussing meanings and the significance of Miles Davis today is a challenge, especially given the multiple representations, musical styles, artistic offerings and descriptions of the artist we have on record. To many, Davis was the embodiment of cool, the visionary jazz innovator who was at the forefront of almost every significant change in modern jazz in the postwar era. Whilst his work from the 1950s to the early 1970s is revered, the merits of his music in the 1980s is debated and, to some, controversial (hence the need for this collection). However, when we consider Miles Davis' lifestyle alongside his artistic output, a more serious controversy emerges. Most problematic, Davis was a misogynist who, throughout his life, was a self-confessed serial abuser of women (Davis with Troupe 1990). Despite explicit examples of abhorrent domestic abuse and attempts to call Davis to account for his crimes against women during his lifetime (Cleage 1994), posthumous representations of Davis continue to sidestep the problematic aspects of his biography. Portrayals of Davis either romanticise his abhorrent behaviour as a necessary feature of his creative genius or fetishise the artist as a violent masculine role model, celebrating Miles as an all-round "bad motherfucker" or simply as "The Man" (Early 2001; Szwed 2003). I argue that the legacy of Miles Davis presents musicians, scholars and fans with multiple problems that need to be confronted head-on. Given these problems, how can the study of the posthumous representation of Miles Davis, particularly in light of the #MeToo movement, encourage us to change our own behaviour and challenge the work of others in order to become better historians, musicians and, ultimately, human beings? Can thinking about Miles differently encourage a new kind of jazz appreciation and mode of working, a *new* new jazz studies?

Mediating Miles

In an interview conducted five years prior to Davis' death, the journalist Nick Kent describes the way in which the "demonic" and "chilling" voice of Miles Davis made him feel unable to rebut some of his statements about using drum machines. Kent reflects on how he felt during the interview itself: "Good God almighty. This is after all *Miles Davis*. The legendary Miles Davis. The *indefatigable* Miles Davis. The *wickedest, canniest, deepest, slickest, baddest* musician this century will ever see" (2009, 255). Kent was clearly awestruck and overwhelmed to meet Miles in person, to the point where he lost his ability to ask difficult questions. Encounters such as these were common and were clearly affected by the mediated persona of Miles Davis, how the artist had achieved an almost mythical status through the stories that had circulated about his life on and off stage. Given these interviews, and different types of writing that circulated during Davis' lifetime—including Miles' own autobiography—it is perhaps unsurprising that posthumous representations largely follow a similar mythical path.

In my book *Jazz Icons* (Whyton 2010), I explored the way in which mythologies play an important role in the dominant narratives of jazz, the way the music is constructed, articulated and understood by historians, artists, critics and filmmakers. Dominant narratives often promote notions of jazz and an unmediated form of expression; they avoid contradiction and contestation in offering simplified accounts of the music and its tradition and romanticise heteronormative masculinity as the lifeblood of the music. In the opening of *Jazz Icons*, I described the way in which Miles Davis is used as a symbol for the jazz life in Michael Mann's 2004 film *Collateral*. During a scene where the trumpeter and bandleader character Daniel (Barry Shabaka Henley) is interrogated by hit man Vincent (Tom Cruise), Miles Davis is used as a means of testing the jazzman's authenticity as an artist. In recounting his life in music, Daniel describes a night when he shared the bandstand with Miles and how this was the most frightening yet awe-inspiring moment in the jazzman's life. The narrative uses Miles to create a sense of awe coupled with hysteria, promoting a jazz life bound up with unpredictability and danger. Although fictional, the scene plays on the hyperbolic masculine rhetoric seen in a number of representations of Miles and draws on the artist as the embodiment of cool. The scene incorporates real-world—albeit possibly apocryphal—stories about Miles and integrates them into the scene. For example, jazzman Daniel describes the way Miles aggressively responds to some fans at a gig when they try to strike up a conversation: "Get out of my face you jive motherfucker and take your silly bitch with you". This exchange riffs on an anecdote shared by several writers wherein Miles describes the way he deliberately treated a female fan with contempt but then suggested that his meanness (or misogyny) would incentivise the woman to buy more records (Crouch 2006, 247). The scene also uses the persona and biography of Davis to perpetuate several mythologies of jazz, from his portrayal as a musical genius detached from his social environment ("he was focused", "in his own musical space", "You don't just go up and talk to Miles Davis") to the assertion that true educational value can occur only on the street or bandstand. Indeed, Daniel's ultimate downfall is triggered by his suggestion that the Juilliard School was the place where Miles learned music. Here another trope is presented, with formal education portrayed as completely incompatible with living an authentic jazz life. The story of Davis dropping out of Juilliard to pursue Charlie Parker on 52nd Street is one of the most romantic and well-trodden narrative devices to explain his coming of age and pathway to genius. However, the story of Davis' departure from Juilliard is not as sudden or romantic as it is often portrayed; indeed, rather than simply dropping out, as narratives such as these suggest, John Szwed points out that Miles achieved pretty good grades during his first semester at Juilliard, averaging a B in his studies overall. Having failed a couple of courses during his second semester, Miles actually returned for the summer session to make up for his bad grades during the previous semester. Eventually he managed to pass two of the three courses he took during the summer and had options to continue with his studies (Szwed 2003, 106–121). There was perhaps, at times, an ambivalence towards his education, although Szwed also gives several examples of Miles talking about the value of his studies at Juilliard. Contrary to popular myth-making, Szwed suggests that Miles demonstrated a commitment to completing his first-year studies and thought long and hard about suspending his formal education and discussed the pros and cons of this decision with his father. Whilst Davis' autobiography plays down the significance of his time at Juilliard (and there is no discussion of retaking examinations), there is mention of a detailed conversation with Davis' father and an acknowledgement that, before he left Juilliard, Miles obtained some additional lessons in piano and symphonic trumpet playing which would support his subsequent work (Davis with Troupe 1990, 64). Overall, therefore, this story is not as dramatic as it is often portrayed.

Whilst many biographers strive to identify correct dates, details and objective truths, we perhaps ignore the point that narrating someone's life often involves more than just getting the facts right. Even when we know the facts, as in the Juilliard example, we may still feel drawn to the mythology or the romance of storytelling when describing the life histories of our idols. In many respects, facts can make us feel uncomfortable, especially when they destabilise the mythic foundations of jazz past and present. Furthermore, drawing on the work of folklorist Alan Lomax, Nicholas Gebhardt proposes that what we think of as "the story of jazz" is often inseparable from our method of telling it, that the different media through which we record the past do not simply reflect, but actually create, what we take that past to be about (2017, 190–203). Histories of artists, whether presented in biographical or documentary form, often conform to established codes and conventions of the media through which the story is told. With this in mind, we should consider how artists are represented and how their personas are constructed, not only how others engineer or frame depictions of artists but also how artists themselves play a role in how they would like to be represented, both during their lifetime and posthumously.[1] Krin Gabbard, for example, has explored the complexities of Miles Davis' autobiography and the extent to which large portions of the manuscript either

[1] Indeed, this point also relates to Gebhardt's study of Alan Lomax and Jelly Roll Morton. In an important sense we could say that Mr. Jelly Roll was the creation of both Morton and Lomax, even though Lomax may shift on his sense that it is both Morton's story and the story about what happened.

were ghostwritten or, following the investigative claims of Stanley Crouch, were lifted directly from Jack Chambers' biography of Miles and other sources. In his chapter 'How Many Miles: Alternate Takes on the Jazz Life', Gabbard refutes the notion that a singular voice is possible to find; when considering Miles Davis, we may have a desire to know his 'real' character, but given the range of mediating influences, it is almost impossible to know one true Miles (2009, 184–200). To illustrate the way in which artists' voices are mediated, framed and constructed, Gabbard shows how the original manuscript of Davis' autobiography had been changed and adapted at several editorial stages to sound more vernacular and aggressive. For example, Gabbard demonstrates the way Miles' original description of Sarah Vaughan was changed from "she used to sing" to "she be singing" to subsequently appearing as "she'd be singing", as if to emphasise the vernacular of Davis' language. Miles' characterisation of Vaughan was also embellished by others, with the insertion of the words "and she was a motherfucker too" (190). In effect, either Quincy Troupe or the editorial team at Simon and Schuster changed Miles Davis' own words—or his authorial voice—in order to make him sound *more* like Miles Davis. Or, in fact, they made the text read like how we want Miles Davis to sound, regardless of whether he actually talked or wrote like that.

In many ways, Don Cheadle's 2015 film *Miles Ahead* is a remediated telling of the Miles Davis story that plays with the constructed themes of jazz history and the codified representations of the artist. Cheadle describes the film as a 'metaphorical' (rather than factual or fictional) tale that brings together Ewan McGregor as a bogus *Rolling Stone* journalist and Cheadle as a reclusive Miles Davis. As a work of fiction, the film plays with Davis as a creative signifier and explores the idea that he transcends time and space, as seen in the non-chronological use of music, the role of flashback, and, most significant, the final cathartic scene where the fictional Miles (Cheadle) plays alongside his aged real-life contemporaries Herbie Hancock, Wayne Shorter, and the film's composer Robert Glasper and a younger generation of artists, including Esperanza Spalding and Antonio Sanchez. The final sequence of the film ends with the date and year of Davis' birth, followed by a hyphen and a blank space presented where the year of his death would fall. Here Cheadle suggests that the dates of Davis' mortal life are irrelevant: Miles Lives!

We might consider these creative processes troublesome, given that audiences might interpret the events on-screen as biography or a claim to historical integrity; however, we should be aware that a lot of supposedly objective jazz histories consist of imagined, embellished and/or fictional elements. In this instance, like Gabbard's reading of Miles' documented life, the film perhaps acknowledges that a single version of the Miles Davis story would be impossible to tell, and so the playful use of Miles as a metaphorical voice recognises the mediated nature of iconic representation. Instead, the film attempts to use Miles as a vehicle to express a sense of legacy, a continuity of moving from one generation to the next. As Bjorn Heile (2016) comments, "Although this time shift is confusing at first, a further clue is provided when rapper Pharaohe Monch is heard over the subsequent end titles, testifying to the continuity of black music. The music, we are told, unites past, present and future; it transcends all boundaries of age, race and gender, even that between fiction and reality". Here, when using Davis as a creative signifier, we should perhaps view *Miles Ahead* as having more in common with the symbolic use of jazz artists in literature and poetry than with standard Hollywood jazz biopics. Since John Coltrane's death, for example, the 'Coltrane Poem' has emerged as a vehicle to explore themes that are regarded as core to the African American experience. Kimberley Benston (2000) has shown how the absence created by the death of Coltrane had a symbolic quality that was used by poets to explore themes such as the loss of voice in America and the alienation of black subjects. Poets treated Coltrane's death as a tragedy but also as a means of rebirth—the loss of one voice inspired new voices to emerge. When applying the same logic to Miles Davis, it is worth considering what metaphors are at play in posthumous representations and what Miles comes to stand for symbolically when people pay tribute to him today. If Coltrane came to represent a symbol of empowerment and rebirth, what kind of rebirth or positive action could Miles serve as a catalyst for? For example, in addition to Miles' musical legacy, which is clearly promoted in Cheadle's film, *Miles Ahead* does touch on Davis' abusive behaviour, both to himself and to others. However, like other documentaries and texts discussed below, the film's storyline does not encourage us to interrogate our relationship to problematic figures of the past, nor does it move away from romanticised narratives that ultimately celebrate Miles as a flawed genius, presenting his vices as a necessary part of his creativity. Therefore, if Miles is to serve as a metaphorical voice or symbol of renewal, then I would argue that we need to ask more questions of Miles and of ourselves. Uncomfortable questions. Questions that have been raised before but that have been left unanswered, sidestepped or ignored.

Miles and the Masculine Myth

Whilst Miles Davis' violent and abusive acts have been documented and criticised to some extent, there remains a limited body of work on the problematic constructions of masculinity in both the representation of Miles and broader jazz discourse.[2] As seen in the reviews, tributes and representations above, Davis is often portrayed as an idealised masculine icon, an uncompromising personality who engenders a sense of awe in people through his uncompromising attitude, his charisma and his willingness to undertake acts of violence at any moment. He is represented as aggressive, intuitive and emotion-filled, and these aspects of his character are said to fuel his creative energies; they also inform his sensuality and sexual persona alongside his frustrations and vulnerabilities (see, for example, Early 2001; Crouch 2006).

Surveying the literature on Miles and his broader representations, we become acutely aware of the complex discourse surrounding modern masculinity and problematic constructions of blackness. As scholars such as Herman Gray (1995) and Hazel V. Carby (1998) demonstrate, masculine constructs—including concepts of black masculinity—change and adapt over time and remain socially and culturally produced. Within this context, the ongoing portrayal of Miles Davis strikes to the heart of racialised gender roles in jazz; indeed, accounts of Miles Davis past and present are fuelled by problematic constructions of masculinity which inevitably feed into many of the social problems we face today. George Mosse has made a convincing argument about the way in which ideas of modern masculinity helped to construct normative patterns of morality and behaviour and how, in turn, the creation of a masculine 'Other', which demonised blackness, was key to this process:

[2] See Cleage (1994), Carby (1998), and Nisensen (1996) for examples of studies that examine the relationship between Miles Davis and different conceptions of masculinity. More recently, Nichole Rustin-Pascale's (2017) work on Charles Mingus has opened up a space for a more nuanced understanding of masculinity in jazz, and stresses that black 'jazzmasculinity' is both varied and contradictory in character, being a problematic aesthetic expression of heterosexual power and pleasure on the one hand, yet also having the potential to open up a space where concepts of freedom, emotion, and experience can be voiced and performed by both men *and* women. Rustin-Paschale examines the performative nature of masculinity and stresses that "jazzmasculinity is a habitable space both theoretically and experientially for women" (15). By adopting this approach as a feminist strategy, Rustin-Paschale disentangles maleness and manhood from masculinity and attempts to broaden the understanding of masculinity and the way it permeates everyday life; jazzmasculinity shapes our emotions, frames our experiences, and feeds directly into discourses of power and freedom.

> The masculine stereotype was strengthened . . . by the existence of a negative stereotype of men who not only failed to measure up to the ideal but who in body and soul were its foil, projecting the exact opposite of true masculinity. Groups marginalised by society, such as Jews or blacks, fulfilled this role, and indeed racism was based upon stereotypes and stereotyping. Those who were said not to fit into settled and respectable society were transformed into countertypes to the ideals that society cherished and that manliness represented so well. They were supplied with all the features that in an unambiguous manner told everyone who had eyes to see of the evil they portended. (1996, 6)

Whilst negative stereotypes such as these continued to inform representations of black subjects—and do so to this day—we could consider the postwar period as fostering an atmosphere of change, where ideas of black masculinity were challenged, confronted, exaggerated and embellished. Building on Mosse's point, if masculinity was believed to reinforce normative patterns of morality and behaviour, then the concept of black masculinity revealed much more about white power structures and the role black bodies performed in both playing out fantasies and preying on fears. In the postwar era, black masculinity became integrally linked to the fetish and romance of the jazz life, wherein, in certain contexts, black musicians were celebrated and revered for displaying nonconformist attitudes in a world of violence, deviancy and degeneracy. Indeed, the appeal of jazz can be understood in the context of broader writings within the period, from Howard Becker's (2018) examination of deviancy and the outsider status of musicians to Norman Mailer's (1999) conception of 'the white Negro'. Artists were either perceived as outside of power structures or as growing in political awareness and were portrayed as inhabiting dangerous spaces riddled with vice and violence. For some, black men, and their music, encapsulated nonconformity, hysteria, sexuality and resistance.

Writers such as Gerald Early and John Szwed have idealised Miles Davis as a figure who embodied and reconciled the contrasting, and at times contradictory, masculine constructs of the postwar period. Indeed, Szwed suggests that Miles Davis' persona responded well to the social anxieties of the 1950s, when general concepts of masculinity were being negotiated and reconfigured. In an interlude in his biography of Davis, Szwed attempts to capture the complexity of Davis' sound and lifestyle and its relationship to postwar negotiations of masculinity: "The fear was that a new postwar economy was creating a society in which people were externally motivated, too well adjusted, too sociable. Scarcely concealed behind the jargon of social science was the fear that it was not women who were changing, but men, who were becoming soft, emotional and expressive—that is, more like women rather than like the rational and task oriented patriarchs who had built and protected America" (2003, 204). Szwed describes how *Playboy* magazine would promote a particular kind of male hedonism as a response to such anxieties, which included the bachelor lifestyle, imported cars, the objectification of women, and top-of-the-line stereos that would play the essentially male sounds of jazz. Szwed continues, "In the midst of this maelstrom of ideas, these crisscrossed, heightened sensibilities and exaggerated claims for male selfdom, in walked Miles: inner-directed to a fault and authentic as hell, with the material aspirations of a *Playboy* man and the drive for self-expression of the Beats" (204).

Miles is portrayed as a focused musician with drive, determination and attitude alongside a clear sense of purpose and competition. He had suffered injustice but responded by having a style and confidence in the way he carried himself—the physical prowess of a prizefighter—and was viewed as a musician who wouldn't shy away from confrontation. As a masculine composite, he is described as focused and driven, at the same time as being physically strong, charismatic and attractive. To some, he was endearing and chivalrous, romantic and sensuous, even effeminate at times, and yet he was capable of extreme violence, to himself and to others.

I would suggest that masculinity could also be constructed through Davis' sound, both vocally and musically, as his raspy voice in itself became a signifier of excess, the result of physical stress, mistreatment and abuse: masculinity sonified. Musically, Szwed described Miles' use of the harmon mute as a way of creating a voice-like sound that was also raspy yet understated, not brash and bold, and suggested that this new sound challenged and recast the idea of virility in jazz as being linked to brashness and the production of high notes. Instead, Davis created a new sound bound up with the coolness of the era, described by Krin Gabbard (1995) as 'post-phallic'. And yet Szwed's description does not portray Miles and this 'post-phallic' sound as impotent. Instead, we are presented with a new kind of man—'The Man'—as the closing statement of Szwed's interlude asserts. Miles' sound has been described by both men and women as having seductive qualities, which move beyond the sensual to provide a space for self-identification among listeners. Amiri Baraka, for example, suggested that the seduction of Miles' sound was born from its clarity, which, in turn, led to a form of separation, an "aesthetic distance" and "sensuous alienation" that enabled people to project their own feelings and desires onto Miles' musical sound space (1987, 156).

Whilst I would question the relationship between the clarity of musical sound and aesthetic distance outlined here, this type of self-identification through the experience of listening to Miles is expressed very clearly by Farah Jasmine Griffin, who states, "Perhaps this is what women, particularly black American women, especially creative black American women, hear in Davis' horn. Perhaps we hear something akin to our own voices" (2001, 182). For Jasmine Griffin, Miles' music "promises a feather bed upon which to fall while taking the risks required of a multidimensional womanhood" (184). These comments may seem surprising, especially given Davis' abusive relationship to women. However, Jasmine Griffin addresses this tension and suggests that the complexities and contradictions of Miles' sound are what make his music appealing to women: "His horn is seductive not because it is harshly masculine but because it is not. In the sounds that emanate from Miles there is space for women's tears, vulnerability, anger, love, sexuality, creativity: a space simply to be. Perhaps this is why many felt so betrayed by his admission of emotional, verbal and physical violence against women" (182). Whilst I discuss the paradox between the appeal of Davis' music and his abusive behaviour below, we should consider violence—or a willingness to undertake acts of violence—as a central tenet of modern masculinity and the problems it engenders. Within Miles' lifestyle, this is not only evident in his abuse of himself and others but also in the way he drew on both the discipline and the aesthetic of boxing as a way of performing masculinity. Drawing on accounts from Miles' autobiography, Gerald Early has discussed the way Miles constructed a "mythology of black masculinity" by modelling himself on the boxer Sugar Ray Robinson (2001, 6). Several writers argue that the discipline of boxing enabled Davis to align his musical practice with the "destructive accuracy" of revered pugilists (Crouch 2006, 42). Comparisons to boxing extend to the way Davis would apparently shut people out before concerts and refuse food and sex before playing in order to stay hungry for performances. Boxing comparisons extended to his playing technique. Drawing on Early's work, Szwed says the athletic dimension of boxing informed Miles' approach to performance, suggesting that playing from the legs and bending the knees, mirroring the technique of boxers, protected his embouchure. Szwed writes that "boxers and musicians are both itinerant workers in the arena of individualism, both pay the dues of a brutal meritocracy, and though public figures, both are embedded in a shadowy elite with its own code of values under the spotlight" (2003, 196). Whether emulating the style and attitude of Sugar Ray Robinson or embodying the techniques of the pugilist in performance, embracing the boxing aesthetic reflects a desire to construct an idealised masculine persona that links style, charisma and control to one's discipline. Borrowing from Robinson, Miles is said to articulate knowledge of both his commercial and artistic worth and demonstrates a command of the stage like a champion boxer would dominate the ring. Ultimately the boxing aesthetic points to the desire for power and control over one's environment as well as displaying preparedness for violence.

Early stresses that within Davis' own mythic construction of black masculinity, he saw himself as operating within a black male heroic tradition, but his heroes were not typical leaders, such as W. E. B. Du Bois and Martin Luther King, but figures such as Jack Johnson and, later, Muhammed Ali (2001, 11). Linking masculinity to uncompromising creative practice is not new; myths of the heroic male genius' nonadherence to social norms producing great art permeate histories of Western art (see, for example, Wolff 1993). Yet Early's description of Miles' own construction of a masculine myth is conspicuously devoid of any critical reflection or interrogation. As readers, we are left with a sense of familiar awe and reverence and the impression that there is something inevitable about Miles' construction of masculinity and its links to violence, misogyny and abuse. Following his detailed description of Miles' masculine aesthetic and abusive behaviour, Early simply states, "Great flaws and great contradictions are often the marks of great people" (2001, 16).

Contrary to Early's lack of engagement with the problems of mythmaking, it is important to consider how mythic presentations of black male subjects often exaggerate and skew constructions of masculinity. Black men are often demonised, portrayed as having threatening physical and sexual demeanours. When blackness emerges as resistant to previous modes of control, of dehumanisation and problematic racial representation, assertions of masculinity often continue to perpetuate established conventions, normative values and patriarchal structures. Indeed, even when black lives are perceived as powerful and resistant to white control, power is most often predicated on a willingness to perform violent acts, on ingrained and supposedly naturalised constructions of masculinity.

This point forms the central argument of the late influential feminist bell hooks, in her general critique of modern masculinity: "Showing aggression is the simplest way to assert patriarchal manhood. Men of all classes know this. As a consequence, all men living in a culture of violence must demonstrate at some point in their lives that they are capable of being violent" (2003, 46). hooks continues, "Male violence is a central problem in our society. Black male violence simply mirrors the styles and habits of white male violence. It is not unique. What is unique to black male experience is the way in which acting violently often gets both attention and praise from the dominant culture. Even as it is being condemned black male violence is often deified" (61). Here hooks stresses that, by adopting violence—even as an emblem of struggle and resistance—one expresses allegiance with the values of white patriarchy.[3] In discussing Miles and his willingness to perform acts of violence, Crouch and other writers have argued that similar power dynamics are at play in Davis' attitudinal shift and antagonism towards white audiences, who, in effect, develop a fetish for bad behaviour. To illustrate the point, Crouch draws on Ralph Ellison's description of the irony of Miles Davis' antagonistic gestures and antisocial behaviour on stage and the way his abusive and aggressive behaviour was embraced and eagerly anticipated by audiences: "The result was a grim comedy of racial manners, with the musicians employing a calculated rudeness, treating the audience very much as many white merchants in poor Negro neighborhoods treat their customers. . . . Then comes the comic reversal. Today the white audience expects the rudeness as part of the entertainment. If it fails to appear the audience is disappointed" (Ellison quoted in Crouch 2006, 246). Whilst Crouch is at pains to critique Miles for his abhorrent treatment of women, he does continue to draw on constructions of heteronormative masculinity in critiquing artists who supposedly lack authenticity in jazz.[4]

When we celebrate Miles today, I argue that we can no longer brush over the problematic aspects of his lifestyle, superficially condoning violent acts and then explaining them away as an integral part of his flawed

[3] This point is mirrored by Herman Gray in relating jazzmen such as Miles Davis to present-day constructions of black masculinity: "Like their jazz predecessors, contemporary expressions of black masculinity work symbolically in a number of directions at once; they challenge and disturb racial and class constructions of blackness; they also rewrite and reinscribe the patriarchal and heterosexual basis of masculine privilege (and domination) based on gender and sexuality" (1995, 402).

[4] Here we can observe homophobic language and themes in Crouch's work on Miles, ranging from the description of Miles as "turning butt to the beautiful" (2006, 240) to suggesting that rumours of Miles' bisexuality were merely born out of jealousy, "the gossip joy of his inferiors" (59). Even Davis' admiration for Prince leads Crouch to describe the popular artist as "a Minneapolis vulgarian and borderline drag queen" (240). For Crouch, it seems, it would be extremely distasteful to conceive of Miles—or any authentic jazz musician—as being capable of having a bisexual relationship or swaying from normative constructions of heterosexual masculinity.

genius or excusing these acts by stressing that his music played a formative role in the experiences of so many men and women. If violence is part of the mythic make-up of Miles' masculinity, the characteristics that make writers and musicians celebrate him as The Man, then we need to confront these constructs head-on. If we continue to pay tribute, to idolise Miles, we need to ask: Who does Miles speak for today? What values does he represent?

Miles & #MeToo

In their book *The Dark Side of the Tune* (2009), Bruce Johnson and Martin Cloonan describe the need to consider the role of violence in popular music from a range of perspectives. The authors argue that there is an assumption that popular music is therapeutic and that case studies and historical narratives are often written from the position of fans or sympathisers. Music clearly has the power to seduce, to transform lives, and to convey a genuine sense of magic and otherworldliness to listeners. As jazz researchers, we have a tendency to write only about music that inspires us and focus on the musicians we feel passionate about. It is perhaps because of these reasons that we do not want to tarnish our listening experience with the acknowledgement of violence or to consider our love of music alongside the abhorrent acts carried out by artists whose music we adore. This, in part, could explain why dominant histories tend to foreground notions of 'the music itself' when the relationship between abusive acts and creative practices is raised as an issue. However, I argue that these issues run much deeper than simply not wanting to spoil our enjoyment of music.

Despite several attempts to bring the problematic aspects of Miles Davis' life to the fore, any such intervention has resulted in no more than a mild ripple. The dominant discourse continues to separate Miles' music from his abuse of women. Defences of this position range from accepting violence as a necessary part of genius to accounting for Miles' violence as a by-product of having to work in abusive and racialised contexts (Early 2001). Relatedly, George Lipsitz's obituary of Ike Turner examines the relationship between violence and the racialised contexts within which popular music is made. Lipsitz states that we judge Turner without paying attention to the "vexed contradictions and conditions that shaped his life and deeds," and he suggests that Turner's abusive behaviour is often singled out without any contextual understanding (2009, 117). Lipsitz argues that Turner is the product of a racialised society where black men are simultaneously singled out as abusers in disproportionate numbers to their white counterparts and represented in such ways that they are encouraged to conform to such stereotypes: "Yet while people were and are absolutely correct to condemn Ike Turner's assaults against Tina and the other women he professed to love, we have to ask if the public outcry would have been the same if Ike Turner had been white, and if Tina had not left rhythm and blues music for pop music and embraced the producers and musical forms most pleasing to white audiences" (118). This statement alone opens up a number of questions about intersectionality, race and its relationship to fandom and the marketplace, yet I argue that, when the same logic is applied to Miles Davis, a very different outcome emerges. In the majority of biographical accounts and documentaries, the "vexed contradictions and conditions" of Davis' life are used to explain away his violence, not condemn him. For example, in Stanley Nelson Jr.'s 2019 film *Miles Davis: Birth of the Cool*, Davis' violence towards women is treated as episodic—linked only to two incidents in two relationships—and is portrayed as being the result of drug and alcohol abuse alongside a behavioural legacy from his father. Whilst a racialised society might well have contributed to Davis' psychological state, race does not lead overtly to persecution in the same way Lipsitz describes the frequent attacks on Ike Turner. Instead, in broader representations, Davis' violence is often presented as an inevitable feature of the artist's genius or, as we have seen, the essence of his masculinity.[5] As such, violence is tolerated in order for us to experience his greatness. In true modernist fashion, Miles is portrayed as a type of expressionist; artistic ideas, frustrations and passions need to come out of him with a sense of urgency, whether through sound, painting, acting or his fists. He is uncompromising because his art is authentically pure.

Unlike Lipsitz, Pearl Cleage's *Mad at Miles* moves the focus away from black men as victimised to focus more on the violence inflicted on women themselves. In perhaps the most direct confrontation of the relationship between fandom and Davis' misogyny, certainly during the artist's lifetime, Cleage stresses that it is the tolerance of violence towards women that is the problem, not the construction of racialised stereotypes: "I can't stop

[5] Genius narratives tend to emerge even when writers are critical of Miles. For example, consider the following statement about Miles by Jasmine Farrah Griffin: "I want to suggest that these men should not be our heroes and they ought not to be our leaders. We need to reserve those roles for those who provide protection for our needs, interests, and physical selves. But unfortunately, they are often our friends, brothers, fathers and yes, they are our geniuses. Because genius is quirky like that—it can appear in the oddest places" (2001, 183).

wondering what we would do if the violence was against black men instead of black women. . . . I can't stop wondering what our reaction would be if, say, Kenny G . . . was revealed to be kicking black men's asses all over the country in between concert appearances and recording sessions? What if Kenny G wrote a book saying that sometimes he had to slap black men around a little just to make them cool out and leave him the fuck alone so he could get some peace and quiet?" Cleage continues:

> Would Kenny G be the music we would want to play to relax and focus the person we love on romance? Would Kenny G be the music we would play when our black male friends came to call? And if we did and they questioned us about it—and you know they would question us about it!—would we explain our continuing support of Kenny G's music by saying: "Yeah, I know he's beating black men and all that, but this white boy is a musical genius! I don't let personal stuff get in the way of my appreciation of his music. After all, the brothers probably asking for it. You know how it is when y'all start naggin' and shit." (1994, 42–43)

Here, by simply substituting Kenny G for Miles and inverting the role of black men and black women, Cleage draws attention to the hypocrisy of idol worship and the ingrained misogyny that forms the bedrock of dominant modes of representation in jazz. This simple inversion forces us to consider our values in jazz. Why should Miles continue to resonate with us when we come to understand the stark realities of his violent misogyny, and what problematic role does race play in our ongoing relationship to male jazz heroes?

Cleage's text has taken on a renewed significance in recent years, following the emergence of the #MeToo movement. I propose that it is essential to reconsider Miles Davis' violence and abusive behaviour in light of #MeToo in order to attempt to redress the balance of representation and to encourage musicians, scholars and fans to reflect on their own behaviour and complicity in continuing to romanticise the work of artists whilst excusing abhorrent behaviour. #MeToo provides us with an opportunity to rethink our values, how music—and the artists who produce it—speak to and for us, and to revisit historical moments that have been deliberately obscured, played down in significance or considered separate from the production of 'the music itself'.

Sociologist Michael Flood (2019) provides a useful mapping of men's responses to the #MeToo movement and outlines common forms of resistance among men to anti-violence and sexual harassment campaigns. Despite the widespread coverage of #MeToo in the news and on social media, Flood's study highlights the continuation of patriarchal norms and the preservation of power structures that continue to deny the fact that sexual harassment and violence towards women is an issue that involves all of us. Within his mapping exercise, Flood identifies common attitudes to #MeToo among male groups that, whether intended or not, serve as forms of denial or modes of resistance to social change. First is the suggestion that violence and sexual harassment towards women occurs only in the extreme and that they do not form part of everyday life. Second, and linked to the first point, is the claim that violence is perpetrated by a deviant minority. This is the argument that there are too many false allegations against the behaviour of men, signalling that #MeToo has gone too far. Flood suggests that these attitudinal trends indicate that men's understanding of violence and harassment differs drastically from women's. In countering these responses, Flood argues that the #MeToo movement demands we take collective action to address the social and structural roots of men's violence against women and asks men "to challenge the abusive behaviour of other men and the attitudes and behaviours which sustain this" (294). As part of a mobilisation strategy, Flood outlines three primary tasks to counter men's typical responses to #MeToo. I consider these tasks in relation to posthumous readings of Miles Davis and explore how they can help us engage more critically with jazz discourse and, ultimately, our own behaviour.

1. For men to listen to women—to recognise that violence is common and wrong.

Flood argues that the position of women is not always framed as significant and that men need to recognise that violence and sexual harassment towards women are commonplace. Within a jazz context, several recent publications point to compelling examples of widespread sexual harassment and systemic barriers to inclusion in different jazz scenes which respond directly to this task (see, for example, Buscatto 2021; Raine 2019).

As jazz scholars, we need to do more to make explicit the commonplace nature of male violence in our work and the ways in which jazz representations often deliberately obscure the female voice by placing it alongside opinions and perspectives that deliberately undermine the significance of violent acts. This can be evidenced through numerous writings and representations where Davis' violence towards women has been downplayed in favour of a more sensitive, feminine-conscious portrayal of the artist and his legacy.[6] For example, reading the press release and subsequent press reviews for the *Birth of the Cool* documentary, it would be easy to assume that, as one critic claims, the film is "a masterful and compelling work that tells the whole unvarnished story of the mercurial Miles as a musician and a man" (Mergner 2017). However, whilst the blurb for and press responses to the film promise to engage directly with the myths and controversies of Miles' life, the documentary downplays acts of violence and sidesteps arguments made by feminists such as Cleage, to focus again on Davis as a flawed genius, style icon and embodiment of masculine cool. Miles' violence is noted within the film through the somewhat muted testimony of Miles' former wife Frances Taylor, yet, surprisingly, there is no deep interrogation of the problematic aspects of his life by the cultural and critical commentators featured in the documentary. For example, scholar Tammy Kernodle states, "He was the personification of cool. The mythological hero. He becomes our black superman". In describing Miles, Kernodle sidesteps the violent aspects of his life by describing these characteristics as an essential part of his art: "There were all these personality quirks he had. He was angry, anti-social. But oftentimes those insecurities and those demons are the very things that are the basis of art. So that art becomes a way of healing. It gave him the opportunity to show a vulnerability and to show a side of him that, in the real world, he could not show" (Kernodle quoted in Nelson 2019).

All of these observations are perhaps typical of the medium where established romanticised genius tropes are provided as structuring elements of documentary filmmaking and the voices of experts are often mediated, with meanings constructed through the work of directors and film editors. Within this context, one of the most powerful examples of a revised portrayal of Davis can be seen in the late Greg Tate's contribution to the documentary. Rather than talk about Miles as a problematic character where women are concerned, Tate heralds Miles as a black feminist sympathiser when discussing the album *Some Day My Prince Will Come*. The music on

[6] Consider, for example, Farah Jasmin Griffin and Salim Washington's fairly typical scant description of misogyny in an otherwise hagiographic depiction of Miles Davis' life and music: "It is important to note that Miles, for all of his notorious profaneness, brashness, misogyny, and just plain cold-bloodedness, was also capable of the kind of generosity that has endeared him to band mates. The man who could be cool and confident, and who could play with the openness and vulnerability that Miles did, was a complex, bold, and pioneering version of midcentury masculinity" (2013, 23). Again Miles' construction of masculinity is presented in heroic and unproblematic terms.

the album is portrayed as somehow expressing a feminine sensibility, but more important, Miles is seen to be representing the voices of black women through his determination to change the initial cover of the album (which featured a white woman) to feature his wife Frances instead. Tate stresses, "He was standing up for the beauty of black women. You know, he was saying 'this beauty here is the beauty that I'm projecting'" (Tate quoted in Nelson 2019).[7] In the broader context of the documentary, this passage is used as a softener for what is to follow; a section that describes Miles being jealous of Frances and of his controlling personality. Whilst temper outbursts are discussed, they are explained away as being the result of alcohol, pain killers and cocaine. This sequence is followed by a statement from Miles saying that Frances was the best wife he ever had; this serves as a signifier of remorse, something that was never expressed by Davis during his lifetime.

In a critique of the *Birth of the Cool* documentary written for the *New Yorker*, Richard Brody (2019) comments on the strategic use of women's voices within the film:

> In a trio of clips that end the film, Cantú[8] and Taylor speak admiringly of Davis—"I don't regret, I don't forget, but I still love," Taylor says—and Davis' friend, the artist Cortez McCoy, remembers him tearfully, saying, "Of course I loved him. He was like a brother who did dumb things, and you accepted it." Brody argues that, while facing up to Davis' violence toward women, Nelson relies on these comments as a sort of benediction, if not a kind of absolution, as if suggesting that, if the women who were among his victims still speak of Davis with love, so may we all.

Miles' violence is acknowledged, but it is seen as an anomaly; there is never a sense that he was a serial offender who abused women throughout his life.[9]

[7] In many ways, Tate may well have been paraphrasing Miles Davis' own words. Referring to the image of Cicely Tyson on the cover of *The Sorcerer*, Miles states, "I have this thing about helping black women, you know. Because when I was using dope it was costing me a couple of grand a day and I used to take bitches' money. So when I stopped to clean up, I got mad at *Playboy* and I wouldn't accept their poll because they didn't have no black women in their magazine, you know. So I started putting them on my covers" (Carr 1984, 206).

[8] Marguerite Cantú (nee Eskridge) was a former girlfriend of Davis and the mother of his youngest son, Erin Davis.

[9] The downplaying of the severity of violence against women could also reflect broader tensions between antiracist and feminist movements. In seeking to avoid the problematic racial stereotyping of black men, examples of violence within the African American community can be played down or viewed as a distraction from the antiracist cause. Kimberlé Crenshaw, for example, examines how antiracial debates can often marginalise intersectional identities such as women of colour within these contexts: "Within communities of color, efforts to stem the politicisation of domestic violence

2. To reflect change in their own behaviour and everyday relations with women and other men.

Flood argues that downplaying the significance of violence in this way is no longer acceptable in the post–#MeToo era and that men need to change their own behaviour, to call out examples of harassment, and to think about their complicity in supporting patriarchal systems of power and control. Both men and women clearly find it difficult to acknowledge the severity of the crimes Davis committed, to the extent that we might reappraise our relationship to him. In many ways, an impasse remains between the love and romance of the music of Miles Davis on the one hand and a broader sense of our humanity, morality and ethical responsibility on the other. Defenders of Miles may point to the fact that the artist contributed to the creative labour of several generations, inspiring artists and fans alike.[10] Davis' crimes against women have the potential to uproot these formative experiences and challenge people's identification with jazz. Whilst this dichotomy cannot be easily resolved, it is important for us to continually resist the seduction of flawed genius narratives, to question the symbolic and metaphorical function of iconic representation and how it fuels our values and desires, and to be explicit and consistent in calling out artists for their crimes.

Although the majority of biographical and documentary accounts of Davis continue to downplay issues of violence and misogyny, one example of reflective change can be seen in the writing of the late Eric Nisensen, who was the only writer to get close to Miles during his reclusive period from 1975 to 1981. In the first edition of Nisensen's book *'Round About Midnight*, published during Davis' lifetime, Davis is presented mostly in uncomplicated terms. In his preface to the second edition of the book, however, Nisensen admits that he had deliberately omitted information about Miles' drug use

are often grounded in attempts to maintain the integrity of the community. The articulation of this perspective takes different forms. Some critics allege that feminism has no place within communities of color, that the issues are internally divisive, and that they represent the migration of white women's concerns into a context in which they are not only irrelevant but also harmful. At its most extreme, this rhetoric denies that gender violence is a problem in the community and characterises any effort to politicise gender subordination as itself a community problem" (1991, 1253). Crenshaw suggests that the solution to the problem is not so much the portrayal of violence within black communities as it is the absence of other narratives and images that portray a fuller range of black experience. For Crenshaw, suppressing examples of violence against women of colour in pursuit of broader anti-racism campaigns imposes real costs on society (1256).

[10] This was one of the main points raised in defence of Miles Davis' legacy cited in the York University 'Gender in Jazz: Narratives, Practice and Justice' panel discussed below.

and mistreatment of women in the original publication as he felt this would have been an intrusion on the artist's privacy. In opening up about Miles' 'dark moments', Nisensen provides a shocking account of Miles breaking a girlfriend's jaw, sending her to the hospital. Reflecting on his own complicity in championing Miles' music whilst ignoring the artist's abusive behaviour, Nisensen states, "I obviously greatly admired Miles despite his despicable treatment of women. It is a great human dilemma—can we love parts of a person and simply ignore that which is repugnant? Now I believe Miles' brutality towards women simply cannot be avoided" (1996, 169). Here we have a rare example of a writer and historian reflecting on their own practice and admitting they were wrong. Yet despite this admission, Nisensen's words go only so far in engaging with themes of violence and in condemning Davis' abusive acts. Indeed, his preface concludes with the statement, "[D]espite his inexcusable treatment of women . . . Miles changed my life for the better, and changed the lives of all who were moved by his music" (171). Here Nisensen again separates Davis' abhorrent behaviour from his creativity and continues to promote him as a figure who demonstrates "the way of the artist" (170). Reflecting on behaviour is one thing, but actually changing it is another.

By engaging with these issues, taking Miles to task posthumously, we can begin to reflect on our own behaviour. To openly criticise our idols might make us uncomfortable, as we are criticising not only the artists but also our own values, our formative experiences and our creative pasts. However, we need to understand that this is not character defamation but a strong dose of realism, for which we are morally and ethically responsible. As Flood states, many men view the solution to violence against women as solely a women's issue. This position is not tenable.

3. To contribute to social change, both by challenging other men and by contributing to wider efforts to shift the systemic gender inequalities that form the foundation of sexual harassment and abuse.

"[Miles Davis] is guilty of self-confessed violent crimes against women such that we should break his albums, burn his tapes and scratch up his CDs until he acknowledges and apologises and agrees to rethink his position on The Woman Question" (Cleage 1994, 36). Cleage's repeated calls "to break his albums" until Miles "rethinks his position" offer an early example of a call to arms, an attempt to contribute to social change. Although there will be fans who deny the extent of Davis' treatment of women, his self-confessed violence and misogyny and the testimony of his victims provide evidence for everyone to see. Given the prevalence of genius tropes and the downplaying of violence in posthumous representations of Miles, it is important for jazz scholars to develop a strategy for social change that engages directly with these themes. Following a broad overview of abhorrent acts in popular music history, Catherine Strong and Emma Rush (2018) draw on the field of applied ethics to explore how best to construct a history of music that doesn't ignore violence against women. In seeking to contribute to social change, Strong and Rush map out some tentative guidelines for historians and stress that, when violence against women is admitted by the perpetrator (as in the case of Miles), these facts should always be noted in discussions:

> [W]here VAW [violence against women] has been legally proven or admitted by the perpetrator, our view is that it should be acknowledged, clearly and accurately—that is, there should be no attempt to hide, minimise or explain it away. This is important because shying away from discussion of violence sends a message that such behaviour is really not that bad, or that there may be acceptable excuses for it. Failing to hold famous and successful men to account for VAW when the fact is on the public record suggests to other potential perpetrators that they will be "let off lightly" and to survivors of violence that "they shouldn't make a fuss." This plays into historical tendencies for VAW to be minimised, excused, blamed on the woman or treated as a private "domestic" issue that outside parties should not intervene in. The increasing acknowledgement that VAW is highly damaging means that these types of excuses are being found less and less acceptable. Equally, "artistic genius" is also neither an excuse for the behaviour itself nor for not discussing the behaviour: artists or those associated with them should not be held to a lower standard than other people. (575)

In offering an ethical way forward for scholars, Strong and Rush advocate a separation of the artwork from the artist. They stress that, by rejecting the artist as well as their works, we would be losing access to important shared cultural heritage and ignoring the fact that artworks are the product of collaborative practices. Whilst I would not claim that we should stop listening to Miles Davis—indeed, it would be impossible to avoid Davis' cultural influence in jazz—I would argue that, as outlined at the start of this chapter, we should be careful in separating music from the people who make it, as this can potentially serve to reinforce romantic ideas where music is treated as if it exists in a vacuum and is taken out of the social and political context of its production. This point is taken up by Carby in response to *Miles: The Autobiography* (Davis 1990): "I think it is very important to challenge the apparent distance between Davis' violence against women and the 'genius' of his music, as if they were enacted on different planes of existence. . . . [T]his division reproduces the material/spiritual divide that Davis himself creates. The various women described in *Miles* are carefully given their place in his material world: they may service his bodily sexual and physical needs, but are albatrosses around his neck when he wants to fly with other men in the musical realm of 'genius' and performance" (Carby 1998, 144).

Clearly, these issues are complex and it is difficult to work out how best to proceed in terms of our ongoing relationship to Miles and his music. Music inevitably takes on a life of its own once produced and circulated in the public domain. However, in striking at the heart of systemic gender inequalities and the cultures of production that continue to excuse artists for acts of sexual harassment and abuse, I would suggest that any reappraisal of the legacy of Miles Davis needs to place his violence directly alongside his music.

Conclusion

"The jazz world has been so wedded to the modernist notion of the artist as a transcendent genius to whom nothing matters but the music that the historical particularity of how the icons of jazz achieved greatness—that presume[s] the source of excellence to be simply talent—ha[s] missed the fundamentally social processes by which a musical voice becomes heard, evaluated, identified with and ultimately takes on symbolic force" (Monson 2001, 95). Ingrid Monson encourages us to think about the social processes by which voices are heard, transformed and made symbolic. As important, I would argue, is to think about the way these same social processes can result in the loss of voice and the erasure of violence from history. If it is impossible to silence Miles Davis or his musical influence within broader jazz discourse and popular culture at large, then we need to work hard not to silence the women who suffered abuse at his hands. In moving towards a more critically engaged understanding of the legacy of Miles Davis and his acts of violence, therefore, I'm mindful of Sherrie Tucker's call for jazz studies to be treated as an unstable object where multiple voices coexist. Tucker reassures us that by treating an object of study as unstable, we do not necessarily lose our desire for the significance of that object, and yet, by enabling different voices to sound simultaneously, "we may open our ears to multiple and unexpected sources" and "listen for their connections and disconnections without rushing for resolution" (2005, 44). This approach advocates a non-patriarchal jazz studies of inclusion that is both critically engaged and open to contradiction and contestation. This perspective offers a vision of future scholarship, although the current reality is somewhat different. As we have seen, posthumous representations of Miles Davis have done little to provide a platform for alternative voices to emerge. As an explicit approach to hearing Davis posthumously, therefore, I would suggest that if his music continues to be heard, then his violence towards women should be sounded in equal measure.

As scholars, musicians and fans, it is important to stimulate discussions of artistic value alongside the politics of race, gender and representation. Equally, when consuming Miles posthumously we should include explicit statements about agency and his abusive behaviour when talking about his legacy or presenting his music in public. As I was concluding this chapter, I attended a virtual seminar, 'Jazz and Gender', hosted by York University Canada, where the figure of Miles Davis was ever present during the discussion.[11] Issues of masculinity and the problems of patriarchy were raised throughout, and the seminar triggered a plethora of responses from the online audience, with Miles providing the stimulus for several questions: Was it possible to cancel Miles? How can we engage in critiques of Miles without losing sight of the impact he had on generations of men and women? Surely art should be separated from the man? The general consensus was that many of these issues were incredibly complex and difficult to reconcile. Interestingly, the seminar began with the chair offering a land recognition statement, acknowledging the Indigenous ground on which York University is situated. Such announcements are used more and more frequently by scholars at conferences—even when they are visiting institutions overseas—as well as by politicians and artists, using introductory words to acknowledge Indigenous groups and leaders. Within this context there is a broader

[11] York University Department of Music hosted a virtual panel on March 18, 2021, titled 'Gender in Jazz: Narratives, Practice and Justice'. The panel was chaired by Noam Lemish and included contributions from Sherrie Tucker, Nichole Rustin-Paschale, Terri Lyne Carrington, and Sean Jones.

political will to take ethical responsibility, to acknowledge and redress former acts of violence and historical erasure, and to pay respects to local tribes. Respectful statements such as these often display a commitment to ethical work and reparative justice, to showing how communities can work better to support Indigenous people alongside research carried out on Indigenous lands. In the same spirit, I started this chapter with a warning, a statement that invites readers to take ethical responsibility for their engagement with Miles Davis and to acknowledge former acts of violence against women. In future, I would encourage others to make similar statements, whether in print or film, on album covers or prior to the performance of Davis' music.

If multiple voices are to sound equally, as Tucker suggests, we will need to dismantle the patriarchal systems, problematic masculine constructs and social processes by which genius figures are both celebrated and excused for their abusive acts. As patriarchal systems are not going to dismantle themselves, we need to take responsibility by acknowledging acts of violence publicly, thinking more about our complicity in sustaining problematic structures of power, and reconsidering our own listening in light of these issues. What *do* we hear when Miles' music is placed on the turntable and we're mindful of the crimes he committed? Perhaps Miles and his music should occupy a more muted place within jazz history, as the voices of the women he abused take centre stage. It's time to take responsibility. Change the record.

References

Baraka, Amiri. 1987. *The Music: Reflections on Jazz and Blues.* William Morrow.

Becker, Howard. 2018. *Outsiders: Studies in the Sociology of Deviance.* Free Press.

Benston, Kimberley. 2000. *Performing Blackness: Enactments of African-American Modernism.* Routledge.

Brody, Richard. 2019. '"Miles Davis: Birth of the Cool" and the Problem of the Archive'. *New Yorker*, August 29. https://www.newyorker.com/culture/the-front-row/review-miles-davis-birth-of-the-cool-and-the-problem-of-the-archive.

Buscatto, Marie. 2021. *Women in Jazz: Musicality, Femininity, Marginalization.* Routledge.

Carby, Hazel V. 1998. *Race Men.* Harvard University Press.

Carr, Ian. 1984. *Miles Davis: A Critical Biography.* Paladin Books.

Cleage, Pearl. 1994. *Deals with the Devil: And Other Reasons to Riot.* Ballantine Books.

Crenshaw, Kimberlé. 1991. 'Mapping the Margins: Intersectionality, Identity Politics, and Violence Against Women of Color'. *Stanford Law Review* 43 (6): 1241–1299.

Crouch, Stanley. 2006. *Considering Genius: Writings on Jazz.* Civitas Books.

Davis, Miles, with Quincy Troupe. 1990. *Miles: The Autobiography.* Picador.

DeVeaux, Scott. 1997. *The Birth of Bebop: A Social and Musical History.* University of California Press.

Early, Gerald. 2001. 'The Art of the Muscle: Miles Davis as American Knight and American Knave'. In *Miles Davis and American Culture*, edited by Gerald Early. Missouri Historical Society Press.

Flood, Michael. 2019. 'Men and #MeToo: Mapping Men's Responses to Anti-Violence Advocacy'. In *#MeToo and the Politics of Social Change*, edited by Bianca Fileborn and Rachel Loney-Howes. Palgrave Macmillan.

Gabbard, Krin. 1995. 'Signifyin(g) the Phallus: "Mo' Better Blues" and Representations of the Jazz Trumpet'. In *Representing Jazz*, edited by Krin Gabbard. Duke University Press.

Gabbard, Krin. 2009. 'How Many Miles? Alternate Takes on the Jazz Life'. In *Thriving on a Riff: Jazz and Blues Influences on African American Literature and Film*, edited by Graham Locke and David Murray. Oxford University Press.

Gebhardt, Nicholas. 2017. 'A Time for Jazz: Narrative and History in Alan Lomax's Mister Jelly Roll'. In *New Jazz Conceptions: History, Theory, Practice*, edited by Roger Fagge and Nicolas Pillai. Routledge.

Gray, Herman. 1995. 'Black Masculinity and Visual Culture'. *Callaloo* 18 (2): 401–405.

Heile, Bjorn. 2016. '*Miles Ahead*: A Film That Remains (Mostly) True to Jazz Legend Miles Davis'. *The Conversation*, April 27. https://theconversation.com/miles-ahead-a-film-that-remains-mostly-true-to-jazz-legend-miles-davis-58353.

hooks, bell. 2003. *We Real Cool: Black Men and Masculinity*. Routledge.

Jasmine Griffin, Farah. 2001. 'Ladies Sing Miles'. In *Miles Davis and American Culture*, edited by Gerald Early. Missouri Historical Society Press.

Jasmine Griffin, Farah and Salim Washington. 2013. *Clawing at the Limits of Cool: Miles Davis, John Coltrane and the Greatest Jazz Collaboration Ever*. Thomas Dunne Books [e-book].

Johnson, Bruce and Martin Cloonan. 2009. *Dark Side of the Tune: Popular Music and Violence*. Ashgate.

Kent, Nick. 2009. 'Lightening Up with the Prince of Darkness'. In *Miles on Miles: Interviews and Encounters with Miles Davis*, edited by Paul Maher. A Capella Books.

Lipsitz, George. 2009. '"What's Race Got to Do with It?" Remembering Ike Turner (1931–2007)'. *Popular Music and Society* 32 (1): 117–121.

Mailer, Norman. 1999. 'The White Negro'. In *Keeping Time: Readings in Jazz History*, edited by Robert Walser. Oxford University Press.

Mergner, Lee. 2017. 'Inside Stanley Nelson, Jr.'s New Miles Davis Documentary'. *JazzTimes*, June 7, 2017. https://jazztimes.com/features/interviews/inside-stanley-nelson-jr-s-new-miles-davis-documentary/.

Monson, Ingrid. 2001. 'Miles, Politics and Image'. In *Miles Davis and American Culture*, edited by Gerald Early. Missouri Historical Society Press.

Mosse, George L. 1996. *The Image of Man: The Creation of Modern Masculinity*. Oxford University Press.

Nisensen, Eric. 1996. *'Round About Midnight: A Portrait of Miles Davis*. Da Capo Press.

Raine, Sarah. 2019. 'Keychanges at Cheltenham Jazz Festival: Issues of Gender in the UK Jazz Scene'. In *Towards Gender Equality in the Music Industry: Education, Practice and Strategies for Change*, edited by Catherine Strong and Sarah Raine. Bloomsbury Academic.

Rustin-Paschal, Nichole. 2017. *The Kind of Man I Am: Jazz Masculinity and the World of Charles Mingus*. Wesleyan University Press.

Strong, Catherine and Emma Rush. 2018. 'Musical Genius and/or Nasty Piece of Work? Dealing with Violence and Sexual Assault in Accounts of Popular Music's Past'. *Continuum* 32 (5): 569–580.

Szwed, John. 2003. *So What: The Life of Miles Davis*. Arrow Books.

Tucker, Sherrie. 2005. 'Deconstructing the Jazz Tradition: The "Subjectless Subject" of New Jazz Studies'. *The Source: Challenging Jazz Criticism* 2: 31–46.

Whyton, Tony. 2010. *Jazz Icons: Heroes, Myths and the Jazz Tradition*. Cambridge University Press.

Woolf, Janet. 1993. *The Social Production of Art*. Macmillan.

Filmography

Cheadle, Don, dir. 2015. *Miles Ahead.* Sony Pictures Classics.
Mann, Michael, dir. 2004. *Collateral.* Paramount Pictures.
Nelson, Stanley, Jr., dir. 2019. *Miles Davis: Birth of the Cool.* Davis Raynes Productions/Mad Dog Pictures.

2

"Just Kickin' That Doo-Bop Sound"

Miles Davis, Jazz and Hip-Hop

Roger Fagge

Jazz has had a long relationship with the human voice, most obviously through the great jazz vocalists including Louis Armstrong, Billie Holiday and Ella Fitzgerald. However, when hip-hop emerged in the late 1970s, and with its popularity exploding in the following decades, this seemed to many a dramatic musical and cultural break in jazz history and occasioned disagreements in the jazz and wider community. This was in spite of the fact that there were many examples of spoken or rhythmic vocals within jazz prior to this, including scat singing. For example, Iain Ellis (2005) has suggested Cab Calloway could be seen as one of the precursors for rap: "In style, persona, lyrical purpose, and rhythmic priority, a bricolage of hip-hop ingredients can be discerned in this Baltimore maverick from the 1930s swing era". And of course Armstrong, Fitzgerald and Louis Jordan, among others, used vocal verbal variety in their output.

As Elijah Wald (2014) has shown, the 'Dozens' saw verbal sparring and rhythmic use of language on the street from the early 1900s that could be traced back to African rituals and can be seen as a precursor for rap. Jazz also had a history of interlinking with poetry, most particularly during the Harlem Renaissance and the later Black Arts Movement. A good example of this is the poet Langston Hughes, whose 1925 poem 'The Weary Blues' had a musician as the subject matter and was performed live with a jazz band. The 1958 performance with the Doug Parker Band on CBS Vancouver has been viewed nearly 250,000 times on YouTube (Hughes 1958). Similarly, popular writer Jack Kerouac, the so-called King of the Beats, was influenced both culturally and stylistically by jazz, including calling his writing style 'Spontaneous Bop Prosody'. In December 1957, following the publication of *The Dharma Bums*, Kerouac planned a three-week residency at the Village Vanguard in New York, backed by jazz musicians. However, the

Roger Fagge, *"Just Kickin' That Doo-Bop Sound"* In: *Rethinking Miles Davis*. Edited by: Roger Fagge, Nicolas Pillai, and Tim Wall, Oxford University Press. © Oxford University Press 2026. DOI: 10.1093/9780190085834.003.0002

residency ended prematurely due to the author's drinking and liberal use of Benzedrine. Three albums were subsequently recorded, the first of which, *Poetry for the Beat Generation* (1958 released 1959), included 'October in the Railroad Earth', which had Steve Allen accompanying on piano. The second album, *Blues and Haikus*, saw Kerouac accompanied by Al Cohn and Zoot Sims (Clark 1997, 166–170; Fagge 2019, 7–18).

By the end of the 1960s, further explorations in the spoken word and jazz took place, including through the Black Arts Movement. As Dorian Lynskey has pointed out, "The Last Poets, like the Watts Prophets and Gil Scott-Heron, operated at the nexus of black America's two most radical art forms: poetry and jazz" (2011, 232). The Last Poets and Scott-Heron experimented along similar lines, mixing rhythmic poetry and jazz-influenced music, and bringing in politics, more revolutionary in the case of the former. Whilst both have been seen as precursors for hip-hop, the latter has sometimes been seen as the Godfather of rap, although others have rightly pointed out he was much more than this (NME Blog 2011; Hamilton 2011, 213; Dalton 2000).

Despite these precedents, the emergence of hip-hop and its relationship with jazz was controversial, not least when an idiosyncratic and important figure like Miles Davis engaged with it. Matters were further complicated by the fact that the resulting album, *Doo-Bop*, was released posthumously on 30 June 1992, and was in the conventional sense Davis' final album. It was recorded whilst he was experiencing ongoing illness and remained unfinished at the time of his death in September 1991, subsequently completed by producer Easy Mo Bee. The issue of 'lateness' is discussed in the introduction to this book, but there are additional considerations for albums completed after an artist's death. Issues of authenticity and artistic vision, as well as, for some, morality, are relevant here. Albums released in similar circumstances are often treated with a slightly lighter touch by critics, out of respect for the artist concerned and in some cases as an attempt at providing a longer perspective on an artist's career. For example, Johnny Cash's 'American Series', which was started towards the end of his life, with releases continuing after his death, received strong reviews and awards which took into account the fact that they were final recordings by the artist (Wilde 2004). Jim Morrison's *American Prayer* (1978) also had a resetting of an artist's work after their death. The latter album placed spoken-word recordings from 1969–1970 with later recordings by the Doors (although this received mixed reviews) (Tosches 1979). Other posthumous albums by artists who died at the height of their career include Notorious B.I.G.'s *Life After Death*, which not only drew acclaim but helped underline Biggie's role as one of the most significant figures in hip-hop (Fadele 1997). Joy Division's *Closer* and Elliott Smith's *From a Basement on the Hill* likewise passed into history as important works, in part due to the fact that Ian Curtis, lead singer of Joy Division, and Smith both took their own lives after recording the albums (Murray 1980; Rogers 2004). As technology has moved on and sampling and related technology has become more widespread, this issue has become less significant than in the 1990s. Hip-hop has of course been influential in this regard and illustrates the more complex meanings of authenticity in popular music.

Doo-Bop was always going to be controversial, given its content and as the culmination of the career of one of the most important figures in American musical history. As we shall see, the reviews were mixed, although perhaps inevitably the album won a Grammy in 1993 for the best R&B instrumental performance. The rest of this chapter will explore the making of the album, the critical reaction to it, and the wider critical climate surrounding Miles Davis and hip-hop which may have impacted the contemporary and historical view of the album. It will also consider the broader issue of the connection between jazz and hip-hop, and the significance of generational differences in this regard. The aim is to place *Doo-Bop* in context.

The Album

By 1991 Miles Davis' health was worsening, and he remained musically restless as he had done since his return from his late 1970s hiatus. Most writers suggest that Miles was still keen that his music reach the black community and especially black youth, Martha Bayles writing that in his later years his "final gambit was to market himself as a black youth idol" (2001a, 163). George Cole (2005) has suggested that *Doo-Bop* came out of a "creative" surge at end of Davis' life, encouraged by others in jazz who were beginning to explore hip-hop. Other factors also came into play, including Davis' desire to rekindle his broader popular appeal as well as to create music that would get radio plays and provide an income (307–309).

In many ways Miles' interest in hip-hop was not unexpected given his willingness throughout his career to work with contemporary strands of black popular music. Hip-hop had of course emerged during the 1970s, and rapidly became a global force in world music. Popular with young people, both black and white, the generational division was widened by the emergence of gangsta rap in the mid- to late 1980s with Schoolly D, Ice T and NWA's influential album *Straight Outta Compton* (1988). Conservative and liberal critics, including from within the black community, joined in on an attack on hip-hop, and the press attention encouraged generalisations and a gross simplification about what hip-hop actually was. From its earliest days hip-hop drew on various sources and took a variety of forms, and many MCs were not 'gangsta'. There was a failure to understand rap lyrics, which were often read as autobiography rather than fiction, and the lyrical dexterity and artistic and political ambition at work in certain numbers were lost in the media-fuelled hysteria. Public Enemy and De La Soul were just two of the artists who rejected gangsta and explored lyrical and artistic complexity. Others, including MC Easy Mo Bee, who would eventually work on *Doo-Bop*, were doing likewise.[1]

Miles stepped into this mini culture war, seeing hip-hop clearly as the music of the streets. In his *Autobiography* he noted that in the early 1980s, "some of the most interesting stuff was happening" in rock, and that he also particularly liked Prince, who he had first heard around 1982 and was "playing the most exciting music" at that time. He also saw the potential in hip-hop: "I thought some of the things being done in rap music might get to be real interesting, but that was a little ways off" (Davis with Troupe 1990, 343). By the end of the decade he was keeping "artistic juices flowing" and was considering writing a play or musical; he had also "been experimenting with some rap songs as there's some heavy rhythms up in that music". He noted that Max Roach said the next Charlie Parker would come from rap, and that "sometimes you can't get those rhythms out of your head". He also noted that musicians could draw on great music in recent decades from Coltrane and Davis himself, and from Stravinsky and Bernstein, "but it's still a black thing that is leading the way, like breakdancing, hip-hop and rap" (380, 390). The fact that hip-hop was definitely music with black origins in some ways answered criticisms of his earlier electric work which had suggested he was pandering to white rock music.

Miles wasn't the only jazz artist who was looking at hip-hop. There had been a number of interactions, reciprocated by hip-hop artists who were looking at sources of musical inspiration other than the funk that was most

[1] On the debates around hip-hop, see Dyson (2010), Neal (2002), Rose (1994, 2008), and Watkins (2005). Public Enemy were openly critical of gangster rap and also presented an articulate line on black nationalism, including musically ambitious songs like the lyrical and musically complex 'Black Steel in the Hour of Chaos' from the album *Fear of a Black Planet* (1989).

prevalent in this period. In 1983, Herbie Hancock's single 'Rockit' used scratching, and Roach was working with Fab Five Freddy, who was helping the older jazz musician understand the world of hip-hop. Indeed Roach would later get Freddy to rap over Miles' late 1950s quintet at a memorial to the trumpeter, which "raised the hackles of some of Roach's peers in the jazz world" (Jenkins 2019; Guilliatt 1993). Stetsasonic also began exploring the link between jazz and hip-hop in the mid-1980s, including 'Talkin' All That Jazz' (1988), with Daddy O noting that "the way jazz musicians created then is how hip-hoppers create now. They would go with a feeling and take pieces from here and there. And so do we" (McAdams and Nelson 1992). Similarly, Mike Carr's jazz fusion band Cargo released 'Jazz Rap' on *History of Jazz* (1985). Later, Gang Starr's (including the influential MC Guru) *No More Mr. Nice Guy* (1989) was followed by a collaboration with Branford Marsalis on 'Jazz Thing' for the soundtrack of Spike Lee's 1990 movie, *Mo Better Blues*. As Tom Perchard has pointed out, it is ironic that this track has jazz history as its subject but was mostly based on Kool and the Gang's 'Duji' (2011, 296). Tentative moves in the direction of hip-hop by Quincy Jones on *Back on the Block* (1989) included hip-hop artists Ice T, Melle Mel and others, and Miles played on 'Jazz Corner of the World'. Furthermore, the critically acclaimed A Tribe Called Quest's *People's Instinctive Travels and the Paths of Rhythm* (1990), followed by *The Low End Theory* (1991), both had jazz elements. They included guest Ron Carter playing bass on the track 'Verses from the Abstract'. (Carter had of course played in Miles Davis' second "great quintet'.) The album has jazz inflections, and the single taken from the album, 'Jazz, We Got It', used Blue Note iconography on the sleeve. However, the jazz connections on the album have been overstated, including the idea that Carter's appearance provided a form of jazz validation of hip-hop. Indeed, when he was asked to appear, Carter had to check with his son about who the band was. He agreed to join so long as there were no profanities on the track, illustrating perhaps a sign of cultural differences between the purveyors of jazz and hip-hop (Batey 2011).[2]

Miles' interest in hip-hop was also encouraged by conversations with his friend Russell Simmonds, co-founder in 1984 with Rick Rubin of the influential Def Jam label. Miles and Simmonds had discussions about how hip-hop records were produced, and Cole suggests this appealed to Miles after

[2] There's an interesting interview with Carter (2020), where he describes getting involved with the album.

his doubts over aspects of recording *Amandla*, including the control of production, limits on his own playing, and the cost of making the record. Davis, he suggested, wanted something "simpler" (Cole 2005, 307–309).

Ian Carr pointed out that Gordon Meltzer was much more than Davis' tour manager by this point, overseeing his career and becoming executive producer on the project (1998, 259). Davis was seeking a collaborator to fulfil the role played by Marcus Miller in putting the tracks together. After talking with various figures, including Chuck D and Flavor Flav of Public Enemy, Davis decided on Easy Mo Be, as he liked "True Fresh MC" on GZA *Words from the Genius* album. Easy Mo Be recalled, "Miles kept playing that again and again". He was only vaguely aware of who Davis was and became nervous about Davis' reputation and behaviour after meeting him. It worked out fine, though, as the two got along well (Carr 1998, 529; Cole 2005, 311–316).

Davis initially had thoughts about doing a double album of hip-hop and R&B, but was turned down. He had talked to producer Sid Reynolds and John Bingham, as well as Chuck D and Flavor Flav. There was also consideration about using some of the unfinished tracks Prince sent Davis in January 1991. Davis had used some of these in a live setting (most notably 'Penetration'), but not in recordings (Cole 2005, 313–320; Carr 1998, 329; Szwed 2002, 398).[3] The *Rubberband* sessions, recorded between October 1985 and January 1986, remained unfinished after Warner Bros. weren't impressed and decided not to release them (Cole 2005, 205–225). *Rubberband* was eventually released in September 2019 and, like *Doo-Bop*, drew mixed reviews. That album raises similar questions about work being completed after an artist's death, in this case 28 years later. Davis' nephew Vince Willburn Jr. worked with original producers Randy Hall and Attala Zane Giles, and the vocals were by Lalah Hathaway and Ledisi in place of Chaka Khan and Al Jarreau (Fordham 2019).

The recording sessions for *Doo-Bop* were held at Unique recording studios. Carr suggests that Miles listened to Easy Mo Bee's tracks and then, "when the spirit took him", played over the top, rather like a vocal line (Carr 1998, 329; Cole 2005, 314–315). Six tracks were completed before Davis' death on 28 September 1991, but only the 'Doo-Bop' song was in its final mix; the others were in an earlier, rough mix. Davis also left two unaccompanied solos (Cole 2005, 316). After Miles' death, Easy Mo Bee and others were

[3] Cole suggests that Prince wasn't happy for the tracks to be used for *Doo-Bop* "because [the] relationship between Prince and Warner Bros had deteriorated badly" (2005, 313–320).

keen to continue with the project, but there was not enough music for a full set, so the latter put together 'High Speed Chase' and 'Fantasy' from parts of two tracks on the *Rubberband* sessions. The album tracks included various samples and influences, including Chocolate Milk on 'Mystery', Kool and the Gang on 'Doo-Bop', James Brown on 'Blow', Gene Ammons on 'Duke Booty', and Donald Byrd on 'High Speed Chase' (Cole 2005, 322–340).

Critical Reaction to *Doo-Bop*

After the release of *Doo-Bop*, Easy Mo Bee said, "The album fell under the heaviest criticism", drawing mixed reviews from both jazz and hip-hop critics and fans (Cole 2005, 334–335). The reviews, however, were more mixed than this comment suggests. In *The Independent* in July 1992, Richard Williams, pointing to the fact the album was completed after Davis' death, asked, "Who knows what Miles would have thought about the way his playing is placed over the samples, the bragging raps . . . and the synthetic drum tracks. And, to be blunt, these pieces provoke trumpet improvisations displaying a rhythmic banality that was never remotely discernible in Miles' pre-electric playing". Conceding that Miles "wanted to stay connected to the street, and this is a logical chapter to add to his extraordinary story", Williams concluded, "If you're happy to stick with what he did between 1945 and 1969, don't touch it".

Don Snowdon (1992) in the *Los Angeles Times* was more mixed in his views; he gave the record two and a half stars out of four and suggested that *Doo-Bop* "succeeds only in fits and starts", although that was "probably more a result of this being a first-time venture than of the strength of Davis' playing or the appropriateness of the hip-hop context". Snowdon zeroed in on the what he saw as the "colorless" nature of some tracks and criticised the "seriously lame delivery of a rap extolling Davis' virtues", which he claimed severely undercut the title track. The *Time* review in August 1992 was even more critical, calling the album "a miss by miles" and noting that the "*unfinished* album, Doo-Bop, recorded with the rapper Easy Mo Bee, merely skims the rich possibilities of a synthesis. . . . [T]he numbers have a slapped-together, disconnected feeling, like a long-distance correspondence between strangers". Greg Sandow (1992) in *Entertainment Weekly* wrote that "all too quickly the album starts to *sound* like elegant aural wallpaper, background music for the VIP room of a sleek new night spot". He also focused on the raps: "Dorky added raps—one of them limply calls Miles 'a multitalented and gifted musician / Who can play any position'—hardly help".

The critical opinion was generally negative in later reviews as well, with Martha Bayles (2001a) suggesting that *Doo Bop* "impresses neither as hip-hop nor as jazz", although she did point out that, "to Davis's credit, neither does it pander to the gangsta image then grabbing the headlines". Bayles was later more positive about *Doo-Bop*, calling it "a worthy finale" even though it wasn't a masterpiece (2001a, 169). John Szwed in his *So What* biography paid little attention to the album; he said Davis' playing was good, but "it was an undistinguished hip-hop album and despite some later remixed versions, it never caught on" (2002, 398). Reviewing the Warner Years collection in 2012, Jeff Dayton-Johnson offered a more balanced view; after singling out once again the raps on *Doo-Bop* as "mostly fawning panegyrics to Davis [that] have not aged well", he credited Easy Mo Bee's production and Davis' playing for being surprisingly strong, calling 'Chocolate Chip' "a particularly effective mixture of sampling, beat and trumpet soloing".

Not only did some of the reviews have positive remarks; some saw the album from a broader perspective. Mark Rowland (1992) in *Musician* magazine suggested that whilst it had the "feel of an unfinished project" at times, that didn't undermine its significance: "For younger ears weaned on modern beats, it's also an inviting opening into one of the great cornucopias of American music. Which could be just as the master of timing planned it. Like most everything Miles Davis played, the music of *Doo-Bop* is cool and warm, beautiful and true". In *The Black Collegian* in 1992, J. Reynolds declared, "*Doo-Bop* brings with it some of the funkiest grooves a jazz album has ever offered". There was no mention of the quality or not of the raps, but Reynolds commented, "Well Miles was always one to stretch the bounds of music, and this album perhaps demonstrates this best". The review concluded, "The only down side of this CD is that there aren't enough cuts". Here was someone who would have enjoyed the proposed double album that was turned down.

Richard Cook suggested that the fact that Miles left only about 30 minutes of music made this "a cadaverous exercise" and that, whilst there were some good points, even when Davis was seemingly engaged, "no one can know how much of this is down to astute editing and overdubbing". An example of this was the way Easy Mo Bee used elements of two tracks from the *Rubberband* sessions to create new tracks for the album, 'Fantasy' and 'High Speed Chase'. On the latter Cook pointed out that "little did any listener know that it was actually a solo he had played six years earlier", although it was "one of the best things on the record" (2005, 308). This raises the issue of authenticity, as Davis' death meant that he was unable to listen to the new tracks as well as the finished album. Cole suggests that Meltzer consulted the Davis family about reusing the *Rubberband* tracks, and that Miles would have been okay with the tracks being released in this fashion. Meltzer told Cole, "As regards stuff coming out without Miles approving the finished tracks, I swear that Miles would have loved it because that's where he was going and that's what he wanted. He would have been fine about it" (Cole 2005, 332). Meltzer knew Davis well, and the latter had used various production techniques on recent albums, including Miller's work on *Tutu*. Davis was in some ways a collaborative player, and when Cook asked him in 1985 about band performances, Davis responded, "I keep playing and editing and playing and editing myself out . . . and I try and stop on a high point to leave someone else something to do". Davis continued, "When I'm playing, I'm never through. It's unfinished. I like to find a place to leave for someone else to finish it. That's where the high comes in". Davis was talking about the band at live performances, but arguably this represented part of his philosophy of working in a group (Cook 1985).

Critical Climate

The negative response to *Doo-Bop* was not surprising, given the reaction to Davis' albums since the comeback in 1980, and indeed criticisms dating back to fusion and *Bitches Brew*. If we recall, Williams suggested in his review that Davis circa 1945–1969 may be the only period worth listening to. This was a common argument by the 1990s. Part of the problem was the long-standing debate over commercial versus art music and, as David Ake has pointed out, cultural hierarchies in music which privileged jazz over other music, like hip-hop (2010, 4–5). Stanley Crouch put this point powerfully in his *New Republic* review of Davis' autobiography, when he wrote that "beyond the terrible performances and terrible recordings, Davis also became the most remarkable licker of moneyed boots in the music business" (Crouch 1990, 30–37). And if fusion was at the heart of this sell-out, seen as dancing with the rock audience, there was even more antipathy and jealous guarding of the genre boundaries by members of the jazz community, who watched with dismay Davis' collaboration with hip-hop. Hip-hop was seen as a crass music form that had abandoned the aesthetics and political values of black America, and the use of sampling and electronic drum machines underlined what was seen as a difference between authentic and inauthentic, commercialised music pandering to the lowest common denominator.

Within jazz, Wynton Marsalis and Stanley Crouch were two of the most open and long-standing critics of the cultural and musical impact of hip-hop. Of course, this is probably not surprising as their dislike of more recent free jazz and fusion was well known. In an interesting interview occasioned by the release of *Plantation to Penitentiary* (2007), Marsalis spoke at length about his antipathy towards hip-hop. Interviewer John Lewis (2007) noted that they were "10 minutes into an angry denunciation of hip-hop, and he's just hitting his stride", when Marsalis replied, "I call it 'ghetto minstrelsy.' Hip-hop substitutes the plantation for the streets. Now you have to say that you're from the streets, you shot some brothers, you went to jail. Rappers have to display the correct pathology". He continued, "Rap has become a safari for people who get their thrills from watching African-American people debase themselves, men dressing in gold, calling themselves stupid names. like Ludacris or 50 Cent, spending money on expensive fluff, using language like 'bitch' and 'ho' ". The discussion that followed was made more interesting by the fact that the Marsalis album had a spoken-word/rap final track, 'Where Y'all At', which has a dig about rap, suggesting it has undermined political discourse: "even the rap game started out critiquin' / but now it's all about killing and freakin'" (Marsalis 2007, track 7). Marsalis differentiated his use of rap from hip-hop, suggesting it dated back to an earlier form of street rhyming (Lewis 2007).

Crouch kept up his attack on hip-hop, writing in the *Jazz Times* in 2002, "Rap is finally being recognised as the minstrel update that it is. . . . Its popularity among white suburban kids has nothing to do with 'hip-hop culture'; it has to do with what I have called 'audio safaris.' . . . [T]here had always been whites willing to pay Negroes top dollar if they dedicated their careers to proving the inferiority of black to white". About hip-hop artists who were reaching out to jazz, he said dismissively, "[W]e should not care for some rapper who claims to be influenced by jazz. But we should laugh at those who make artistic claims for fusion". As Tricia Rose has pointed out, such criticisms of hip-hop echoed the resistance to jazz earlier in the 20th century, when critics saw it as " 'jungle music,' a primitive, dangerous African-based influence on American society", before it was recognised as a creative art form (2008, 66–67).

As was mentioned earlier, Miles walked into the sometimes acrimonious debate over hip-hop, and it is important to remember that many saw hip-hop as a much broader and complex music than these criticisms suggest. The album became embroiled in these debates, and it was viewed within this prism. Despite the fact that hip-hop had been around since the late 1970s, the debate rumbled on, usually with more heat than light, into the 21st century. Some contested more specifically the arguments made by Marsalis and Crouch. Touré (2017), for example, responded to similar comments by Crouch in a later debate, suggesting that Crouch was trading in stereotypes and generalising for a whole movement from the actions of a few: "It's easy to point at a segment of any culture, especially the basest part, and make a derisive point about the whole group". He offered a more nuanced argument, conceding that "of course there's pathetic buffoonery and modern minstrelsy inside the big tent called hip hop", including a problematic approach to gender: "The greater misogyny is that hip hop as a whole (industry and fans) is too comfortable with women being at the periphery of the conversation". However, hip-hop was "also like a teen . . . sometimes surg[ing] toward a more mature place", including an engagement with politics: "Though hip hop isn't always the most evolved culture, it is the most politically involved musical culture in modern history". This last point has been taken up by various writers in the growing field of hip-hop studies, including Michael Eric Dyson, who pointed out that the criticism of hip-hop was in part generational; an older generation with different cultural values see hip-hop as celebrating materialism, violence and street fashions, compared with civil rights–era soul music and jazz, collective politics and elements of respectability. Dyson suggested that this argument missed the diversity in hip-hop, including 'conscious' rap that had a political angle through consciousness-raising. Dyson was critical of aspects of hip-hop but pointed out the way the media focused on violence in hip-hop, when violence was a much wider issue in US culture (2010, 61–120). Rose has similarly written widely and powerfully about the problematic aspects of hip-hop, but also its social and cultural significance (2008, 113–132).

There were other factors which affected the critical climate around Miles Davis by the early 1990s. As Eric Porter has shown, many saw Davis as the archetypal black genius, who some, including Crouch, accused of selling himself and the black community short. Rather than seeing his last years as signs of restless creativity, they saw his efforts as the embrace of commercial values. Porter suggested Crouch had moved away from a more radical 'unity music' view of jazz, instead looking at Armstrong, Ellington and Marsalis as key figures in articulating the democratic message of jazz. Davis was likewise in the past, and Crouch saw him as abandoning that message—as the "licker of moneyed boots" comment implies. Porter argued that for Crouch, *In a Silent Way* "marked the moment when Davis sold out". He continued, "By infusing his records with rock and funk rhythms and instrumentation Davis symbolised the ways African American artists, intellectuals and the black middle class in general rejected bourgeois convention, embraced cultural and moral relativism and bought into stereotypical images that the culture industry used to sell Black America". In these ways, Porter suggests Crouch saw Davis as representing "an unmitigated failure of black male genius" (2001, 142–143).

On a related note, Davis' unapologetic admission in his autobiography that he had been violent towards women dented his reputation. Pearl Cleage's *Mad at Miles*, published in 1990, linked Davis' violence against his partners to more general violence against women. This was taken up by others, including Crouch and journalist Greg Tate, who wrote about Davis, hip-hop and culture more generally. Shortly after Davis' death, Tate pointed out the musical and cultural importance of the man, quoting a friend who said, "Miles Davis was the black aesthetic". However, having read about his violence towards women, Tate wrote, "[M]uch as I loved Miles, I despised him after reading those incidents". Mimicking his autobiography, Tate added, "because I'd loathe any mufukuh who violated women the way he did and relished the way he did and relished the opportunity to tell the world about it. Miles may have swung like a champion but on that score he went out like a roach" (1992, 85–90).

Making Sense of *Doo-Bop*, Jazz and Hip-Hop

Doo-Bop is an interesting album which raises certain questions of genre and authenticity, as well as about Miles Davis' role in jazz and as an icon of black America. Whether it is a good album or not depends on the listener; it is a late album made by an artist who was unwell, and it should be viewed in that light. Similarly, the critics of the raps may overstate their case. As with lyrics more generally, raps are not poetry as such, as they are performed with a rhythmic backing track. Certain tropes (including bragging and bigging up) are part of hip-hop, as are tropes in other forms of music. Taking a lyric out of context and without its musical backing is somewhat reductive, whether in hip-hop or any other type of vocal performance.

Authenticity is also a subjective issue and is affected by the cultural climate surrounding music at the time. The fact that Miles died before he heard the music or had a chance to approve it would be significant to some but not to those used to production practices in other forms of music.[4]

Amid the debates over hip-hop and the questioning of Davis' role as an icon, jazz and hip-hop in the late 1980s were, as we have seen, making connections, and there were parallel debates about the musical compatibility of jazz and hip-hop. This was not a static debate, however. In the early 1990s, when Davis stepped onto the scene, some saw the gap between the two genres as unbridgeable. However, as the two genres developed, and different generations moved into both, the connections have been enhanced and also become less controversial. Branford Marsalis worked with hip-hop artists from the late 1980s, including playing on the longer version of Public Enemy's 'Fight the Power' and, as we saw earlier, with Gang Starr on 'The Jazz Thing' for *Mo Better Blues*. Marsalis told Cole that "jazz and hip-hop don't really mix but sensibilities occur, like a lot of shit we do has hip-hop sensibilities, but we're not playing hip-hop" (2005, 334–340). Marsalis elaborated on this theme when talking to the *Los Angeles Times* in early 1993, saying, "[M]ost rap groups and DJs don't even play live; most of it's done on tape. . . . [T]he reality is that most of these guys can't play music and don't have a musical sensibility, which is why they can take three harmonically opposed tracks and stick them together on the one thing". This was brought to a head when Marsalis "discovered the dangers of this balancing act when he got up on stage to jam with Gang Starr and realised that DJ Premier was scratch-mixing in a nebulous pitch somewhere between G and G-sharp. 'It was a train wreck,' recalls the saxophonist" (Guilliatt 1993). Cole quotes Stuart Nicholson when discussing the musical impact of hip-hop on jazz, the latter writing in 1997 that hip hop "robbed" jazz musicians of their "storytelling role" and the jazz musicians only added "ingredients of decoration rather than (being) an integral part of the music's overall construction" (Cole 2005, 336–337). Nicholson, an influential jazz scholar, in 2001 pointed out in the *New York Times* that whilst US jazz was stuck in a retro phase, European jazz was reaching out to drum'n'bass, techno and related dance music, with what he described then as "European new jazz", with figures like Nils Petter

[4] On authenticity, see Moore (2002).

Molvaer, Julien Lourau and the Esbjörn Svensson Trio. He contrasted this with the previous decade's jazz–hip-hop collaborations, writing, "Whilst there have been experiments by American Jazz Musicians in combining jazz and hip-hop, like Miles Davis' *Doo-Bop* . . . the results merely confirmed the seeming incompatibility of jazz and rap". The "seeming" may be significant, and Nicholson argues that musically drum'n'bass "is not too far removed from driving jazz rhythms and can easily accommodate jazz improvisation" (Nicholson 2001).

With hindsight, the suggestion of the musical incompatibility of jazz and hip-hop is too prescriptive and ignores the more fluid nature of the musical genres, with both jazz and hip-hop changing, adapting and including aspects of a widening palette of musical influences. A broader view of hip-hop as a cultural force also informs those who see things differently from the critics and others more sceptical of the music. For example, Williams also underlined the variety in hip-hop and suggests that some hip-hop artists saw jazz as a way of reaching out to a more intellectual and artistic form of music which differentiated them from both gangsta-rap and pop-rap (2010, 435–459). Perchard has also discussed the different motivations of hip-hop artists, some of whom sought to rescue jazz from what they saw as its popular oblivion, as well as fitting hip-hop into the canon of African American music (2011, 283–295).

Whatever the motivation, several artists followed this path in the 1990s: Ronny Jordan's *The Antidote* from the same year at *Doo-Bop* (1992), Digable Planets' *Reachin* and Guru's *Jazzmatazz* (1993), which was probably the most thoughtful and well-realised jazz–hip-hop album of the period. Jazz musicians involved in the project included Donald Byrd, Roy Ayers, Ronny Jordan, DC Lee, Courtney Pine and Branford Marsalis, and for the second album Guru added others, including Kenny Garrett, who was "a pleasure to work with. He used to play sax with Miles Davis, but is a cool young cat. Smooth man". There were clearly musical crossovers and a compatibility at work here, and a major aim of the project was to bring the older generation from jazz together with the younger hip-hop world. Guru said, "[T]he older jazz cats that we sampled for so long, we're bringing them to life letting people see who they really are. And we're letting the older crowd know that rap music isn't just a bunch of violent noise; that it's essential; that it's a tool; that it's a safety valve for society". Guru talked about working with Ramsey Lewis on the second album, and their discussions helped Lewis see hip-hop in a more positive light: "Ramsey had a lot to say about how jazz has evolved. And how rap evolved for him to have respect for it. He said before he just didn't know what it was about". Things didn't always work out this way with the jazz musicians. Guru commented, "It's funny, a lot of those same musicians who were cynical have changed their views since then. . . . [However,] some still haven't, but I'm not working with the ones who haven't". Musically his interest in working in jazz and hip-hop was based upon combining the "jazz method of improvising and hip-hop's freestyling" (Broughton 1995; Nicholson 2001; Cole 2005, 336). There would be later *Jazzmatazz* albums, which continued with collaborations. The mixing of generations, when it worked, was an important way of building a realistic acceptance for hip-hop in the jazz community and vice-versa.

Others collaborating in jazz–hip-hop in the early 1990s included Greg Osby and '3D Man'; some were involved in the acid-jazz movement that emerged in late 1980s London clubs. This included hip-hop as one of a variety of influences. Among others, The Brand New Heavies and Incognito, along with US3, were from the British scene, and Buckshot LeFonque and Digable Planets were part of the US scene (Snowboy 2009).[5] The late 1970s through to the 1990s saw the coming together of a number of music strands which influenced each other and had a tendency towards being more electronic, and to sometimes using forms of sampling. Funk, disco, house, dancehall and reggae from the 1970s linked to acid house and techno, jungle, UK garage, drum'n'bass, though to trip-hop, all of which drew from a wide musical vocabulary, including jazz and hip-hop among the mix of influences (Lawrence 2004; Farrugia 2012; James 2020; Hall 2018).

Jazz was also influential on hip-hop in less obvious ways. Jazz musician Donald Harrison recalled meeting the younger Christopher Wallace (who became famous as the Notorious B.I.G.); they started talking about music, and in the process became friends. Harrison described how Biggie became a jazz fan after hearing Cannonball Adderley and others, and told him that it influenced his rapping style (Michaels 2010).

The links between jazz and hip-hop were noted by the influential trade journal *Billboard* in August 1992, which argued that jazz–hip-hop was becoming a major force. What *Billboard* called "new jazz swing" (a name initially associated with Ronnie Jordan) included a variety of collaborations and cited *Doo-Bop* as influential. However, whilst jazz remained an influence, it turned out that producer Ali Shaheed Muhammad of A Tribe Called

[5] On the origins and early days of British acid/jazz, see Snowboy (2009).

Quest was partly right when he commented in the article that "this is the next phase that's gonna phase itself out" (McAdam and Nelson, 1992).

Jazz and hip-hop didn't disappear, though, and jazz remained part of the musical landscape of hip-hop, but with the proliferation of styles that emerged in the 1990s and beyond, as hip-hop became more successful and more complex. Soul and funk were the most common sources, and it is well known that James Brown is the most sampled artist. Jazz also became more outward-looking, and a generational shift occurred which saw a less structured approach to genre.

More recently the jazz and hip-hop link has become more prominent again, including in the award-winning, best-selling work of Kendrick Lamar, particularly the important *To Pimp a Butterfly* (2015). Kamasi Washington was musical director, and the bassist Thundercat, Robert Glasper and others jazz musicians played on the album. The point about later generations having a different musical horizon is important here. Washington (who has become a successful jazz figure in his own right) told the *Guardian*, "We've now got a whole generation of jazz musicians who have been brought up with hip-hop. We've grown up alongside rappers and DJs, we've heard this music all our life. We are as fluent in J Dilla and Dr Dre as we are in Mingus and Coltrane". Saxophonist Shabaka Hutchings has also pointed out the way that concepts around genre have become more fluid for this generation of musicians: "Guys like Wynton Marsalis were young players who were keen to be taken seriously by an older generation of jazz musicians, and keen to assert that jazz was a high art form. Mentioning reggae or hip-hop might seem to dilute that commitment. So you ended up with a somewhat dogmatic genre, one that was quite self-contained". He continued, "The difference now is that my generation don't feel the need to solely identify ourselves with one genre. We've grown up with rave and electronica and hip-hop, and have no qualms about integrating that into our music. And those artists who have collaborated with Kendrick Lamar are perfect examples of that" (Lewis 2016).

Electronics and samples are also now an established part of popular music and don't raise the same issues of authenticity. Rob Turner of Go Go Penguin noted that drummers often incorporate hip-hop beats: "It shows you how jazz musicians have thoroughly internalised the hip-hop they've grown up with". Alongside Lamar and Washington, other examples are Badbadnotgood, who have worked with Ghostface Killah from the Wu Tang Clan on *Sour Soul* (2015), and Robert Glasper's *Everything's Beautiful* (2016) on Miles Davis, linking jazz soul and hip-hop. The recent wave of British jazz, spearheaded by the likes of Hutchings, Nubya Garcia, Alfa Mist and Moses Boyd, illustrates a mixing of various influences, including hip-hop. And this is only scratching the surface, as hip-hop, jazz, house and various other music continue to share a wide musical palette (Hutchinson 2018).

Conclusion

Miles Davis was restless, and it is no surprise that he worked with hip-hop musicians both because of an interest in attracting a younger audience and the fact that there were musical synergies. Although he was unwell, and died before the album was completed, *Doo-Bop* attracted a lot of attention and had an influence on other musicians and fans thinking in similar ways. Once again, therefore, Miles was there at an important juncture in the development of popular music. Of course, jazz and hip-hop collaborations were already happening and would have developed anyway, and although *Doo-Bop* may not have been a classic album, it raised and sometimes answered questions about the relationship between the two genres. The way the album was recorded and finished and notions of authenticity were more significant when it was released than in the years that followed. Perhaps fans and critics were always too precious about these issues, as Miles had often worked collectively and sometimes let others develop and even finish his work. In that sense *Doo-Bop* was less unusual than some critics suggested. It wasn't even a final word, for in contemporary music there is an ever-increasing series of 'official' bootlegs, outtakes, and different versions among later releases. When Miles told the NME in 1985, "When I'm playing, I'm never through. It's unfinished", he was right in more than one sense (Cook 1985). *Doo-Bop* will be worth 'digging' for many years to come, both for what it does and for what it doesn't say.

References

Ake, David A. 2010. *Jazz Matters: Sound, Place, and Time Since Bebop*, 4–5. University of California Press.

Bayles, Martha. 2001a. 'Miles Davis and the Double Audience'. In *Miles Davis and American Culture*, edited by Gerald Early. Missouri Historical Society Press.

Bayles, Martha. 2001b. 'Miles Davis: The Chameleon of Cool. An Innovator with Duelling Ambitions. (A Look Back at the Life of the Controversial Jazz Trumpeter)'. *The New York Times*, May 13, 2001. (0362-4331)AR1.

Batey, Angus. 2011. '20 Years On: A Tribe Called Quest's *The Low End Theory* Revisited'. *The Quietus*, October 10. Rock's Back Pages. http://www.rocksbackpages.com/Library/Article/20-years-on-a-tribe-called-quests-ithe-low-end-theoryi-revisited-.

Broughton, Frank. 1995. 'Guru: Reality Bites'. *Hip-Hop Connection*, July. Rock's Back Pages. http://www.rocksbackpages.com/Library/Article/guru-reality-bites.

Carr, Ian. 1998. *Miles Davis: The Definitive Biography*. Rev. ed. Harper Collins.

Carter, Ron. 2020. 'Bassist Ron Carter Talks About His Work with a Tribe Called Quest'. YouTube, March 16. https://youtu.be/SMXQCwmaU5Q.

Clark, Tom. 1997. *Jack Kerouac: A Biography*. Plexus.

Cole, George. 2005. *The Last Miles: The Music of Miles Davis, 1980–91*. Equinox.

Cook, Richard. 1985. 'Miles Davis: Miles Runs the Voodoo Down'. *New Musical Express*, July 13. http://www.rocksbackpages.com/Library/Article/miles-davis-miles-runs-the-voodoo-down.

Cook, Richard. 2005. *It's About That Time: Miles Davis off and on the Record*. Atlantic Books.

Crouch, Stanley. 1990. 'Play the Right Thing'. *The New Republic* 202 (7): 30–37.

Crouch, Stanley. 2002. 'Four Letter Words: Rap and Fusion'. *Jazz Times*, March. http://jazztimes.com/articles/20011-four-letter-words-rap-fusion.

Dalton, D. 2000. 'The Last Poets: Progenitors of Rap'. *Gadfly*. http://0-search.ebscohost.com.pugwash.lib.warwick.ac.uk/login.aspx?direct=true&db=edsrbp&AN=edsrbp.228&site=eds-live.

Davis, Miles, with Quincy Troupe. 1990. *Miles: The Autobiography*. Picador.

Dayton-Johnson, Jeff. 2012. 'Miles Davis: 1986–91 The Warner Years'. *Jazz Times*, January 18. https://www.allaboutjazz.com/miles-davis-1986-1991-the-warner-years-by-jeff-dayton-johnson.php.

Dyson, M. E. 2010. *Know What I Mean? Reflections on Hip-Hop*. Basic Books.

Ellis, Iain. 2005. 'Cab Calloway: Original Rapper'. *Pop Matters*, November 17. https://www.popmatters.com/ellis051118-2496099263.html.

Fadele, D. 1997. 'The Notorious B.I.G.: *Life After Death* (Arista)'. *New Musical Express*, April 12. Rock's Back Pages. http://www.rocksbackpages.com/Library/Article/the-notorious-big-ilife-after-deathi-arista.

Fagge, Roger. 2019. 'The Politics, Aesthetics and Dissonance of Music in Everyday Life'. *Jazz Research Journal* 13: 7–13.

Farrugia, R. 2012. *Beyond the Dance Floor: Female DJs, Technology and Electronic Dance Music Culture*. Intellect.

Fordham, John. 2019. Review of *Rubberband*. *The Guardian*, August 30. https://www.theguardian.com/music/2019/aug/30/miles-davis-rubberband-review.

Guilliatt, Richard. 1993. 'Jazz and Rap Take the Plunge'. *Los Angeles Times*, January 31. https://www.latimes.com/archives/la-xpm-1993-01-31-ca-800-story.html.

Hall, J. 2018. *Boys, Bass and Bother: Popular Dance and Identity in UK Drum 'n' Bass Club Culture*. Palgrave Macmillan.

Hamilton, Jack. 2011. 'Pieces of a Man'. *Transition (Kampala, Uganda)* 106: A112–A168.

Hughes, Langston. 1958. "The Weary Blues' on CBUT, 1958'. YouTube. https://www.youtube.com/watch?v=uM7HSOwJw20.

Hutchinson, Kate. 2018. 'The British Jazz Explosion: Meet the Musicians Rewriting the Rule Book'. *The Guardian*, April 8. https://www.theguardian.com/music/2018/apr/08/british-jazz-invasion-moses-boyd-matthew-halsall-nubya-garcia?CMP=share_btn_link.

Jenkins, Willard. 2019. 'Fab 5 Freddy: The Max Roach Influence'. *Jazz Times*, April 26. https://jazztimes.com/features/interviews/fab-5-freddy-the-max-roach-influence/.

James, M. 2020. *State of Bass: The Origins of Jungle/Drum & Bass*. Velocity Press.

Lawrence, T. 2004. *Love Saves the Day: A History of American Dance Music Culture, 1970–1979*. Duke University Press.

McAdams, J., and H. Nelson. 1992. 'Hip-Hop Puts Fresh Spin on Jazz'. *Billboard* 104: 34.

Lewis, John. 2007. 'The Shock of the New'. *The Guardian*, March 2. https://www.theguardian.com/music/2007/mar/02/jazz.

Lewis, John. 2016. 'How Kamasi, Kendrick and Co Gave Jazz a New Groove'. *The Guardian*, October 6. https://www.theguardian.com/music/2016/oct/06/new-cool-kamasi-kendrick-gave-jazz-new-groove.

Lynskey, Dorian. 2011. *33 Revolutions per Minute*. Faber and Faber.

Marsalis, Wynton. 2007. *From the Plantation to the Penitentiary*. Blue Note.

Michaels, Sean. 2010. 'Revealed! Notorious BIG's Secret Jazz Education'. *The Guardian*, August 3. https://www.theguardian.com/music/2010/aug/03/notorious-big-secret-jazz-education.

Moore, A. 2002. 'Authenticity as Authentication'. *Popular Music* 21 (2): 209–223.

Murray, Charles Shaar. 1980. 'Joy Division: *Closer* (Factory)'. *New Musical Express*, July 19. Rock's Back Pages. http://www.rocksbackpages.com/Library/Article/joy-division-icloseri-factory.

Neal, M. A. 2002. *Soul Babies: Black Popular Culture and the Post-Soul Aesthetic*. Routledge.

Nicholson, Stuart. 2001. 'Europeans Cut in with a New Jazz Sound and Beat'. *New York Times*, June 6.

Nicholson, Stuart. 2014. *Jazz and Culture in a Global Age*. Northeastern University Press.

NME Blog. 2011. 'More Than the Godfather of Hip-Hop: Gil Scott-Heron Remembered'. May 28. https://www.nme.com/blogs/nme-blogs/more-than-the-godfather-of-hip-hop-gil-scott-heron-remembered-763662.

Perchard, Tom. 2011. 'Hip Hop Samples Jazz: Dynamics of Cultural Memory and Musical Tradition in the African American 1990s'. *American Music* 29 (3): 277–307.

Porter, Eric. 2001. "It's About That Time': The Response to Miles Davis' Electric Turn'. In *Miles Davis and American Culture*, edited by Gerald Early. Missouri Historical Society Press.

Reynold, J. 1992. 'Music Reviews'. *Black Collegian* 23 (1): 50.

Rogers, Jude. 2004. 'Elliott Smith: *From a Basement on the Hill* (Domino)'. *The Word*, November. Rock's Back Pages. http://www.rocksbackpages.com/Library/Article/elliott-smith-i-from-a-basement-on-the-hilli-domino.

Rose, Tricia. 1994. *Black Noise: Rap Music and Black Culture in Contemporary America*. University Press of New England.

Rose, Tricia. 2008. *The Hip Hop Wars: What We Talk About When We Talk About Hip Hop—and Why It Matters*. Basic Civitas.

Rowland, Mark. 1992. 'Miles Davis with Easy Mo Bee: *Doo-Bop* (Warner Bros.)'. *Musician*, June. Rock's Back Pages. http://www.rocksbackpages.com/Library/Article/miles-davis-with-easy-mo-bee-idoo-bopi-warner-bros.

Sandow, Greg. 1992. 'Doo-Bop'. http://www.ew.com/article/1992/08/21/doo-bop. visited August 19, 2016.

Snowboy. 2009. *From Jazz Funk and Fusion to Acid Jazz: The History of the UK Jazz Dance Scene*. Chaser.

Snowden, D. 1992. 'Miles Davis Leaves a Hip-Hop Finale'. *Los Angeles Times*, July 26. http://articles.latimes.com/1992-07-26/entertainment/ca-5112_1_miles-davis.

Szwed, J. F. 2002. *So What: The Life of Miles Davis*. William Heinemann.

Tate, Greg. 1992. *Flyboy in the Buttermilk: Essays on Contemporary America*. Simon & Schuster.

Time. 1992. 'At the End, a Miss by Miles—*Doo-Bop* by Miles Davis and Easy Mo Be 1992. August 10.

Tosches, Nick. 1979. 'The Doors: *An American Prayer*'. *Rolling Stone*, January 1. Rock's Back Pages. http://www.rocksbackpages.com/Library/Article/the-doors-i-an-american-prayeri.

Touré. 2017. 'The Daily Beast Hip-Hop Battle'. *Daily Beast*, July 14. https://www.thedailybeast.com/the-daily-beast-hip-hop-battle.

Wald, Elijah. 2014. *Talking 'bout Your Mama: The Dozens, Snaps, and the Deep Roots of Rap*. Oxford University Press.

Watkins, S. C. 2005. *Hip Hop Matters: Politics, Pop Culture, and the Struggle for the Soul of a Movement*. Beacon Press.

Wilde, Jon. 2004. 'Johnny Cash: *Unearthed* (American Recordings/Lost Highway)'. *Uncut*, January. Rock's Back Pages. http://www.rocksbackpages.com/Library/Article/johnny-cash-iunearthedi-american-recordingslost-highway.

Williams, J. A. 2010. 'The Construction of Jazz Rap as High Art in Hip-Hop Music'. *Journal of Musicology* 27 (4): 435–459.

Williams, Richard. 1992. 'Records'. *The Independent*, July 25. http://www.independent.co.uk/arts-entertainment/records-jazz-miles-davis-doo-bop-warner-bros-7599-26938-1535726.html.

3

Locating *Tutu*

Tim Wall

Released in 1986, *Tutu* was Miles Davis' first record on his new major label, Warner Bros.[1] It signalled the maturity of a creative working relationship with multi-instrumentalist and producer Marcus Miller, as part of a significant shift in the way Davis would be understood as a contemporary musician. In this chapter I explore the landscape of meaning in which the record emerged, an activity which enables us to understand Davis' continuing creative ambitions outside the jazz world and to place the recording's meaningfulness beyond the narrow scope in which it has most often been critically located. As many have subsequently noted, when compared with the detailed dissection afforded to Davis' recordings in the first 35 years of his career, *Tutu* and (even more noticeably) the music of his final years remain neglected in terms of scholarly attention.

The analysis in this chapter entwines with two other discussions in which *Tutu* emerges as significant within this book. The first relates to my analysis in chapter 4 of the meaningfulness of Davis' move from Columbia to Warner Bros. set within an exploration of the meaning of record labels within jazz music industry and culture. In both chapters, I utilise the idea of a 'map of meaning':[2] here to locate the *Tutu* album synchronically in the field of mid-1980s popular music; in the other chapter, to locate the move to Warner diachronically within the map of the US music industry over the four-decade length of the trumpeter's career as a band leader. The other discussion in which *Tutu* plays a significant part comes from my dialogue with Bobbie-Jane Gardner about ideas of collaboration, orchestration and the

[1] *Tutu*, Warner Bros. Records, 9 25490-2. Recorded at Le Gonks West, West Hollywood, CA, February 6, 1986; Capitol Tower, Los Angeles, February 10, 12, 13, 1986; Clinton Recording Studios, New York City, March 12–25, 1986. Released September 29, 1986.

[2] In using the term 'map of meaning', I reference ideas of semantic mapping, extended to music as a meaningful activity built around the relationship of one instance of music to another. I do not intend any connection to the work of clinical psychology or the study of belief. As will be apparent, I draw on wider ideas from semiology and critical discourse analysis in the approach I take in this chapter.

Tim Wall, *Locating* Tutu In: *Rethinking Miles Davis*. Edited by: Roger Fagge, Nicolas Pillai, and Tim Wall, Oxford University Press. © Oxford University Press 2026. DOI: 10.1093/9780190085834.003.0003

black aesthetic through which we explore Davis' collaboration with Miller and Tommy LiPuma, contrasting that with his work on *Miles Ahead* with Gil Evans and George Avakian 30 years before. In combination, these chapters offer three trajectories through which we can understand how a single recording, and a musical lifetime, are positioned within the intersecting relationship of music as contemporary cultural sound and traditions of musical production and distribution.

While focusing on *Tutu*, I aim to provide a model to rethink the trumpeter's career as a whole and to offer some indications on how we could reconceive the way we think about jazz and the musicians who produce it. To achieve this, I explore the *Tutu* album's location in a map of meaning of mid-1980s popular music. *Tutu* is both particularly open to such analysis and specifically in need of a rethink because of the way it has been located in Davis' recording catalogue. In spite of some recent attempts at reconsideration, *Tutu* remains a critically controversial recording. The album is often deployed to make the case for the trumpeter's later recordings as examples of his musical decline, as part of an argument that jazz had an earlier classic period in which Davis' contribution is canonical. *Tutu* certainly received mixed reviews on its release and in the decade beyond. In *The Last Miles*, George Cole's selected quotes of critical responses to the new LP neatly summarise the main positions: that it is really a Marcus Miller record (Milkowski 1987); that it is glossy and lacking in musical substance (Cook and Morton 1996, 366); that it would not survive the judgement of posterity (Chambers 1998, xiv); that Davis had lost interest in music of quality (Crouch 1990); that *Tutu* was disappointing, anonymous and determined by commercial awareness (McRae 1988, 70).

Ultimately, though, there is no way to simply box *Tutu* in. *Tutu* takes its place in a very diverse string of releases that include three studio albums, the Caribbean and go-go-flavoured *Amandla*[3] and Nordic jazz *Aura*[4] from 1989 and the 1992 posthumous release of the hip-hop-infused *Doo-Bop*;[5] two movie soundtracks, the 1987 *Music from Siesta*[6] jointly credited to Davis

[3] *Amandla*, Warner Bros. Records, 925 873-1. Recorded at Clinton Recording, New York City, December, 1988; Right Track Recording, New York City, early 1989; and Le Gonks West, West Hollywood, CA, early 1989. Released in US May 18, 1989.

[4] *Aura*, Columbia, C2X 45332. Recorded at Easy Sound Recording, Copenhagen, January 31–February 4, 1985. Released September 12, 1989.

[5] *Doo-Bop*, Warner Bros. Records, 9 26938-1. Recorded at Unique Recording Studios, New York City, January 19–February, 1991. Released June 30, 1992.

[6] *Music from Siesta*, Warner Bros. Records, 1-25655. Recorded at Studio Sigma Sound, New York City, January 1987; Minot Sound, White Plains, NY, January–March 1987; Amigo, North Hollywood, CA, March 1987. Released November 1987.

and Miller, the trumpeter's contribution to Michel Legrand's 1989 *Dingo*[7] soundtrack; and finally, two posthumous live recordings on 1993's *Miles & Quincy Live at Montreux*[8] and 1996's *Live Around the World*.[9] The Warner 2019 release of remixed music from 1985's *Rubberband*[10] sessions provide further insight into Davis' musical interests and the record company's sense of his legacy and position in 21st-century music culture. However, we should not simply understand these Warner recordings as part of the trumpeter's diachronic career. Using the frame of contemporary black American music of the early 1980s, we can reveal far more about the meaningfulness of *Tutu*, and of Davis' other later career recordings. I do return to questions of the reinvention of jazz that engaged Davis as an artist for over 30 years in my companion chapter, but again by utilising ideas of maps of musical meaning rather than more conventional frames of biography.

I start the chapter by establishing the dominant ways in which *Tutu* has been framed in relation to the music and those who created it, and what discursive resources they provide for a new model of understanding the recording in its place in 1980s musical culture. In applying the model of maps of musical meaning, I examine three intersecting areas of 1980s music practice which define *Tutu*: 'electric pop', smooth jazz and Marcus Miller's own music. These observations become a way to rethink *Tutu* as a contemporary vehicle for a jazz veteran. Finally, I make some suggestions for the ways these musical and cultural resources become a powerful means for Davis' performance of change and how the trumpeter incorporated these into his sense of agency as a musician and into his identity as a progressive black American man.

Critical Conventions

Something of the perceived contemporary importance of *Tutu*, and an indication of the way the recording was received, can be found in a concurrent

[7] Miles Davis and Michel Legrand, *Dingo*, Warner Bros. Records, 9 26438-2. Recorded at Crystal Studios, Los Angeles, early March 1990. Released November 5, 1991.

[8] *Miles & Quincy Live at Montreux*, Warner Bros. Records, 9 45221-2. Recorded at Montreux Casino, Switzerland, July 8, 1991. Released August 10, 1993.

[9] *Live Around the World*, Warner Bros. Records, 9 46032-2. Recorded in 11 international venues between 1988 and 1991. Released May 14, 1996.

[10] *Rubberband*, Warner Records, R2 599464. Recorded at Ameraycan Studios, Los Angeles, October 22, 1985; remixed Utopia Studios; vocals at The Village, Los Angeles. Released September 6, 2019.

review from Robert Palmer, the influential American popular music critic. Palmer (1986) devoted all of one of his *New York Times* Pop Life columns to reviewing the CD, concluding that "'Tutu' is fusion music for the hot tub". The review contains a number of the tropes used more generally to assess Davis in the 1980s. The trumpeter, asserts Palmer, "has been content to be a follower" and *Tutu* "already sounds curiously dated". He describes the synthesisers as having "the glutinous textures so overly familiar from the mainstream of late-70's pop jazz" and the drum-machine rhythms as "politely harmless". There's some damning with faint praise for the deftly dancing muted trumpet-playing and "some interesting cross-rhythms" and an acknowledgement that 'Don't Lose Your Mind' "sounds reasonably fresh". Readers at the time may have expected Palmer to have received the record more warmly. The former *Rolling Stone* journalist had a deep interest in black music forms, championed contemporary rock music and, at the same time he wrote this review, was writing the script for the celebratory documentary *The World According to John Coltrane* (1990).

However, beyond the critic's personal preferences, his insightful knowledge alerts us to two important factors about, on the one hand, the way *Tutu* enters into the meaning map of mid-1980s popular music and, on the other, the semantic map of critical interpretation of both Miles and (then) contemporary jazz. The first sentence of Palmer's review positions the music as Davis' "first full-scale foray into electronic pop". While Palmer later in the article comments that this constituted grounds for the recording's dismissal, this nuanced observation points to how we should frame our insights into what Davis and Miller had produced musically. While Palmer may have been using an older map of popular music in which *Tutu* could only be understood as positioned in the margins, we should not simply commit ourselves to the same process. If Davis is entering a new musical world, it is the meaningfulness of this world that should guide our understanding rather than the reference points of the music in which Davis had previously immersed himself.

Equally, it is Palmer's assertion that the recording represented Davis as a follower, rather than the leader of old, that should alert us to a central question that goes begging rather than the simplistic answer provided in the article: Just how could jazz musicians, and Davis in particular, realise their agency as a progressive musician in the mid-1980s? In posing this question in this way, I reference a similar question Scott DeVeaux (1997, 45) asked about Coleman Hawkins and the birth of bebop in the late 1940s and early

1950s. If it is a question worth posing for Davis' work through to the 1960s, it is worth asking of his later recordings, too. If we refashion Palmer's subjective denunciation as a question about agency in 1980s popular music, rather than the myths of the genius jazz soloist and band leader that dominated post-war jazz criticism, we start to see the recording in a different light.

Perhaps because of this sort of critical reception, the music of *Tutu*, along with the final decade of Davis' music and career, have only slowly been documented in print. While such attention has started a more measured assessment of this recording, and such assessments have increasingly offered more detail on the origins of the recording, these existing discussions really do not do more than set a scene for our understanding. It is noteworthy that it took a decade after Davis' death in 1991 for a consolidated appraisal of this period to emerge. Ian Carr, typically, led this critical reconsideration in 1998, with additional chapters to his 1982 biography that explored Davis' later work. Since then there have been new studies of Davis' career that included commentary on his 1980s work (see, for instance, Cook 2005, 285–320; Szwed 2002, 281–407) and even book-length studies of his 'electric' period (Tingen 2001) and, probably the most developed at 20 years' remove, George Cole's *The Last Miles* (2005).

Among the existing studies, the accounts of Carr, Cole, Cook, Tingen and Szwed construct an almost identical narrative, using a common set of sources, reinforced with references to each other, as evidence. Cole's study is especially worthy of note for its richness of participant anecdote and the thoroughness of its research, and this detail remains one of the best ways to master the events around the recording of *Tutu*. Too often, though, these accounts are less successful at explaining what was happening: their narratives are merely asserted, and then, rather obviously in what follows, the stories presented are undermined by the particulars of the very events that are being narrated.

It is notable, in both the contemporary assessments and 21st-century accounts by journalists and jazz studies academics, that Miles' music of this period is positioned against the neoclassical jazz of Wynton Marsalis and mainstream rock forms. The idea of a neoclassical moment in mid-1980s jazz, and the personification of this idea as embodied in Marsalis as a player, was championed in the criticism and essays of Stanley Crouch (see, for instance, Crouch 2006a). While Crouch's critical positions were rooted in the Black Arts Movement, he later rejected the avant-garde leanings of the most voluble music that emerged from this movement, but his definitional framing of jazz reimagined the music as "America's classical music", a form seen as determined and developed by African Americans (see Wall 2007, 197–198).

This conception of jazz as America's classical music is most often associated with Billy Taylor, in whose doctoral dissertation the idea is first advanced, then more widely disseminated in book form, and subsequently used by Taylor as a platform for jazz education and public and private funding initiatives (Taylor 1975, 1982; Arnold-Forster 2017). Crouch, though, positions his own views at the intersection of Ralph Ellison's cultural theories, Albert Murray's very literary sense of jazz as an American art form, and Martin Williams' notion of the jazz tradition (for exemplars, see Crouch 2006b; Murray 1976; Murray and Thomas 2016; Williams 1970). For Crouch, Ellison and Murray were influential because they were "each a man who saw very clear connections between the sensibilities and the structures of jazz artists and any serious artists from the wide world at large" (2006b, 5). By the time Davis was struggling with the idea of moving record labels and making a new form of music, the 'jazz as classical music' notion was in wide circulation. Grover Sales (1984) adopted the idea for his jazz primer, although it offers little beyond a standard history built around Williams' 'Smithsonian Collection of Classic Jazz' and the proposition that jazz demanded the same attention as Bach and Beethoven. These shifts toward a new frame for proselytising jazz certainly chimed with a wider early 1980s retro interest in the fashion, design and iconography of jazz from 1930 to the early 1960s.

Palmer's own journalism had championed the idea of a classic period of rock in the 1970s that reproduced many of the tropes of the later neoclassical jazz narrative, often writing about jazz in these terms as well (see articles anthologised in Palmer 2009). While he had eclectic tastes and enthusiasms and a genuine commitment to earlier musics of black origin, he often framed these discussions through the notion that commercialisation was ruining popular music, a frame that pervades his assessment of *Tutu*. This frame, that post-disco R&B forms of the 1980s are symbols of the decline of a lost classic rock and black music of an earlier generation, also permeates the later analyses of jazz writers who discuss *Tutu*.

To provide an alternative frame, I start with *Tutu* as a recording, and then work outward to its significance using the idea of a synchronic map of meaning. On this map, *Tutu* is situated within the other Warner recordings Davis made and those the company released. In the companion chapter, I detail how Davis' music was very precisely positioned within the codifying organisational structure of jazz and progressive music departments at the Columbia and Warner labels. As I indicate in chapter 4, in its record company context *Tutu* represents something of the awkwardness of a record industry trying to classify and badge a fast-moving music culture in order to allocate resources in proportion to the perceived value that different genres of music have to record companies.

Reflecting on my paraphrasing of DeVeaux's question about how progressive musicians realise their agency, the 'progressive music' which is aligned with jazz by the organisation of the Columbia and Warner labels is equally important. With its origin in the 1970s, the term 'progressive music' makes a claim for the potential to reproduce the cultural and economic coup d'état against the popular music establishment that rock music was perceived to have made in the 1960s. As such, it discursively constructs musics outside the mainstream, perhaps more demanding for listeners and innovative for its musical artists. That jazz was the genre most able to be named within record company discourse, and so confidently marked as dominant over the musics coded as 'progressive', is itself interesting. At the time these departments were named, jazz was both traditional and progressive, qualities to which the other, unnamed musics aspired. By the mid-1980s, though, the relationship between signifier and signified of 'jazz and progressive music' had drifted considerably. The perceived new audience for jazz was the expanding, maturing, affluent middle-class and, significantly, African American audience who had grown up on soul, funk and disco; the progressive nature of jazz was seen as residing (perhaps paradoxically, or even as a contradiction for its critics) in its 'smoothness'.

Perversely, then, I argue that it is the matters around jazz and progressive music that are addressed by *Tutu*'s critics that can provide us with a structured way to understand what *Tutu* meant (and means). A reappraisal of *Tutu* does not demand a rejection of the objects of the critics' ire (as Cole seems to imply) but an opening up of their propositions to the wider discursive currents in which both Davis and his critics were operating. That is, we should not seek to find the truth between the negative and positive assessments but to understand all the maps of meaning in which Davis' agency, the music and its evaluation are positioned and operate in relation to each other.

Locating *Tutu* in Mid-1980s Popular Music

Mapping out the sensibilities of mid-1980s popular music in order to locate Davis' period of creativity, and its realisation in *Tutu*, is a more speculative activity than the one mostly taken in the interview-based evidence approach of biography to which I have so far pointed. It should, though, bring with it the idea that musicians make decisions about their music, career and identity, even when the choices they are afforded are also determined by other factors. Such a semiotic cartography enables us to locate the music made by individual artists within the wider landscape of popular music made available at the time. It makes more meaningful the decisions made by Davis and Miller by highlighting the music culture fields of discourse in which they chose to operate. At the same time, it provides a frame in which to grasp how Davis' critics were positioned and so made equally meaningful (but no more valuable) critiques.

Three overlapping territories are relevant here: the fusion of post-punk and disco, which formed an emerging electronic pop sound that came to dominate 1980s popular music; contemporary jazz, especially those recordings that related to radio-friendly smooth jazz; and the post-disco R&B forms in which Miller had become particularly successful. It is worth taking each in turn before looking in detail at key tracks on the *Tutu* recording.

'Electronic Pop'

While Palmer's broad familiarity with popular music rooted in a black American aesthetic did not help the critic see the innovations in *Tutu*, let alone enamour the record to him, it did allow him to understand that Davis and Miller were exploring what he termed 'electronic pop'. Rhetorically, it is Palmer's coding of the recording as pop that is as significant as designating it as electronic. After all, electric instruments, amplification and studio recording techniques had been characteristic of both the rock music and the Miles Davis recordings after *In a Silent Way* that Palmer had championed. More substantially, Palmer's analysis, however broad and progressive, is fixed within a critical frame that emerged in his early adult years. This may well explain why Palmer chose the term 'electronic pop', which was not widely used at the time, and may reflect his own lack of detailed familiarity with the very music he was trying to explain. That frame had allowed

Palmer to embrace Davis' late 1960s and early 1970s innovations—usually designated as jazz-rock—for the way they linked black-informed white popular music and counterculture politics to an experimental black jazz aesthetic. However, these were the very certainties which were undermined by 1980s studio-based, dance-oriented popular music and shifted the critical coordinates which had guided Palmer's work to this point.

In truth, later critics understood Davis' embrace of what Palmer calls electronic pop, even when their allusions were crude and dismissive. For instance, Cook and Morton (2008, 351–352) describe the music of *Tutu* as "drab cop-show funk" with "a high production gloss that camouflaged a lack of real musical substance". In Cole's (2011) more recent and supportive analysis, "*Tutu* was a product of the 80s, a decade where music was often in danger of becoming subservient to technology", although he added that "while much of the music from this era is now long forgotten[,] Tutu continues to thrive". More generally, jazz critics found it difficult to grasp Davis' later experiments in music because they did not possess a sensitivity to the nuances of new forms of popular music that emerged in the 1980s. This was particularly so because their comprehension of the trumpeter was embedded in much more sophisticated insights into the earlier phases of his career and a personal commitment to the music of that period. In a typical denouncement, Crouch declared in 1986, "Desperate to maintain his position at the forefront of modern music, to sustain his financial position, to be admired for the hipness of his purported innovations, Davis turned butt to the beautiful in order to genuflect before the commercial" (collected in Crouch 2006a, 240). As is often the case, Crouch dresses his sharp insights in an irascible rhetoric, which often clouds the discernment, and the nuanced details are lost in the polemic.

Looking beyond the critical rhetoric of 'sell-out', it is easy to grasp that it was Davis who wanted to work with Miller because of the latter's ability to position the trumpeter in a conjunction somewhere between his recent work on Columbia and that of his new (near) label stablemates Madonna and Prince, and to become part of a wider stream of contemporary black aesthetic-infused popular music. It is the market success of this music, a result of its resonance with a broad range of US and international audiences, in which Davis was eager to participate. Both Madonna and Prince had major records released in 1984, which would have been clearly in focus as the jazz star looked beyond his long stay at Columbia for a new record company. Davis' regard for Prince is well documented in the biographies, but little is said about the success of Madonna on the Warner Sire label. Davis does cite both Madonna and Prince in his 1989 autobiography, giving them as a reference point for understanding his former wife, Betty Mabry, in the 1960s (Davis and Troupe 1989, 280).

Madonna's *Like a Virgin*,[11] her second LP, was released on the Warner label Sire in 1984. The record was produced by Chic's Nile Rodgers using New York's Power Station Studio's state-of-the-art digital recording and synthesiser technology. An update on the girl group sound of the 1960s, Rodgers' production builds rhythmic patterns from the contributions of his Chic bandmates Bernard Edwards and Tony Thompson, melodic elements driven by digital keyboards. Edwards' and Thompson's contributions capture something of the bass and drum patterns from Louis Johnson and Ndugu Chancler on the Quincy Jones–produced Michael Jackson recording 'Billy Jean'.[12] Madonna's *Like a Virgin* deviates from this R&B lineage in the way it incorporates many post-punk devices into the vocals. (I hear Devo, Scritti Politti and Sire stablemates Talking Heads in particular.) This treatment of vocals is unusual in Rodgers' productions, which understandably usually derive from black R&B traditions, but Sire records—which was a solely owned subsidiary of the Warner label from 1978—was significant in promoting British and US post-punk bands in the US, including the Cure, Depeche Mode and Soft Cell, who fused punk sensibilities with electronic rhythm and melodic forms derived from disco.

This connectivity of post-punk and contemporary dance R&B is explicit in *Tutu*'s sixth track, a cover of Scritti Politti's 1985 track 'Perfect Way'.[13] Miller's musical bed for Davis' playing is an almost perfect copy of the opening units created by Scritti Politti's David Gamson, and Miller had been a contributor to other tracks on the album. Probably by coincidence, as they do not follow the same structure throughout, the original and Miller versions are almost exactly the same length. Miles' playing does not reproduce Green Gartside's singing on the vocal track, instead weaving through the up-tempo ballad in a manner distinctive to Miles. It is also hard not to hear this cover as part of a wider reinvention of the jazz standard in which jazz soloists use well-known songs as themes for their improvisations. Davis had already done this with

[11] *Like a Virgin*, Sire, 1-25157. Recorded at the Power Station, New York City, April–September 1984. Released November 12, 1984.

[12] 'Billy Jean', Epic, AS 1596. Recorded at Westlake, Los Angeles, in 1982. Released January 3, 1983.

[13] 'Perfect Way', Warner Bros. Records, 7-28949. Released August 27, 1985.

Cyndi Lauper's 'Time After Time'[14] and Michael Jackson's 'Human Nature'[15] on Davis' Columbia album *You're Under Arrest*.[16]

It is in Prince, though, that we find more explicit musical and role models for Davis' new music. It is easy to see why the label that had supported Prince's career as a black male performer to international stardom would have had positive appeal for Davis. In his autobiography, in a wider discussion of funk, black rock and go-go performers, Davis writes, "[F]rom 1987 I was really getting into the music of Prince" (Davis and Troupe 1989, 374), although elsewhere in the book he suggests Prince was going to contribute a track to *Tutu* in 1986 (362) and that he had followed Prince since 1982 (343). More important, the jazz trumpeter locates Prince as coming "from the school of James Brown", with some "Marvin Gaye and Jimi Hendrix and Sly in him, even Little Richard. He's a mixture of all those guys and Duke Ellington. He reminds me, in a way, of Charlie Chaplin, he and Michael Jackson, who I also love as a performer" (374). Unsurprisingly, Davis' suggestion that Prince could be connected to Duke Ellington enraged Crouch, who railed against any such proposition "that the Minneapolis vulgarian and borderline drag queen 'can be the new Duke Ellington of our time if he just keeps at it'" (2006a, 240).

Prince's *Purple Rain*,[17] released in 1984, sold so well across US markets that it achieved number 1 ranking in Billboard's 200 (pop) and R&B/hip-hop listings in the same year. The self-produced album was created in the same way as *Like a Virgin*, but with Bobby Z's drumming extensively supported by drum machine rhythms—more elements strongly derived from contemporary R&B dance music—and a far greater range of rock devices, especially in Prince's lead guitar work. The debt to Jimi Hendrix, who had long preoccupied Davis, is clear in Prince's guitar style. Davis' autobiography explicitly links Prince's treatment of the bass line with Miller's approach: "You don't hear a bass line in Prince's music because he takes keyboard bass and doubles it with regular bass just like Marcus Miller does" (Davis and Troupe 1989, 313).

[14] 'Time After Time', Portrait, 37-04432. Recorded at Record Plant, New York City, June 1983. Released March 1984.

[15] 'Human Nature', Epic, 34-04026. Recorded at Westlake Studios, Los Angeles, 1982. Released July 4, 1983.

[16] Miles Davis, *You're Under Arrest*, Columbia, CK 40023. Recorded at Record Plant, New York City, January 26, 1984–January 14, 1985. Released April 1985.

[17] *Purple Rain*, Warner Bros. Records, 25110-1. Recorded at First Avenue, Kiowa Trail Home Studio and The Warehouse, Minnesota; Record Plant, New York City; Sunset Sound, Hollywood, CA, July 1983–March 1984. Released June 25, 1984.

As the quotes from his autobiography signal, Davis valued Prince's performance persona as much as the musical influences in instrumentation and recording technique. The official record company video of the 'Purple Rain' single is intriguing in this respect. Built on the conceit that Prince is nervously playing a small college gig, only to be transformed by the music and engaged with the diverse, young audience who are equally mesmerised by the experience. This scene is also central to the film *Purple Rain*, a new venture for Prince, from which the video footage was taken. One can imagine the shy Davis being enamoured by this idea of an African American man's success in adversity and personal confidence emboldened by playing music live. The core music was recorded in live performance, but with significant editing and dubbing of parts to produce the final recording. This idea of a musician at the centre of a multimedia world, with the recording studio, live stage and film sound stage as equals as tools in a collaborative creativity, was clearly enormously powerful for Davis. (These are ideas picked up by Nic Pillai in chapter 6.)

Smooth Jazz in the Jazz and Pop World

None of this important mapping of Davis' new interests on the terrain of post-punk-meets-post-disco-funk-and-R&B should disguise the important place of *Tutu* in jazz of the 1980s. In fact, Davis' *Tutu* can be revealingly located in the then emerging, and later dominating, radio format and music genre of smooth jazz. For Barber (2010, 52), smooth jazz is essentially "instrumental music, led by saxophones or guitars, that combines some jazz improvisation with the harmonic and rhythmic conventions of pop, rock and R&B". And Nicholson (1998, 222) usefully locates smooth jazz in the US radio market as "airplay-friendly instrumental pop-jazz" featuring "slick production values and musical hooks from contemporary popular music". Washburne (2004, 104), along with Barber's later article, locates the term in US radio formats: "[T]he label 'smooth jazz' is a conspicuously fabricated construct that originated in consumer research studies conducted by Broadcast Architecture, a radio consulting firm. The company found that 'smooth' was the most frequently used term listeners employed to describe this mainly instrumental musical style, whose defining elements include R&B, Latin and soul-infused grooves, heavy use of synthesisers, easily recognisable melodies, slick pop-like studio productions, and jazzlike soloing". Barber's (2010) own analysis presents the form as a case study in the relationship of commercial radio programming formats, audience research and music production. He locates its immergence in the mid-1970s Quiet Storm evening broadcasting featuring "mellow R&B, soul and R&B-influenced jazz offerings aimed at the urban, African-American adult" (52), through Wave format stations of the late 1980s, to stations formatted by the consulting business Broadcast Architecture in the 1990s (53–60).

I do not mean to suggest that *Tutu is* smooth jazz, although dismissive online consumer reviews of the record often pejoratively assert it is just that. In fact, the album struggles to get air play on smooth jazz stations even though music from the 1970s and 1980s features prominently in such broadcast output, probably because it would be seen to conform insufficiently to the archetype. Rather, I want to argue that it should, in part, be understood as emerging from the same cultural and economic currents that produced the smooth jazz radio format and musical genre. The tracks on *Tutu* certainly fit the characteristics described by Charles Carson (2008, 3) as emblematic of smooth jazz, including covers of contemporary songs, straight playing of the key melody and variation on that melody through "characteristic ornaments and gestures", and backing tracks that are premixed before the soloist records using an "R&B aesthetic" "that foreground the instrumental soloist similar to the manner in which the vocalist is featured in popular music".

However, as I have tried to stress, *Tutu* is not simply understandable as part of any one locale on a map of 1980s popular music. Just as much as it is not simply 'electronic pop' or post-disco R&B, it is not reducible to the formatting mathematics of US radio, and it is some distance from the core production techniques developed by Dave Grusin and Larry Rosen for releases on their GRP label. For Barber, GRP Records was crucial to the development of smooth jazz (2010, 60–67), and elsewhere he has explored the use of synthesisers and recording technology in fashioning the GRP sound (Barber 2009).

Marcus Miller as a Waymarker

This musical world of studio R&B and smooth jazz productions is exactly the one in which Marcus Miller entered as an emerging performer, studio musician and producer. As a young studio musician, Miller worked on a whole range of recordings in this same tightly focused space at the overlap of contemporary R&B, jazz and pop. These included soul singers Aretha Franklin and Luther Vandross, crossover keyboardist and singer Bernard Wright, soft rock king Donald Fagen and jazz instrumentalists Dave Grusin, David Sanborn and Grover Washington Jr., including the latter's big-selling *Winelight*. Washington's record would become a staple of smooth jazz repertoire.

Miller had secured a Warner Bros. recording contract for himself, and his two solo records, 1983's *Suddenly*[18] and 1984's *Marcus Miller*,[19] foreground his bass playing, but they also used a strong commercial R&B sound and production techniques. For both records, Miller built a music bed of his own drum programming, bass guitars, keyboards and guitars on top of which he added his own lead and background vocals and some clarinet parts, along with contributions from a couple of handfuls of musicians that added percussive richness and musical variety. His debt to Prince, and to some extent Michael Jackson and Stevie Wonder, is apparent throughout, in the compositional structure, production and performance style, but also in the star persona to which he aspires and which is presented on the album covers. The music is mainly funk-orientated dance, but with a strong emphasis on song form and high-level musicianship. It is, therefore, into these very same genre contours and musical ravines that Miles Davis entered when he took up his Warner contract.

As all the tracks on *Tutu*—with the exception of 'Backyard Ritual'—were created initially by Miller, it is instructive to look at how he fits into a number of the trajectories I have set out so far. Miller had been the bass player in the Miles Davis band on the trumpeter's comeback recording *The Man with the Horn*,[20] playing live on the 1981 sets that were released as *We Want Miles*[21] and all but one of the studio and live numbers that became 1983's *Star People*.[22] Miller's bass was certainly an important part of the sound of the

[18] *Suddenly*, Warner Bros. Records, 1-23806. Recorded at Minot Sound, White Plains, NY; Celebration Recording Studios, New York City, October, August–December 1982. Released March 23, 1983.

[19] *Marcus Miller*, Warner Bros. Records, 9 25074-1. Recorded at Mediasound, New York City; Minot Sound, White Plains, NY; Warner Bros., North Hollywood, CA, October 1983–March 1984. Released June 26, 1984.

[20] *The Man with the Horn*, Columbia, FC 36790. Recorded at Columbia 30th Street Studio, New York City, June 1, 1980–May 6, 1981. Released July 1981.

[21] *We Want Miles*, Columbia, C2 38005. Recorded live at KIX in Boston; Avery Fisher Hall, New York City; and special stage in Nishi-Shinjuku June 27, July 5 and October 4, 1981. Released May 1982.

[22] *Star People*, Columbia, FC 38657. Recorded at Columbia Studio B, New York City; live at Jones Beach Marine Theater, Wantagh, NY; The Record Plant, New York City; live Cullen Auditorium, University of Houston, August 11, 1982–February 3, 1983. Released April 1983.

post-sabbatical Davis band, but neither his instrument nor his personality are particularly determining in the music. This familiarity with Davis' music, though, must have been an important part in the trumpeter's accepting an offer from the bass player to produce some tracks for a Warner release. Miller was a young but seasoned studio and commercial musician, arranger and producer before he played with Davis. He was one of the key musicians on Tom Browne's *Browne Sugar* debut album produced by Dave Grusin and Larry Rosen for GRP Records in 1979.[23] Miller is much more prominent on *Browne Sugar* and his playing is more driven and almost experimental, especially when teamed with Michael Brecker's solos, even within the highly produced and glossy digital sound. *Browne Sugar* certainly sets out the main elements that were to formulate the classic smooth jazz sound, especially on the Marvin Gaye cover 'What's Going On' and the Miller-composed ballad 'Brother, Brother'.

Tutu as Contemporary Vehicle for a Jazz Veteran

In this context, while the production processes that Miller used on *Tutu* built upon his own solo albums and his work for soul singers and pop jazz instrumentalists, it is some distance from the danceability of his R&B work and the black rock aesthetic Davis had been working on in his last few Columbia records. The evidence we have suggests that Miller did not get a specific brief to produce the tracks that made up his contribution to *Tutu*, so we can assume he was imagining music that would be appropriate to Davis, using, in particular, the experience Miller would have gained from working with the trumpeter over the previous five years and his knowledge of Davis' recording history.

Miller's explanation, to a group of other former Davis bandmates, of his approach to constructing the 'Tutu' lead track, is enlightening:

> I tried to add a little bit of that 'Birth of the Cool' harmonies. I tried to add a little bit. I wanted Miles' whole history and in the eighties setting. That's what I was trying to do, you know. I want you to hear with the instrument, so I had trombone in there from, for that soft brass, you know, like a trombone playing lightly. I had, um, some of Gil's [Evans] harmonies. I had

[23] *Browne Sugar*, GRP 5003. Recorded at A & R Studios, New York City, 1979. Released 1979.

> those fourths I was telling you about, and a New Orleans beat that Miles had showed us when I was in the band. I just tried to combine everything I knew about them in one track.[24]

This reference to diachronic influences, though, is contextualised by Miller's equal emphasis on the more synchronic music-making practices:

> This is the eighties and we've had Stevie Wonder, who played all the, all the instruments on his own album, you know, he would just play the drums, he rewinds the tape and plays the bass and rewinds the tape and plays the keyboard. He'd just build it up on his own. And then Prince had been doing that a few years later and I was really into that, you know. And so that's how I did 'Tutu'.[25]

Nevertheless, in the same recorded conversation Miller also points to his initial reticence in providing Davis with a multitrack recording: "I was a little nervous because Miles is a true jazz musician and that's not really a jazz concept with the overdubbing and all that, you know".[26]

It is, perhaps, in the work of Bill Laswell, and his band Material, that we can find the reference point to imagine how the contemporary R&B and avant-garde jazz playing and recording techniques could be utilised for an updated Miles Davis track. 'Disappearing' from *Memory Serves* (1981)[27] seems a particularly relevant manifestation. The track was jointly created by Laswell and Material's keyboard player, Michael Beinhorn, along with avant-garde jazz players Olu Dara and Sonny Sharrock and post-punk keyboard player Fred Maher. The propulsive music bed of dense bass, keyboard and drums features weaving improvisations from Dara's cornet, Sharrock's guitar and Henry Threadgill's alto sax. Likewise, Laswell and Beinhorn's production on Herbie Hancock's *Future Shock* must have been a significant influence, especially as Hancock was a former band mate of Davis' who was then achieving the sort of commercial success Davis craved. While most

[24] Transcription of recording of Marcus Miller speaking in Christopher Wilkinson's 2021 documentary *'Round Miles*. 3m 59s to 4m 28s.

[25] 1m 58s to 2m 17s.

[26] Transcription of recording of Marcus Miller speaking in Christopher Wilkinson's 2021 documentary 'Round Miles. 2m 37s to 2m 45s.

[27] Material, *Memory Serves* (1981), Celluloid, 529812. Recorded OAO Studio, Brooklyn. Produced by Material with Martin Bisi.

discussions of the tracks on *Future Shock*,[28] especially the album's most successful single, 'Rockit', focus on the use of Grand Mixer D.ST's DJ turntable scratching, it is the layers of dense rhythm elements, and avant-garde jazz elements from Hancock and Davis band alumnus Pete Cosey on guitar, that were clearly the musical territory Miller was looking for.

"Backyard Ritual"—created for Davis by another successful musician-producer at the intersection of jazz and R&B, George Duke—offers a similar, if different, approach. While initially sounding even more abstract than Miller's tracks—closer, in fact, to the opening of Davis' 1969 *In a Silent Way*[29]—Duke uses exactly the same approach he applied to his contemporaneous *Thief in the Night*.[30] Most notable is the use of the early digital Synclavier II and analog Prophet-5 programmable polyphonic synthesisers. This is much more experimental than any track on Duke's own record, though. With the rhythmic pattern utilising guttural 'umm' vocalisations, a programmatic rather than song-form structure and synthesised sax solos, it can be compared to Brian Eno and David Byrne's (1981) *My Life in the Bush of Ghosts*[31] just as much as Duke's usual danceable jazz funk. This is probably even more the case because the recording was originally conceived as a demo by Duke to communicate his ideas to Davis, but the trumpeter wanted the released track to contain most of the qualities of the rough audio sketch.

Both Miller's and Duke's tracks share something of Davis' contribution to the Artists United Against Apartheid's *Sun City*[32] LP (1985). The track 'The Struggle Continues', produced by Arthur Baker and Steven Van Zandt, offered a model to all concerned in *Tutu* during the months of its gestation. At one level this track unites Davis with Hancock, Ron Carter and Tony Williams but is unrecognisable from their early 1960s jazz group sound on which much of Marsalis' music was modelled. The playing is highly processed and edited by producer Baker and includes contrasting guitar styles from Stanley Jordan and Sonny Okosun. Although Davis' playing is somewhat lost in a typically over-dominant Baker sound processing and production, if nothing else this track would have signalled to both Duke and

[28] *Future Shock*, Columbia, FC 38814. Recorded at OAO Studios and RPM Studios, New York City; Garage Sale Recording, Los Angeles, 1983. Released August 1983.

[29] *In a Silent Way*, Columbia, CS 9875. Recorded at Columbia 30th Street Studio, New York City, February 18, 1969. Released July 30, 1969.

[30] *Thief in the Night*, Elektra, 60398-1. Recorded at Le Gonks West, Los Angeles. Released 1985.

[31] *My Life in the Bush of Ghosts*, Sire, SRK 6093. Recorded at R.P.M. Blue Rock and Sigma Sound, New York City; Eldorado Recording, Burbank, CA; Different Fur, San Francisco, 1979–1980. Released February 1981.

[32] *Sun City*, Manhattan Records, 24 0467 1. Recorded Summer 1985. Released October 25, 1985.

Miller that Davis' muted trumpet playing could sound really effective in such a context.

In closing this section on the musical map of meaning, it is worth pointing to the new insights offered up by the release of other recordings made by Miles with Prince and with Zane Giles and Randy Hall during the same period, on what would come to be called the *Rubberband* sessions. The track 'Can I Play with U?' was speculatively created by Prince in December and January 1985.[33] It is clear that Tommy LiPuma originally imagined that this could be a key track for *Tutu*, as Miller oversaw the trumpet overdubs by Davis while working on the producer's own tracks.[34] In a later interview, Miller said, "Prince heard it again, what we did . . . and even he realised that it didn't sound as if it belonged on *Tutu*, and maybe we shouldn't use it" (quoted in Amorosi 2022). The track really struggles to place Davis' playing with Prince's dominant musical personality. Prince's guitar certainly echoes the sound of Mike Stern on *We Want Miles* (1982), and Davis' trumpet work is remarkably similar to that on the *Tutu* tracks but lacks the musical integration that Miller in particular achieved. Nevertheless, Prince did involve Davis in his production work for Chaka Khan's eighth solo studio album *CK* in 1988. Davis' trumpet playing was overdubbed on the musical tracks created by Prince after Khan's vocals were added. Davis does an effective job in fitting his rhythmic stabbing and melodic playing style to both a dance number and a ballad and they sit comfortably with Khan's vocals while remaining noticeably Davis.[35] I return to some of these issues of collaboration in chapter 8 with Bobbie-Jane Gardner.

The original tracks produced by Giles and Hall, created and subsequently completed with Davis' nephew Vince Wilburn Jr., show exactly the same contemporary reference points and production techniques as the slightly later Miller tracks. The tracks are completed close to the original ambitions,

[33] The princevault.com page for 'Can I Play with U?' says the initial tracks were laid down by Prince on December 26, 1985, at Sunset Sound Studio 3, in Hollywood, with saxophone overdubs by band member Eric Leeds in the same studio the following day, and a basic mix created on 7 January 1986 (https://princevault.com/index.php?title=Can_I_Play_With_U%3F). In an interview, Miller suggested the overdubs were added in February 1986. Amorosi (2022).

[34] Princevault.com indicates these overdubs took place on March 1, 1986 at Capitol Studios in Los Angeles, and also notes additional bass guitar by Miller and synthesiser overdubs by Adam Holzman. Both are audible in the various versions of 'Can I Play with U?' available. https://princevault.com/index.php?title=Can_I_Play_With_U%3F.

[35] The base tracks for 'Sticky Wicked' and 'I'll Be Around' were created by Prince on June 11, 1988, at Paisley Park Studios, Chanhassen, MN, with overdubs from Eric Leeds on saxophone and Atlanta Bliss on trumpet later in June at the same studio. Davis' trumpet work and some spoken passages were added on June 29, 1988, at The Hit Factory, New York.

with vocals from Lalah Hathaway and Ledisi, who take the parts originally intended (interestingly) for Chaka Khan and Al Jarreau (Fordham 2019). The finished *Rubberband* release sounds remarkably coherent, both in terms of a finished CD and as a forum for Davis' playing, and certainly sits comfortably with *Doo-Bop*, the other key posthumous release of 1980s R&B-influenced music. Perhaps, though, in reimagining Davis' career at Warner, the *Rubberband* sessions did not keep enough of the meaningfulness of Miles Davis that his long career had established. This would certainly have been as important to Davis' executive producer LiPuma as the fact that the experiments were taking too long to realise as a coherent musical statement. (Roger Fagge interrogates *Doo-Bop* further in chapter 2.)

The analysis here is not an argument that the alternative map used by many jazz fans and by jazz biographers and critics is wrong. As many of the books cited in this chapter show, they reveal important differences between *Tutu* and previous musical settings in which Davis worked, and some interesting continuities in his soloing. However, as deployed, such points more often serve to support subjective judgements than they provide insights. As important, these were not the maps used by those listeners who came to *Tutu* from contemporary R&B or smooth jazz, including Miller's previous work, and they were clearly not the maps being used by Davis himself. It is to these matters of Davis' motivations and sense of self that we should finally turn.

Miles: Change, Identity and Agency

Part of the rethink proposed by this book is the need to examine how we treat jazz musicians when we talk about jazz. This necessitates that we tackle the issues of agency, identity and determination that lie at the heart of our attempts to understand the jazz musician and the commercial record. In the case of Davis, we need to navigate what he was doing, how that is interpreted or framed by those authors helping us to understand his recordings and who he was as a musician, as well as the wider fields of meaning in which he operated. Davis has a special place within such narratives, and *Tutu* fully makes sense only within these debates.

Paul Tingen (2001), for instance, succinctly articulates the standard narrative about Davis' musical career and motivations. "[F]or Miles, short-term and long-term changes were a way of life", he writes, and he cites a widely reproduced Davis 1969 *Washington Post* quote, "I have to change. It's like a curse" (24).[36] Tingen actually takes the Davis quote from Carr's 1982 biography, but he does not adopt Carr's rich analytical approach. Carr's analysis of Davis' career sustains repeated reading, and the original 1982 subtitle, *A Critical Biography*, is apposite. Certainly Carr is able to offer the multidimensional sense of a musician pushing at the boundaries of jazz, trying to find an artistically satisfying and commercially successful music. In his discussion of *Tutu*, Carr effectively captures the sense that Davis was pushing those boundaries in a moment of crisis for jazz as a popular music and of great change for the recording industry. Carr's insights are all the more interesting because they come from a British trumpeter who had himself broken with the progressive end of British jazz in the late 1960s to create one of the antecedents of jazz-rock with the band Nucleus (see Shipton 2006, 86–107; Farbey 2023, 51–72).

I show in the companion chapter 4 that the start of Davis' career with Warner cannot be understood simply as the result of determinants of a new label. All Davis' statements on his label move are explained as a desire for new artistic freedoms and financial recognition. While he could have been deluding himself, simply seeing *Tutu* as dominated by Miller as collaborator, a failure of artistic vision on Davis' part, or determined solely by commercial factors, does not seem to match the facts of its production or musical identity. Equally, the other common narratives of the published work I have summarised do not adequately explain this change of label either. His move to Warner is much more than a response to things he did not like at Columbia or a management misjudgement.

The agency of a star jazz performer and forceful personality are more significant. However, an emphasis on these factors can also be misleading. The music on *Tutu* should not be seen narrowly as a result of Davis' drive to change, however much this is part of his personal narrative. This moment is far better comprehended as an assertion of a refreshed sense of his cultural identity within the shifting politics of American jazz and popular music culture more broadly.

The standard 'drive to change' narrative of Davis' career is most often presented as a matter of personality set within a biographic story, and while

[36] Originally quoted in West (1969).

most accounts also note his dramatic shifts in sartorial style, change is almost always marked primarily by an emphasis on the idea of musical transformation. In the case of *Tutu*, this is usually presented in terms of the 'influence' of contemporary R&B on Davis' music making, but these remarks merely point our attention in the right direction while failing to follow the analytical trail such an observation opens up. Fundamentally, we need to ask what music outside jazz, and particularly a range of contemporary R&B-derived musics, offered Davis resources to remake his own sense of cultural and musical identity. The meaningfulness of *Tutu* for a black American jazz luminary like Davis only really makes sense in relation to his pursuit of this new identity, and that identity only within the maps of meaning in which he could (and did) position himself within late 20th-century music culture and industry.

We can certainly see this identity realised musically in all his recordings from this period. He is drawn to music outside jazz, not merely because the stars of contemporary R&B-derived music were commercially successful but because they offered him a role model of contemporary black identity and leadership. All Davis' recordings at Warner represent an even more radical change from his post-sabbatical releases at Columbia, and even to his contemporaneous live music, than is accounted for in most biographic analyses. The later releases are heavily producer-led, rely profoundly on studio technology as a creative medium, and utilise approaches of music making, recording techniques and sound that dominated contemporary black music forms that were rooted in urban dance floor culture. Centrally, I argue that his decisions about the form of his new mid-1980s music are based upon what they mean as much as how they sound. In this context, the critical dismissals after Davis' death of the release of *Doo-Bop*, and the jazz journalism reception of the remixed and reconstructed *Rubberband* sessions, often miss the point of both the trumpeter's interest in the project and the posthumous postproduction work.

The title of the album and its lead track are also relevant here, revealing the way Davis engages with his collaborators and the profound implications of black international politics in his sense of identity. As Miller explains:

> We named it *Tutu* because it was that South Africans struggle going on and Desmond Tutu was doing some really important work. And he was a, he was an Anglican, um, bishop, like my grandfather, you know what I mean. So I really felt connected to him, so I named it *Tutu* and, uh, that really gave it extra weight that we, um. That it was . . . just wasn't a tune, but it was connected to that struggle, yeah. And Miles got so into it, man, that he, you

know, his next album he named the South African name as well. He really got into it.[37]

There is an important question about the ability of a 60-year-old jazz musician, schooled in the structures of bebop, to fully understand how such music operated; even a musician as adaptable as Davis. In part, this explains his career-long interest in collaborative partnerships, increasingly with younger musicians the trumpeter saw as 'hip'. (Gardner and I pick up these themes of black aesthetic and collaboration in chapter 8, the ideas for which emerge from our own creative dialogue around ideas of musical arrangement and production applied to Davis' career.)

Music and music making linked to Prince, hip-hop or crossover jazz forms were not the only viable choices available to Davis, and they were far from the most obvious. There was certainly a ready-made model in the highly profitable smooth jazz format, and it is not inconceivable that Grusin and Rosen could have been attracted to provide production duties for the trumpeter. Equally, Davis could have returned to his earlier music as part of the neoclassical strand of jazz that had offered significant commercial rewards for other musicians, including Marsalis. Davis effectively did this himself in 1991, when he collaborated with Quincy Jones to perform material from his past at the Montreux Jazz Festival, recordings from which were subsequently released to impressive sales. Davis already had a ready model in former bandmate Herbie Hancock, who in 1976 left behind the experiments of the early 1970s Mwandishi music to explore the music the keyboard player had made with Davis. Encouraged by his former Warner producer and then manager David Rubinson, this was distilled in the VSOP quintet. This band, with Wayne Shorter, Ron Carter, Tony Williams and the addition of Freddie Hubbard taking Davis' role, explored the music of the mid-1960s Davis group in which the others had been members. Hancock's work with the VSOP quintet fit well in the solidifying jazz neoconservatism, which did prove that it was possible to earn a living playing within the boundaries of jazz set by Ellington in the 1930s and Davis in the 1960s. Hancock cemented his place here in the music and storyline of the 1986 film *Round Midnight*, for which he created the soundtrack and took a role as one of the on-screen musicians.

[37] Transcription of recording of Marcus Miller speaking in Christopher Wilkinson's 2021 documentary *'Round Miles*. 4m 28s to 5m 01s.

Hancock, though, had created a concurrent path rooted in jazz's engagement with then contemporary African American music, most strikingly exemplified in the 1983 single 'Rockit' from the Bill Laswell–produced album *Future Shock* I have already discussed. Hancock's alliance with bass player–producer Laswell was in many ways a precursor to Davis' partnership with Miller, in which the younger, studio-savvy collaborator offered access to new forms of production and a familiarity with urban music forms. Laswell was at the same time more avant-garde and more immersed in contemporary urban music than Miller, and the trumpet player's experiment with street dance music would come with the *Rubberband*, and the later *Doo-Bop*, sessions. Nevertheless, Hancock's commercial success must have encouraged Davis to follow a similar route.

In the chapter of Davis' *Autobiography* that focuses on events after the release of *Tutu*, Quincy Troupe includes a series of the trumpeter's anecdotes about black identity, recognition and white American perception of jazz (Davis and Troupe 1989). Davis' account of a series of exchanges at a Washington dinner to recognise Ray Charles with a Lifetime Achievement Award reveals the way he constructed his own place in American culture. Responding to the questions of 'a politician's wife', Davis says he asserts that jazz is not given credit in the US because white Americans "can't win when it comes to jazz and blues because black people created it". In anger he reports, "I've changed music five or six times, so I guess that's what I've done and I guess I don't believe in playing just white compositions" (370–371). From this perspective, Davis' embrace of contemporary R&B-rooted musics functions powerfully to distance himself from the past of jazz and what he painfully sees as its condescension from white elites and to identify directly with a younger generation of musicians who use their black identity as material for musical and performative meaning. It is no coincidence that in the same chapter Troupe includes Davis' extensive views on Prince and Cameo, contextualising their value in a lineage of black male icons that include James Brown, Marvin Gaye, Jimi Hendrix, Sly Stone, Little Richard and Duke Ellington.

Conclusion

This chapter has focused on *Tutu* to demonstrate how greater reference to contemporary music beyond jazz can inform our understanding of the meaningfulness of jazz recordings. While, as Miller's account to fellow jazz musicians demonstrates, *Tutu* does make sense within the diachronic frame of Miles' own jazz career, it owes just as much to the world of R&B, and its reformulation in smooth jazz, in which Miller had worked as a solo artist and producer. *Tutu* also requires that we rethink some of the certainties of how the jazz musician has been represented, especially the binary between artist and commercial performer that was deployed in much of the critical discussion of Davis' role in *Tutu*. Such positions strangely downplay the idea of collaboration and ignore or marginalise the importance of musical and musician identity in the way musicians decide what to play and how to play. Perversely, in the form it has developed, biography has tended to disempower the agency of jazz musicians, even ones as prominent as Davis. Ultimately the narratives *about* jazz musicians have come from jazz critics, journalists and academics whose frameworks too often are built on discursive narratives which serve their own diachronic engagement with jazz rather than more synchronic interests of musicians as agents in a wider system of commercial music making. And in jazz these questions of identity and agency can never escape the looming issues of race that Davis fought to tackle his whole career.

References

Amorosi, A. D. 2022. 'The Ballad of Miles Davis and Prince'. *Jazz Times*, February 18, 3. https://jazztimes.com/features/profiles/the-ballad-of-miles-davis-and-prince/3/.

Arnold-Forster, Tom. 2017. 'Dr. Billy Taylor, "America's Classical Music", and the Role of the Jazz Ambassador'. *Journal of American Studies* 51 (1): 117–139.

Barber, Simon. 2009. 'Industrial Mediation in Jazz Production: A Case Study of GRP Records'. PhD thesis. University of Liverpool.

Barber, Simon. 2010. 'Smooth Jazz: A Case Study in the Relationships Between Commercial Radio Formats, Audience Research and Music Production'. *Radio Journal: International Studies in Broadcast & Audio Media* 8 (1): 51–70.

Carson, Charles D. 2008. ''Bridging the Gap': Creed Taylor, Grover Washington Jr., and the Crossover Roots of Smooth Jazz'. *Black Music Research Journal* 28 (1): 1–15.

Chambers, Jack. 1998. *Milestones: The Music and Times of Miles Davis*. Da Capo Press.

Cole, George. 2005. *The Last Miles: The Music of Miles Davis, 1980–1991*. Equinox.

Cole, George. 2011. 'How Miles Davis Made *Tutu*'. *Jazzwise*, October 15, 2021. https://www.jazzwise.com/features/article/how-miles-davis-made-tutu.

Cook, Richard. 2005. *It's About That Time: Miles Davis on and off Record*. Atlantic Books.

Cook, Richard, and Brian Morton. 1996. *The Penguin Guide to Jazz on Compact Disc*. 3rd ed. Penguin.

Cook, Richard, and Brian Morton. 2008. *The Penguin Guide to Jazz Recordings*. 9th ed. Penguin.

Crouch, Stanley. 1990. 'Play the Right Thing: Miles Davis, the Most Brilliant Sellout in the History of Jazz'. *New Republic* 202 (7): 30–37.

Crouch, Stanley, ed. 2006a. *Considering Genius: Writings on Jazz*. Civitas Books.

Crouch, Stanley. 2006b. 'Prologue'. In *Considering Genius: Writings on Jazz*, edited by Stanley Crouch. Civitas Books.

Davis, Miles, and Quincy Troupe. 1989. *Miles: The Autobiography*. Simon and Schuster.

DeVeaux, Scott. 1997. *The Birth of Bebop: A Social and Musical History*. University of California Press.

Farbey, Roger. 2023. *Elastic Dream—The Music of Ian Carr: An Annotated Discography*. Jazz in Britain.

Fordham, John. 2019. 'Miles Davis: *Rubberband* Review—Traces of Majesty'. *The Guardian*, August 30. https://www.theguardian.com/music/2019/aug/30/miles-davis-rubberband-review.

McRae, Barry. 1988. *Miles Davis*. Apollo.

Milkowski, Bill. 1987. 'Review of Miles Davis' *Tutu*'. *DownBeat*, January 1987, 27.

Murray, Albert. 1976. *Stomping the Blues*. McGraw-Hill.

Murray, Albert, and Greg Thomas. 2016. *Murray Talks Music: Albert Murray on Jazz and Blues*. University of Minnesota Press.

Nicholson, Stuart. 1998. *Jazz-Rock: A History*. Canongate.

Palmer, Robert. 1986. 'In "Tutu," Miles Davis Goes Fully Electronic'. *New York Times*, October 1.

Palmer, Robert. 2009. *Blues and Chaos: The Music Writing of Robert Palmer*. Simon and Schuster.

Sales, Grover. 1984. *Jazz: America's Classical Music*. Prentice.

Shipton, Alyn. 2006. *Out of the Long Dark: The Life of Ian Carr*. Popular Music History. Equinox.

Szwed, John. 2002. *So What: The Life of Miles Davis*. Simon and Schuster.

Tavernier, Bertrand, dir. 1986. *Round Midnight*. Warner Bros.

Taylor, Billy. 1975. 'The History and Development of Jazz Piano: A New Perspective for Educators'. PhD diss., University of Massachusetts, Amherst.

Taylor, Billy. 1982. *Jazz Piano: History and Development*. William C. Brown.

Tingen, Paul. 2001. *Miles Beyond: The Electric Explorations of Miles Davis, 1967–1991*. Billboard Books.

Wall, Tim. 2007. 'David Murray: The Making of a Progressive Jazz Musician'. *Jazz Research Journal* 1 (2): 173–203.

Washburne, Christopher. 2004. 'Does Kenny G Play Bad Jazz? A Case Study'. In *Bad Music: The Music We Love to Hate*, edited by Christopher J. Washburne and Maiken Derno. Routledge.

West, Hollie. 1969. 'Black Tune'. *Washington Post*, March 13.

Williams, Martin T. 1970. *The Jazz Tradition*. Oxford University Press.

4

Miles on a Second Major

Miles Davis' Career from Columbia to Warner Bros. Records

Tim Wall

George Cole opens chapter 12 of his well-researched and detailed study *The Last Miles* with the statement, "In 1985, Miles shocked the music world by ending his thirty-year association with Columbia Records and signing for Warner Bros" (2005, 197). My contribution to rethinking Miles Davis' career here focuses on understanding what such a 'shocked' reception involved, how jazz writers like Cole have retrospectively narrated this event and how we could more broadly comprehend Davis' decision. As I will show, there is much to build upon the detailed and thorough work of Cole and others, but I seek to stimulate an extended understanding by interrogating the assumptions implicit in such biographical work. My purpose in doing so is not to challenge the factual accuracy of such research, nor simply to doubt the value of the narratives presented. Instead, I make more explicit, then investigate more deeply, how jazz history has dealt with the music industry within which musicians like Davis work. Most biography, of course, includes important references to the social context in which jazz was formed as a distinct music, and the role of record companies has always been included, most often by noting the labels on which the music under scrutiny was released, or highlighting the contributions of record company staff.

My contribution here is to add a layer of insight that uses the idea of maps of meaning[1] to understand the specifics of the Columbia and Warner

[1] In using the term "maps of meaning", I reference ideas of semantic mapping, extended to music-making as a meaningful activity. I do not intend any connection to the work of clinical psychology or the study of belief. As will be apparent, in this chapter I draw on wider ideas from semiology and critical discourse analysis in the approach.

Tim Wall, *Miles on a Second Major* In: *Rethinking Miles Davis*. Edited by: Roger Fagge, Nicolas Pillai, and Tim Wall, Oxford University Press. © Oxford University Press 2026. DOI: 10.1093/9780190085834.003.0004

record companies, but also their semantic place in the wider music culture in which Davis was operating. This allows us a speculative understanding of what Warner meant to Davis in 1985, and what Columbia had meant to him earlier in his career. As such, this chapter acts as a diachronic investigation, complementing work presented in chapter 3 on Davis' 1986 *Tutu* recording. That earlier chapter is based on a synchronic analysis to explore another, intersecting map of meaning related to approaches to music making utilised by Davis' contemporaries in 1985, most notably those artists who released records through labels owned by Warner.

This chapter, therefore, offers a reconsideration Davis' move to Warner Bros. Records. It replaces the story of a 'shock' move with a consideration of how the move made sense, at least to Davis, in that moment. This is not to dispute Cole's statement that such a move seemed like a dramatic change, especially as Davis had been so successful at Columbia for three decades, but to show how we can retrospectively account for the move in more meaningful terms. What I offer here, then, is not new primary evidence that reveals things that others have missed, but a dramatically different way of understanding Davis' career within different stages of the history of the US music record industry. Such a new analysis goes beyond the focus on the biographical Miles in relation to his earlier career, changing tastes in popular music and in recording technology; although all of those remain important to conceiving of Davis and his music. This chapter seeks to prove that while such biographic details are essential to understanding Davis' career, they are not sufficient.

I start by establishing the dominant way Davis' move to Warner is accounted for. This focuses mainly on the most detailed account we have so far, through an engagement with key chapters in Cole's book, but raises questions about the standard biographical account more generally. This allows me to characterise the standard story of this period of Miles' career before offering a distinctive rethink. In what follows, I first position Davis within the late 20th-century music industry, highlighting the relationship of his career to changes in the Columbia record company up to 1985, then contrast that with the way Warner operated in the jazz and rock music worlds. The final section contextualises Davis' relationship to Warner through to his death in 1991. This brings to the fore the way that both Columbia and Warner organised music production and their marketing strategies in the 1980s, along with the roles of industry executives like Clive Davis and George Butler (both at Columbia) and Tommy LiPuma (at Warner).

Examining the Existing Story

The place of record companies in accounts of jazz musicians and their music are most often restricted to discographic detail or biographic references to disputes with record company executives or changing opportunities to release recorded music. Given the emphasis on recorded music as the primary source material for the story of a musician's career, this is no surprise and, at its best, provides important insights. Miles Davis' career is written about more extensively and with greater elaboration than many others, and successive accounts have revealed more detail about his musical life.

Cole's (2005) analysis delves deeply into the operation of Davis' record companies, and so it makes a particularly useful jumping-off point to investigate what more needs to be done. The dramatic opener to chapter 12 of his book, with which I started this chapter, is part of an extensive three-chapter section of his study of Davis' later career (197–231). These chapters examine what the author calls 'The Road to Tutu', the destination being Davis' 1986 recording named in honor of the recently appointed South African Anglican archbishop, Desmond Tutu. In heralding the release of *Tutu*[2] in the book's narrative, Cole calls upon both hyperbole and one of his rhetorical triptychs to articulate the moment: "When *Tutu* was released in September 1986 it hit the music world like a whirl-wind. In every respect, *Tutu* was a milestone recording and everyone seemed to be talking about it. The reason could be put down to the M-factor—Miles, the music and the marketing" (262). Any serious analysis of Davis' change of record company would obviously include the musician and his music, and reference to the promotion activities of record labels points to deeper engagement with the role of the music industry. It would be a mistake not to consider Warner's inspired campaign to promote a strikingly packaged record sleeve. After all, as this chapter explores, this repackaging of his musical identity in contemporary form is exactly what Davis wanted his record label to achieve and exactly what Warner offered the musician when he signed with them as his new recording company in May 1985. As a long-term advocate of examining jazz within its political economy, I can only support Cole's emphasis on the importance of understanding the role of Warner and Columbia in Davis' career. However, Cole's observations

[2] *Tutu*, Warner Bros. Records, 9 25490-2. Recorded at Le Gonks West, West Hollywood, February 6, 1986; Capitol Tower, Los Angeles, February 10, 12, 13, 1986; Clinton Recording Studios, New York City, March 12–25, 1986. Released September 29, 1986.

do not in themselves explain anything about why the new music was received in the way it was, nor in what way it constituted a 'milestone' for Davis and jazz. (No pun seems to have been intended.)

The account of all three drivers fails to substantiate exactly what the importance of a new label was and how this move, along with Davis' first two musical collaborations at Warner, paved a way for what followed. Cole may simply mean that they are the three key events that precede the making and release of Davis' first Warner record, but his account does seem to try to deal with the paradoxical events that unfold. The trumpeter's first attempts at exploring new ways of making recorded music did not find favour at the label, and LiPuma does seem to have tried to negotiate between Davis' desires to explore contemporary black music styles and LiPuma's concept of what a Warner-produced Davis record should be like.

Cole's narrative is based more firmly on the proposition that the change of record company was more to do with leaving Columbia than joining Warner and was motivated by "*Aura*,[3] Wynton and money" (2005, 197). This neatly summarises the proposition he shares with similar biographical approaches from Richard Cook (2005), Paul Tingen (2001) and John Szwed (2002), all three of whom deal with the same issues. However, while the events these index certainly were important, they do not adequately explain the appeal of Warner to Davis at this point in time.

The first part of Cole's new triptych signals Davis' widely documented dissatisfaction with the way Columbia executives had treated the collaborative 1984 Copenhagen recordings he made with the Danish trumpeter, composer and arranger-producer Palle Mikkelborg and the Danish Radio Big Band. The *Aura* recordings did not receive a commercial release by Columbia until September 1989, long after Davis had switched labels. However, Columbia's treatment of this Davis project seems to exactly mirror the disinclination of executive staff at Warner to release Davis' *Rubberband* sessions two years later. This music was not actually released by Warner until 2018, as an EP, and in 2019 as the *Rubberband* album; and, as Cole's account in particular shows, Davis seemed equally annoyed about his treatment here. Either the move to Warner was a total miscalculation on Davis' and his management's part, or this simple narrative does not have the explanatory power it initially seems to have. In fact, as all Davis biographies detail, the trumpeter

[3] *Aura* refers to the Miles Davis LP recording of the same name: *Aura*, Columbia, C2X 45332. Recorded at Easy Sound Recording, Copenhagen, January 31–February 4, 1985. Released September 12, 1989.

had battled for 30 years with Columbia executives over which of his projects would be released and what form that release would take. It is not clear why the delay issuing *Aura* would, in itself, prompt a label move. Plainly, control over his musical releases was important for Davis, but it seems to have expressed itself in semiotic rather than contractual terms. Certainly in the moment of 1985, and given the position Davis had reached as a sales proposition, it is not beyond reason to suggest his managers could have negotiated a contract with greater control on releases with either Columbia or Warner.

The second motivation for change, argues Cole, was that Miles resented the fact that Wynton Marsalis, a jazz trumpeter from a younger generation—and one whose music was rooted in styles Davis was widely perceived to have once perfected but had now left behind—was favoured by George Butler, Columbia Records' Vice President for Jazz and Progressive Artists and Repertoire. However, as much as Davis was clearly irritated by Marsalis in person, it is a more likely explanation that, for Davis, Marsalis represented an 'older' music which the more senior trumpeter constantly asserted he had left behind. Put simply, for Davis, if Columbia was now represented by Marsalis' music (and Davis' past music), the future lay elsewhere.

Actually, many of the sources quoted by Cole provide the evidence the author marginalises in his account. As far more of the detail indicates, Davis positioned himself (and was positioned by Columbia) as aligned with jazz, rock and pop musicians with even stronger sales careers than Marsalis. Most notable here are George Benson, Chicago and Prince. The fact that these musicians released their recordings on the Warner label is as telling in this story as Columbia's strategic prioritisation of Marsalis. Moreover, after moving to Warner, Davis now worked with LiPuma, whose role (and even his corporate title) was almost identical to Butler's at Columbia. LiPuma actually made his corporate reputation by signing jazz guitarist Benson, and this is a more likely explanation for the move than the idea that Davis had a positive view on Warner's approach to jazz as progressive music. The evidence of interviews alone shows that it was the position of black music auteur Prince, and that of other Warner-signed, high-volume stars with roots in black music, that was important to Davis.

Finally, Cole suggests, Davis felt he was not being sufficiently rewarded financially by Columbia. However, as Cole himself recounts, and almost all Davis biographies point out, Davis was dissatisfied with the monetary returns for his work continually throughout his career. To cap this off, as Cole explains at length, the deal Davis' managers struck for him had upfront financial gains but long-term losses. Unless we start to treat Davis solely as a very unsuccessful, or very badly advised, musician-entrepreneur, the change of labels was plainly rooted in a more complex web of less immediate and less tangible factors.

To overcome the limitations set out so far, the approach taken in this chapter represents a significant move away from overt biography as a way of accessing the cultural meaning of recorded music, although I do build on such studies in my discussion. What follows, for instance, shares Cole's position that, in this period, change for Davis was defined by what happened in the recording studio. This is evidenced in the way Davis' recordings determined his live performances. As Cole demonstrates, new musical numbers, developed in the recording studio, became the source for Davis' live stage explorations and, as the approach to making Miles Davis recordings changed, so did the format of his stage work. Although Cole and others are not explicit about this, this privileging of new recordings in live sets follows a standard popular music industry practice in which live appearances form an essential part of the marketing for commercial record release. This was a noteworthy reversal of the standard process for most jazz musicians, and for Davis before his late 1950s Columbia recordings, where numbers developed on the bandstand form the basis for new recordings.

This chapter certainly follows Cole in placing the recorded music at the centre of our attention, but here I draw us back to questions about how the music means what it means. In doing so, I move from biographic concerns with why Miles wanted to move to Warner to questions about what Warner got from Miles economically, musically and semiotically. While doing so, I am not advocating for or against his Warner recordings. Instead, the analysis I present locates these recordings in the popular music and jazz discourse of their time, most notably in the way that the institutionalisation of recorded music relates to the music consumption cultures that constituted ideas of jazz and of other forms of popular music. Such a reconsideration pushes us to ask even harder questions about the extent to which issuing an LP on a particular record label is meaningful in music culture. Likewise, we are forced to consider the place of the organisation of music production and marketing in the creation of his Columbia and Warner albums. Even more fundamentally, these new insights enable us to rethink Miles Davis' long career.

I argue that Warner's approach was attractive to Davis for what it represented in contrast to Columbia, both in terms of their history and in the moment of 1985. As I show, exploring this contrast in both diachronic and synchronic dimensions provides a far more convincing explanation of what Davis and *Tutu* meant in 1980s popular music culture than existing biographies. The operation of record companies like Columbia and Warner have played an important part in forming both the history of jazz and the individual contributions musicians like Davis make. Jazz is as much the creation of the 20th-century entertainment industries as it is the vernacular and commercial musics which were synthesised to form its various sounds and musical practices. Theatrical and nightclub venues played important parts in forming jazz, and radio reframed and disseminated the music widely, but it was sound recording which captured snapshots of the music's sonic form and enabled it to be distributed across the world. That is not to position record companies as the dominant, let alone only force in determining what jazz was like and how it developed. Importantly, jazz musicians have significant agency, and Miles Davis had greater agency over his music than most. So here I aim to focus on the institutionalisation and political economy of jazz production, while keeping a nuanced sense of artistic agency to the fore and setting this within an understanding of how and why recorded music takes the form it does.

There is, at the same time, more to artist agency than a story in which personal grumbles are a motivation, even if such narratives are easier to construct from the personal accounts of the participants in the unfolding events, and they are simpler to reduce to a rhetorical triptych. Certainly accounting for the notion that Warner had connotational differences from Columbia in 1985 is much harder to achieve. However, reducing what was at play here to simply Davis' motivations to be able to spend more money on developing recording projects, leaving behind competition with younger players, and gaining a better deal, however important they were to the star trumpeter, does not actually help us understand what all this meant. That understanding is more clearly found in the map of popular music in which the giants of recorded music take their place. And even more precisely anchored in the realisation that the real giants of mid-1980s recorded music were not Davis or Marsalis, nor Benson or Prince, but Columbia and Warner.

What Did Miles Davis Mean to Columbia and Warner?

An explanation of what Davis' move to Warner signaled can be found in the distinct cultural connotations and associations of the two companies. In the early 1980s Columbia and WEA (Warner's parent corporation), along with European rivals BMG, EMI and PolyGram, dominated commercial music sales as the 'Big Five'. Most estimates suggested between 70% and 80% of all the records sold in the world were produced by just these five major companies. While sharing an ability to connect artists and music to consumers in a way that generated massive record sales, and therefore profits for their owners, each of these dominant companies had a different background and was driven by a different corporate strategy in the market for commercial music recordings. These companies, and their relationship to the hundreds of smaller, so-called independent companies, constituted an important map of meaning for both artist and music fans. There are few studies of the way record companies treat jazz, let alone how they make it meaningful. When this issue is studied in any detail, it is most often in relation to individual small independents, which in their heyday are understood as champions of uncompromised 'real' jazz set against an unstated other: the majors (see, for instance, Gillett 1974; Gray 1988; Cook 2001).

While for the record companies, artists like Miles Davis had a 'brand value', for artists and consumers alike, the companies in themselves, and in relation to each other, were also meaningful. The way each major maps on to the relationships of popular music over time will help us to understand what is at stake when Davis 'jumped ship'. The contrast in history and strategy between Columbia and Warner Bros. was arguably stronger than that between BMG, EMI and PolyGram. While superficially similar as the only remaining US-owned record corporations in the 1985 Big Five, Columbia and Warner Bros. arrived at this dominance through very different trajectories. Warner Bros. Records had its origins as an 'in-house' record label for the film studio business bent on multimedia expansion in the 1950s, and its early releases focused on singing projects from its big screen stars. By contrast, at this time Columbia had enjoyed a nearly 100-year history, had a catalogue which stretched across classical, jazz, rock and pop, and a stability, solidity and confidence, combined with an embrace of new music and technology, that seemed to echo both Davis' personality and his place in jazz. Columbia was the venerable and august record company in the US and globally. The company's president from 1956, Goddard Lieberson, largely secured the company's position, and his own job, in 1957, by overseeing *My Fair Lady*,[4] one of the best-selling examples of the dominant record form: the

[4] Rex Harrison and Julie Andrews, *My Fair Lady*, Columbia Masterworks, OL 509. Recorded at Columbia 30th Street Studio, New York City, March 24, 1956. Released April 2, 1956.

Broadway show album. From such profits, suggests Fredric Dannen (1990, 60), "Lieberson recorded 'important' music that sold poorly, such as Duke Ellington".

It was George Avakian who, in 1955, brought Miles Davis to Columbia from the trumpeter's previous label, the independent jazz company, Prestige Records. Avakian (2000) had established himself at Columbia in 1940, overseeing the Hot Jazz Classics reissue programme of out-of-print recordings owned by the company, which included an impressive back catalogue of Louis Armstrong and Duke Ellington sides. Columbia had launched their new 33⅓ rpm, micro-groove long-playing format and applied it to 12-inch discs in 1948, the same year that Avakian was given the role of introducing the first 100 popular music LP releases as Head of International and Popular Albums. One can conclude that his role was to extend his work on repackaging the back catalogue for the new record format. However, Avakian focused his attention on creating new contexts in which the LP format could create new jazz recordings. For Darren Mueller (2024), both Prestige and Columbia, in their different ways, were central in utilising the long-playing format to transform both the market for jazz and its commercial recording. Mueller focuses on Avakian's role in creating live recordings that would reinvigorate the career of Duke Ellington, including the celebrated but latterly controversial *Ellington at Newport* (see, for instance, Morton 2008; Mueller 2014; Williams 2017). However, it was the three Miles Davis recordings Avakian produced before his departure from Columbia in 1958 that established the model for Davis' output at the label for the next 30 years. Bobbie-Jane Gardner and I further explore Avakian's role as Davis' collaborator producer in chapter 8, including the way the company executive established his own agency at Columbia through his "white, masculine authority" (Mueller 2024, 128).

In many ways, beginning in the mid-1960s, Davis' Columbia career took over from Ellington this leading role in signifying Columbia's strategy around the LP. Columbia was Davis' record company for 30 years, between 1955 and 1985, and the trumpeter seemed in many ways to personify something of the connotational character of the label. In the 1940s and 1950s Columbia positioned itself as defining what, by the end of the next decade, would become known as middle-of-the-road (MOR) popular music. Under producer Mitch Miller, Columbia became the most successful record company of the 1950s, with a sound indexed by some of Miller's most successful signings: Tony Bennett, Rosemary Clooney, Ray Conniff, Johnny Mathis and the defining voice of the decade, Doris Day. In this gaggle of luminaries, Miles Davis was Columbia's star musical innovator, yet he sat safely within the popular musical establishment. Davis' LP records cemented affluent adult jazz record buyers as a key market for these relatively expensive commodities.

Columbia placed Davis at the centre of its attempt to explore new forms of musical composition and improvisation and exploited the idea of studio-based music making, along with the newly established possibilities of high-fidelity stereo recording. His most influential recording, 1959's *Kind of Blue*,[5] in many ways constituted the exemplar of a coherent musical offering that made use of the long-play format of the 12-inch disc, rather than just using its capacity to collect individual pieces together in one place. Davis' records of this time altered what was understood to be jazz and opened up the possibilities of experimentation and the dominance of the LP in the two decades that followed. In Columbia's terms, *Kind of Blue* is bookended by two Davis recordings which successfully brought the other two staples of LP commodification into the domain of jazz. *Porgy and Bess*,[6] recorded in July and August 1958 and released in March 1959 under arranger Gil Evans' direction, applied the idea of jazz improvisation to the existing form of the Broadway show album that *My Fair Lady* had proved could be so successful commercially. Then, in November 1959 and March 1960, Evans took a piece of European art music and produced a jazz version of an orchestral suite for Davis, which Columbia released as *Sketches of Spain*.[7]

By contrast, Warner Bros. Records in the 1950s was a fledgling company building a corporate music unit as a spinoff from its film division by tempting record buyer interest in its screen stars reimagined as recording artists. It was not until the mid-1960s, as the music division started to match its business to emerging markets, that Warner established any presence in the record industry. From this point, its executives brought the company into the mainstream of the music industry through acquisition, first by purchasing Frank Sinatra's struggling Reprise Records, and then profiting by the star's screen and recording career comeback; second by buying Loma Records to focus

[5] *Kind of Blue*, Columbia, CS 8163. Recorded at Columbia 30th Street Studio, New York City, March 2 and April 22, 1959. Released August 17, 1959.

[6] *Porgy and Bess*, Columbia, CL 1274. Recorded at Columbia 30th Street Studio, New York City, July 22, 29 and August 4, 18, 1958. Released March 9, 1959.

[7] *Sketches of Spain*, Columbia, CL 1480. Recorded Columbia 30th Street Studio, New York City, November 15, 20, 1959, and March 10, 1960. Released July 18, 1960.

on the R&B and emerging soul markets among black and white Americans, a strategy consolidated by the acquisition of Atlantic Records in 1967, with its broad black music catalogue. Just a year later Warner completed its transformation into a major company by absorbing another vibrant independent company, Elektra, and renaming the corporation WEA, its music operations organised under three distinct, operationally independent divisions: Warner, Elektra and Atlantic. Initially, Atlantic, with its 20-year reputation for jazz, R&B and (later) soul, became the main provider of jazz within WEA, leaving Warner Bros. to concentrate on the now dominant Adult-Oriented Rock market segments of record consumers. Warner gained a reputation as an 'artists first' record company, ironically on the back of bands like the Grateful Dead, who never achieved the sales their dedicated 1960s following suggested was possible.

While significantly smaller in catalogue and sales than Columbia, WEA in all its subdivisions seemed to be taking the ground away from their more venerable label competition and was certainly better placed to capture the more black music–rooted, rock-oriented future of popular music. By the end of this decade both Columbia and Miles Davis were radically changing in significant ways in response to Warner label artists. On the threshold of the 1970s, as Davis rejected even the idea of jazz and used a new recording, *Bitches Brew*,[8] to reinvent his music as commercially successful black progressive music, Columbia staff were busy reinventing the record company. All accounts of Davis' late 1960s and early 1970s work emphasise this period as a perpetual musical revolution for the trumpeter, but yet again, this is almost always explained using a standard biographical narration of the trumpeter's life and music. Paul Tingen (2001, 43), for instance, rather awkwardly locates Miles' music at this point in broader shifts in popular music from 1967 onward, citing the Beatles' *Sgt. Pepper's Lonely Hearts Club Band*[9] and the Beach Boys' *Pet Sounds*[10] as influences on Davis' producer, Teo Macero. However, both these interpretive frames misposition Davis' work by emphasising simple notions of personal drivers and the absorption of technological innovation.

With far greater insight, Ian Carr (1982, 186–189) argues 1967 offered up to Davis and Macero a far more pressing and important triptych: Clive Davis,

[8] *Bitches Brew*, Columbia, GP 26. Recorded at Columbia 30th Street Studio, New York City, August 19–21, 1969. Released March 30, 1970.

[9] The Beatles, *Sgt. Pepper's Lonely Hearts Club Band*, Parlophone, PMC 7027. Recorded EMI and Regent Sound Studios, London, December 6, 1966–April 21, 1967. Released May 26, 1967.

[10] The Beach Boys, *Pet Sounds*, Capitol Records, DT 2458. Recorded Western, Gold Star, Columbia and Sunset Sound studios, Hollywood, July 12, 1965–April 13, 1966. Released May 16, 1966.

the Monterey Pop Festival and *Rolling Stone* magazine. Clive Davis, who had arrived at Columbia to be part of the company's legal team and then moved swiftly to an administrative role as Vice President, was appointed Company President in 1967 (Dannen 1990). He swiftly refocused the company's recording and marketing activities towards rock artists linked to the American counterculture, including signing bands that drew heavily on black and jazz forms, including Santana, Chicago and Blood, Sweat & Tears. Both Carr and Clive Davis himself cite a visit to the Monterey International Pop Festival as a pivotal moment. As Kubernik and Kubernik (2011) reveal through multiple interviews, the one-off festival gave a platform for a growing West Coast rock music scene inspired by the model of the Monterey Jazz Festival, sharing the same showgrounds venue and some of the jazz business knowhow. For Clive Davis, attending the event was an "epiphany": "I saw a cultural revolution, I saw a musical revolution, a social revolution".[11] In interviews, the main festival organisers, Lou Adler, Alan Pariser and Derek Taylor, all cite the desire to position the emerging music in the same terms in which jazz had become established in American culture (Kubernik and Kubernik 2011). The same philosophy drove San Francisco–based *Rolling Stone* magazine—established by Berkeley dropout Jann Wenner and jazz critic Ralph J. Gleason—whose first edition focused on the Monterey Pop Festival, with an editorial asserting the new magazine was "not just about the music, but about the things and attitudes that music embraces" (Wenner 1967).

Miles Davis seemed to have the same epiphany much earlier, attracting a younger generation of players to his bands, including saxophonist Wayne Shorter, pianist Herbie Hancock and drummer Tony Williams in the early 1960s, and his music became more experimental. From *Filles de Kilimanjaro*[12] in 1968 through 1969's *In a Silent Way*[13] and to 1970's *Bitches Brew*, Davis' LP covers rhetorically asserted the recording's departure from the jazz mainstream, positioning the recordings as "DIRECTIONS IN MUSIC BY MILES DAVIS". The original sleeve notes for *In a Silent Way*, attributed to Frank Glenn (probably producer Macero),[14] pitch Davis and the LP as innovators beyond jazz: "He has come up with something new

[11] Interview with Clive Davis in 2017. *Attending Monterey Pop Festival.* Recording Academy/GRAMMYs. https://www.youtube.com/watch?v=7hVKa2juMmQ.

[12] *Filles De Kilimanjaro*, Columbia, CS 9750. Recorded at Columbia 30th Street Studio, New York City, June 19–21 and September 24, 1968. Released December 1968.

[13] *In a Silent Way*, Columbia, CS 9875. Recorded at Columbia 30th Street Studio, New York City, February 18, 1969. Released July 30, 1969.

[14] See http://www.45worlds.com/cdalbum/cd/ck40580.

in music. The form is free, and from this freedom a masterful outgrowth of composition has emerged. NEW DIRECTIONS by Miles is what it implies". Through this process, the dominant jazz histories tell us, Davis asserted himself in a world of art music as a genius musician, who seemed to transcend place and time, race and culture. And to many, the music on these Columbia recordings 'sounds' this as truth, when of course, as Davis increasingly felt, it was not. Over the next 10 years Davis built upon these new possibilities of extended length, modernist form and studio-based composition, but in a way that rejected the integrationist ambitions of his late 1950s work, and like most African Americans he would demand to be taken as the equal of white Americans; but on his terms, not theirs.

As Clive Davis (1975, 260) relates, from the mid-1960s the record company began to subsidise the trumpeter's expensive tastes through regular advances they knew they would not earn back in record sales income. Miles Davis' symbolic value to Columbia was clearly worth more than his direct financial return. In the Columbia president's own words: "[A]t no time did Miles ever recoup his advances . . . [but] he was good for Columbia in the long run, both on commercial and cultural levels" (263). By the mid-1960s, this value derived from his decade-long string of critically-respected Columbia releases. This financial support from Columbia went way beyond contractual terms and continued through the 1970s and 1980s, and the company even renewed his contract in 1976, just at the point that Davis withdrew from commercial recording and live performance for nearly five years. Carr (1982, 279) has even suggested that in 1980 the record company created a Miles Davis Fund which paid the trumpeter on a regular basis.

However, according to Clive Davis, while the trumpeter was willing to embrace musical changes and incorporate some of the idioms of rock-based music, leaving the small jazz circuit behind seems to have been more difficult. In a tussle about the trumpeter's lower record sales when compared with other Columbia bands like Blood, Sweat & Tears—who in many ways had created a commercial asset out of Miles Davis' experiments with jazz-rock—Clive Davis' (1975, 261) suggestion that Miles should play the 1,000-seat New York Fillmore stadium rock venue led to a threat from the trumpeter that he would do no more recordings for the label. Miles' threat was another he did not act on, and of course the 1970 *Miles Davis at Fillmore*[15] LP located

[15] *Miles Davis at Fillmore*, Columbia, G 30038. Recorded live at Fillmore East in New York City June 17–20, 1970. Released October 28, 1970.

the jazz trumpeter even more firmly into what, in music industry argot, was then called contemporary music. As a best-selling jazz album, *Fillmore* also reinforced in Clive Davis' mind the value of Miles to Columbia. It was *Bitches Brew*, though, that was the touchstone of commercial success. Released in 1970 it sold strongly, quickly reaching half a million retail sales and gained Recording Industry Association of America Gold certification by 1976, going on to platinum status in 2003.[16] The album was of particular importance because it showed Clive Davis how a jazz artist could sell records to avid contemporary music fans on a similar scale to that achieved by leading rock artists.

Having made these points it would be overstating the matter to say that incorporating Miles Davis' recordings into Columbia's 1970s rock marketing strategy was coherent and well-informed. This is made clear by some reflection on that strategy itself. Just as Miles Davis was projecting his own music as a new direction, Columbia's marketing team tried to promote the label as part of the new US youth counterculture. In December 1968 the promotions department took out full-page ads in underground newspapers to promote new releases under the strapline 'But The Man Can't Bust Our Music', and, according to Doggett (2009, 220), in January 1969 the record label started to brand its rock releases "The Revolutionaries Are on Columbia". However, Columbia's position as the venerable company of American recorded music and both Miles and Clive Davis were not in any way obviously aligned with the new ideas of a youth-oriented, alternative music culture. In 1970 Miles was 44, and Clive Davis was only three years younger. The conception of the Columbia marketing strategy, and its perceived relationship to musical experiment and the new alternative culture, was also plainly ill-considered, to say the least. As Doggett has pointed out, 'The Man Can't Bust Our Music' ad promoted recordings of orchestra composers Charles Ives, Karlheinz Stockhausen, and Edgard Varèse, minimalist composer Terry Riley, and some experiments with the Moog synthesiser. A few months later, promotions that covered musicians as diverse as Miles Davis, Thelonious Monk, Bob Dylan, Taj Mahal and (the now long forgotten) Chad & Jeremy were framed by the strapline "Underground . . . Overground. All that matters is that you dig the sound".

16 https://www.riaa.com/gold-platinum/?tab_active=default-award&se=miles+davis#search_section.

Warner seemed less interested in promoting its countercultural credentials using marketing campaigns and focused instead on a policy for rock musicians which looked remarkably like the approach Columbia had taken with jazz musicians Davis, Ellington and Monk. As the WEA Atlantic label—which had originally made its reputation as an independent focused on jazz and black music—expanded its roster firmly into the fields of rock and pop, initially with releases by British progressive rock bands Led Zeppelin and Yes, Warner Bros. Records executives started to look at the possibilities of jazz as part of a label strategy within WEA. In the early 1970s, the model for Warner clearly came from Columbia, whose accomplishments in reimagining jazz for a wider group of more progressive music listeners and, in particular, the success they had with Miles Davis, demonstrated the value of jazz for a major company.

The fit between Miles Davis and Columbia since 1955 seemed unbreakable, and it makes even more sense if we imagine how Davis might have been located at Warner Bros. Records during the 1950s, 1960s and even into the 1970s. As we will see, until the mid-1980s Warner would have offered little to Davis, and Warner executives showed little understanding of what to do with the music that came from Davis' orbit. Up until the late 1970s, on the other hand, Columbia's 'jazz and progressive music' strategy emanated from Davis and the new careers of his former band members and the bands they built.

Davis' musical trajectory remained a good match with the interests and perceived image of Columbia for at least a further 15 years. *Jack Johnson*[17] and *Live-Evil*,[18] both released in 1971, and 1972's *On the Corner*[19] capitalised on the ideas in *Bitches Brew*, while the 1973 releases *In Concert*[20] and *Black Beauty: Live at the Fillmore West*,[21] together with the Japanese concerts on *Agharta*[22] in 1975 and *Pangaea*[23] in 1976 and 1977's *Dark Magus*[24] all

[17] *Jack Johnson*, Columbia Masterworks, S 30455. Recorded at Columbia 30th Street Studio, New York City, February 18 and April 7, 1970. Released February 24, 1971.

[18] *Live-Evil*, Columbia, G 30954. Recorded at Columbia Studio B in New York City, February 6 and June 3–4, 1970; live at The Cellar Door in Washington, DC, December 19, 1970. Released November 17, 1971.

[19] *On the Corner*, Columbia, KC 31906. Recorded at Columbia 52nd Street, New York City, June 1, June 6, and July 7, 1972. Released October 11, 1972.

[20] *In Concert*, Columbia, KG 32092. Recorded live at Philharmonic Hall, New York City, September 29, 1972. Released May 1973.

[21] *Black Beauty: Live at the Fillmore West*, CBS/Sony, SOPJ 39-40. Recorded live at Fillmore West, San Francisco, April 10, 1970. Released 1973 (Japan only).

[22] *Agharta*, CBS/Sony, SOPJ 92~93. Recorded live at Festival Hall, Osaka, February 1, 1975. Released August 1975 (Japan only).

[23] *Pangaea*, CBS/Sony, SOPZ 96~97. Recorded live at Festival Hall, Osaka, February 1, 1975. Released 1976 (Japan only).

[24] *Dark Magus*, CBS/Sony, 40AP 741~2. Recorded live at Carnegie Hall, New York City, March 30, 1974. Released 1977 (Japan only).

repeated the concepts of *Miles Davis at Fillmore. Black Beauty*, *Agharta*, *Pangaea* and *Dark Magus* were initially released only in Japan, reflecting the trumpeter's rising popularity in this international market.

During Miles Davis' exalted period at Columbia, Warner had consolidated its place as one of the Big Five majors and by the mid-1970s was primarily targeting record buyers in their 20s and 30s with high-profile artists selling single recordings at scale. By the turn of the decade both the music on, and market for, jazz commercial recordings was undergoing substantial change.

Progressive Jazz into the 1980s

By the late 1970s Columbia had translated Davis' crossover success into a corporate strategy and appointed one of the industry's most successful champions of the approach. When George Butler became Columbia Records' Vice President for Jazz and Progressive Artists and Repertoire in 1979, he brought with him eight years of experience in transforming the Blue Note label from a niche jazz independent into the crossover subsidiary of United Artists Records. Butler's first notable success at Blue Note was with 1972's *Black Byrd*,[25] which teamed Davis acolyte Donald Byrd with soul producers Fonce and Larry Mizell, promoting the record through strong marketing campaigns. By the time the Blue Note label was shelved (temporarily) by its new owners, EMI, in 1979, Butler had created a commercial asset out of albums by Byrd, Bobbi Humphrey, Earl Klugh and Ronnie Laws, among others, combining strong contemporary production with the 'Blue Note Hits a High Note' marketing strapline. This market success, and the music on which it was based, has been neglected in jazz studies. Even Richard Cook's (2001) thoughtful book-length history of Blue Note gives only four pages to this period and does not even mention Butler's role.

Leading in a new role at a major company and reimagining jazz as a part of a new progressive force of popular music, Butler steered Columbia's engagement with Davis' career and legacy. Butler underwrote the trumpeter's four-year sabbatical from performing and recording and led the efforts to persuade him to return to recording in 1980. Butler enticed Davis to continue in much the same way in the 1980s, mixing studio and live recordings

[25] *Black Byrd*, Blue Note, BN-LA047-F. Recorded at The Sound Factory, Hollywood, April 3–4, 1972. Released 1973.

with bands based upon young innovative musicians rooted as much in rock and funk styles as jazz, releasing *The Man with the Horn* (1981),[26] *We Want Miles* (1982),[27] *Star People* (1983),[28] *Decoy* (1984)[29] and *You're Under Arrest* (1985).[30] Just as important, Butler signed some of the biggest-selling jazz artists of the 1980s to Columbia and guided their recordings through his role as executive producer. These included Billy Cobham, who in many ways consolidated Davis' early 1970s experiments, along with Bob James and Grover Washington Jr., with whom Butler carried forward much of his approach from Blue Note.

Warner's own initial experiments with what became known as jazz and progressive music rather transparently built on the success of *Bitches Brew*, combined with Butler's approach to making soul jazz popular with a wider affluent white audience. The solution at Warner was to find a Miles Davis sideman and get them in the studio with a Columbia producer who had commercial success synthesising black music and rock styles. Their precise answer to this challenge was to take Herbie Hancock's early 1970s Mwandishi band into the studio with producer David Rubinson, who had established The Chambers Brothers, Santana and Taj Mahal at Columbia. Just for good measure, Rubinson brought that symbol of Columbia progressive music, the Moog synthesiser, into the band's second recording, *Crossings*.[31] The results, though, where more successful creatively than they were commercially, and (ironically) Hancock and Rubinson would achieve that combination of musical experiment and major sales with *Head Hunters*[32] just a few years later at Columbia. The value of Hancock's Mwandishi recordings took a long time to receive any retrospective recognition. Initially released on 12-inch vinyl in 1971, a month later than Davis' *Jack Johnson* LP on which Hancock also

[26] *The Man with the Horn*, Columbia, FC 36790. Recorded at Columbia 30th Street Studio, New York City, June 1, 1980–May 6, 1981. Released July 1981.

[27] *We Want Miles*, Columbia, C2 38005. Recorded live at KIX in Boston; Avery Fisher Hall, New York City; and special stage in Nishi-Shinjuku June 27, July 5, October 4, 1981. Released May 1982.

[28] *Star People*, Columbia, FC 38657. Recorded at Columbia Studio B, New York City; live at Jones Beach Marine Theater, Wantagh, NY; The Record Plant, New York City; live Cullen Auditorium, University of Houston, August 11, 1982–February 3, 1983. Released April 1983.

[29] *Decoy*, Columbia, FC 38991. Recorded at A&R Studio, New York City, June 30, 1983; Théâtre St. Denis, Montreal, July 7, 1983; Record Plant, New York City, September 5, 10 and 11, 1983. Released June 1984.

[30] *You're Under Arrest*, Columbia, CK 40023. Recorded at Record Plant, New York City, January 26, 1984–January 14, 1985. Released April 1985.

[31] *Crossings*, Warner Bros. Records, BS 2617 Recorded at Pacific, San Mateo; Different Fur, San Francisco, February 15–17, 1972. Released May 1972.

[32] *Head Hunters*, Columbia, KC 32731. Recorded at Wally Heider and Different Fur, San Francisco, September 1973. Released, October 26, 1973.

performed, Hancock's band recording did not chart, while Davis' Columbia release hit Top 5, and Mwandishi saw only a reissue as late as 1994, while the *Jack Johnson* LP was back in print as early as 1977 as *A Tribute to Jack Johnson*. It is hard to imagine Davis would have thought that this was the moment to move to Warner.

Yet Warner had far greater success with a pure Blue Note crossover 'progressive' jazz strategy focused on the success of a former CTI artist. The CTI label was established by producer Creed Taylor. ('CTI' stood for Creed Taylor Incorporated.) He had formerly produced jazz–bossa nova at independent label Verve, and then spun out the CTI imprint at indie A&M, before establishing it as one of the most successful 1970s jazz labels, building on first guitarist West Montgomery, and subsequently his musical acolyte, George Benson. Charles Carson (2008, 5) effectively defines the CTI sound as "a style of jazz that would attempt to use the familiarity of popular songs to 'crossover' to mainstream audiences, while at the same time relying on the credentials (and presumably, the musical talents) of these artists to retain a connection to 'authentic' jazz". Under Taylor's guidance, often set in Don Sebesky's jazz orchestral arrangements, Benson produced a string of strong-selling recordings, including the 1970 Beatles cover album *The Other Side of Abbey Road*,[33] 1972's *White Rabbit*,[34] with a title track cover of the Jefferson Airplane song, and 1973's *Body Talk*.[35] Using the same approach, with richer orchestrations set in Tommy LiPuma's glossy production, Benson re-created the Gábor Szabó and Bobby Womack performance of 'Breezin', which LiPuma had produced six years before for his own Blue Thumb company. Along with a very different rendition of Leon Russell's 'This Masquerade' and four other tracks, the records secured LiPuma's prominent place at Warner.

It is hard to overstate the importance of Benson's *Breezin'*,[36] for both Warner and the wider American music industry. The recording won six prizes at the 1976 Grammy Awards, covering Album of the Year, Record of the Year for 'This Masquerade', Best Engineered Album, Best Pop Instrumental

[33] *The Other Side of Abbey Road*, CTI Records, SP-3028. Recorded at Van Gelder Studio, Englewood Cliffs, NJ, October 22–23, November 4–5, 1969. Released June 1970.

[34] *White Rabbit*, CTI Records, CTI 6015. Recorded at Van Gelder Studio, Englewood Cliffs, NJ, November 23, 24, 30, 1971. Released 1972.

[35] *Body Talk*, CTI Records, CTI 6033. Recorded at Van Gelder Studio, Englewood Cliffs, NJ, November, July 17–18, 1973. Released August 23, 1973.

[36] *Breezin'*, Warner Bros. Records, BS 2919. Recorded at Capitol Studio, Hollywood, January 6–8, 1976. Released March 19, 1976.

and Best Male Pop Vocal Performance.[37] In October 22, 1984, *Breezin'* was certified a million-seller in the US by Recording Industry Association of America.[38] It certainly convinced the Warner top brass that jazz recordings that combined jazz with pop and R&B productions like this would be an important area for the future. In 1979 LiPuma was appointed Vice President of Jazz and Progressive Music at Warner Bros. Records to execute this very approach. At Warner, Lipuma initially worked with a number of artists who, like Benson, had recorded records for CTI. Most notably, South Americans Eumir Deodato, Antônio Carlos Jobim and João Gilberto. He also developed artists as diverse as Bill Evans, Al Jarreau and Stuff. Evans, of course, had played on Miles' *Kind of Blue*.

There is irony to this moment of success modelled by Butler and LiPuma, and copied widely across the industry, because it led to all the major US companies initially neglecting a rising interest in the back-history of jazz among a younger generation coming to adulthood in the 1980s. This is most often associated with the 'neoclassical' jazz recordings of Wynton Marsalis released by Columbia from 1982 and with the renaissance of Blue Note as a reissue and contemporary releases label from 1985. Intriguingly (especially given Cole's story about Davis' dissatisfaction with Butler's privileging of Marsalis), Cook suggests Butler procrastinated about finalising a contract with the young pretender (2001, 212). In retrospect, it seems ridiculous that a corporate record company VP for jazz would not jump at securing Marsalis in this moment but, so strong was the sense that jazz could pay its way only through the model of Davis' jazz rock or Blue Note crossover 'progressive' jazz, that contracting Marsalis was seen as a risk.

This new mid-1980s jazz map of meaning is oft noted but infrequently examined. Perhaps because jazz commentators were themselves participants in what was to become a struggle over exactly what jazz was and had been, we have not yet explored what was at play here with a clear head. Stuart Nicholson's (1990) *Jazz: The Modern Renaissance* is important because it sets out much of the detail but utilises such a strong division between what Nicholson sees as a jazz culture and media and pop's mainstream that he misses the very changes he seeks to explain. The notion that the 1980s was a decade in which the truth and vitality of jazz were restored is, in reality, just

[37] https://www.grammy.com/grammys/awards/19th-annual-grammy-awards-1976.

[38] https://www.riaa.com/gold-platinum/?tab_active=default-award&se=george+benson+breezin#search_section.

one partial position within a debate, and it sits some distance from being an insightful account of this intriguing new twist to the history of jazz.

Music critic Stanley Crouch led the most sustained attack on Miles' post-late 1960s music. In a memorable but excoriating essay in the *New Republic* (1990), Crouch castigated Davis for being "the most brilliant sellout in the history of jazz". The essay was later reproduced in a compendium of Crouch's writing, *Considering Genius* (2006).[39] The whole period of music is evaluated as "progressively trendy and dismal" (251), "an abject surrender to popular trends" (252), with "a sound so decadent that it can no longer disguise the shriveling of its maker's soul" (240). This position, in which Davis' later 'commercial', 'trend-driven' and 'empty' work is contrasted with the 'transcendence', 'genius' and 'brilliance' of his earlier music, sets the framework for much discussion of the trumpeter's career and music. Even those who champion Davis' recordings through the *Kilimanjaro–Silent Way–Bitches Brew–Fillmore* period draw upon the same discursive constructions to vilify examples of his releases on Warner. For instance, Nicholson was happy in 2011 to distance himself from the 'self-aggrandisement' of the Crouch thesis and to frame the music on a repackaged *Tutu* in terms of change and redefinition and champion it as "a bona fide Davis classic and an album that numbers among the best jazz recordings of the last 25 years". However, in his review of what he positions as jazz's 1980s resurgence, *Tutu* appears only in terms of Davis' move to Warner and a collaboration with Miller, and by 1998 Nicholson hardly mentions the album in his book on jazz rock, even though Davis is the defining musician of the book. In the latter, Nicholson presents *Tutu* as interchangeable with the later *Doo-Bop*, whose hip-hop base he argues is incompatible with jazz: "[J]azz and hip-hop could never be anything more than an uncomfortable liaison between man and machine' (231). Three years later, propounding a new thesis that jazz in the US was dead, Nicholson (2001) "confirmed the seeming incompatibility of jazz and rap". Focused on *Doo-Bop*, he asserts, "Never part of the music's internal construction, the collage of beats and samples assumed an independent existence as a rhythmic, rather than musical medium, thus musical considerations are subservient to the message. The jazz musician, robbed of his storytelling privilege, remained apart, an outsider never central to the performance (the machine), his role that of an occasional participant with a solo here, a solo

[39] Confusingly, the book does not cite the original source of the essay but dates it as from 1986. This seems unlikely as the essay references *Siesta* from 1987 and *Amandla* and *Aura*, both released in 1989.

there or an obbligato, ingredients of decoration rather than an integral art of the music's overall construction" (1998, 231). Aside from the rather striking similarity of Nicholson's proposal to arguments that were made against 'hot" jazz in the 1920s, it also highlights the sort of analysis that emerges from the application of a critical frame built out of the idea that jazz is somehow a transcendental form of art music. While Crouch and Nicholson are just two theorists who use such frames (they are dominant, close to universal even, within jazz criticism), such positions have required some considerable ideological work to construct. In the 1970s Crouch was, of course, one of the great advocates for free jazz and the New York loft scene, before he discovered Albert Murray and Wynton Marsalis and reimagined jazz as black America's classical music. Likewise, Nicholson provided a spirited argument for locating jazz rock within a longer jazz tradition, before championing European musicians as the inheritors of jazz as art and contrasting this with what he sees as the commercialism of contemporary jazz musicians in the country of jazz's birth. Both position jazz as a form created outside commercial determinants, when, of course, it is a music that emerged from commercial, mediated, mass entertainment.

The more productive way into this is heralded, yet again, by Carr, who emphasises a very different aspect of the label change: "In 1985, Miles Davis had once more wiped the slate clean . . . in order to join Warner Bros and start afresh . . . looking for new musical visions as well as different modes of procedure in the recording studio" (1998, 449).

As I show in more detail in chapter 3, Davis' first commercial release with Warner, *Tutu*, provides us with a case study in the relationship between the agency of an artist and the institutional forces of a major record company. As Davis started to consider that he should leave Columbia behind, in the early 1980s the Warner's big sellers were some of the icons of American popular music: Christopher Cross, Chicago, Elvis Costello, ZZ Top, Madonna and Prince. Together the case study and cultural semiotic analysis provide a greater sense of how *Tutu* took the form it did and, given its distinctiveness, how it emerged from the new company and not from Columbia.

Conclusion

The focus of this chapter, on Miles Davis' long recording career through the meaningfulness of his contracts with his two main recording companies, acts as a model for wider studies of jazz musicians and their music. Doing so in no way detracts from the agency of the musician. As the example of Davis demonstrates, musicians of this status make decisions and are not simply driven by larger forces over which they have no control. They do, however, make such decisions with a field of meaning that relates directly to their self-identity and the way they position themselves in wider senses of jazz. At one level jazz musicians are no different from any other creative worker in the way they negotiate the political economy of the music business, and yet at another level they are a special case of the point at which creativity must find resonance with the economic and cultural drivers of profit-driven businesses.

While Jed Rasula (1995) long ago alerted us to "the seductive menace of records in jazz history", recorded music and the businesses in which jazz musicians operate are major strands of professional careers and, ultimately, the decisions they make about music. For a musician like Davis, who made so much money from record sales (and advances on those sales), this is many times more important. However, jazz studies has not yet produced a sophisticated model of the meaningfulness of the record companies to which musicians sign. Attentive writers like Mueller and Cole offer important detail that is often missing in more immediate critical responses to recordings. Mueller's exploration of the role of key record company executives and the cultural capital they amass to be successful in both independent and corporate companies provides a model for future analysis. Cole, in studies of later musicians like Davis, demonstrates how important it is to build from the detail of primary sources. The historical detail really matters. And yet biography tend to emphasise temperament and personality over meaning and identity as frames from which stories about musicians are constructed. While it is the musician who has agency, record companies are not just employers of creative and managerial talent; they are also meaningful entities in a wider cultural landscape.

The range of commercial Miles Davis recordings that are traced in this chapter was created within the wider semiosis of the company that recorded, released and promoted them. The recordings are as much the creation of Columbia and Warner, and the position of these companies within the field of jazz and popular music, as they are Davis' and his musical collaborators. Further, almost all Davis' Columbia recordings would not have been produced at Warner at the time; Davis moved labels to be able to make records like *Tutu* (1986), *Amandla* (1989), *Doo-Bop* (1992) and *Rubberband*

(2019), and then spurred Columbia to retrospectively release *Aura* in 1989. That record companies have 'personalities' and their staff make meaningful decisions about artists and repertoires, and that these are part of the motivation for musicians to sign a contract with a particular label, is commonplace in the discourse of musicians. Strangely, we have not yet developed approaches that extend these observations into useful analytical frameworks to study the history of jazz. I hope this is a useful contribution to such a development.

References

Avakian, George. 2000. 'The First Reissue Program: The Story Behind the Original Hot Fives & Sevens Reissues and More'. *JazzTimes*. https://www.jazztimes.com/archives/the-first-jazz-reissue-program/?v=7885444af42e.

Carr, Ian. 1982. *Miles Davis: A Critical Biography*. Quartet.

Carson, Charles D. 2008. '"Bridging the Gap": Creed Taylor, Grover Washington Jr., and the Crossover Roots of Smooth Jazz'. *Black Music Research Journal* 28 (1): 1–15.

Cole, George. 2005. *The Last Miles: The Music of Miles Davis, 1980–1991*. Equinox.

Cook, Richard. 2001. *Blue Note Records: The Biography*. Secker & Warburg.

Cook, Richard. 2005. *It's About That Time: Miles Davis on and off Record*. Atlantic Books.

Crouch, Stanley. 1990. 'Play the Right Thing: Miles Davis, the Most Brilliant Sellout in the History of Jazz'. *New Republic* 202 (7): 30–37.

Crouch, Stanley. 2006. *Considering Genius: Writings on Jazz*. Civitas Books.

Dannen, Fredric. 1990. *Hit Men: Power Brokers and Fast Money Inside the Music Business*. Muller.

Davis, Clive. 1975. *Clive: Inside the Record Business*. Morrow William.

Doggett, Peter. 2009. *There's a Riot Going On: Revolutionaries, Rock Stars, and the Rise and Fall of the 60s*. Open Road+ Grove/Atlantic.

Gillett, Charlie. 1974. *Making Tracks: Atlantic Records and the Growth of a Multi-Billion-Dollar Industry*. W. H. Allen.

Gray, Herman. 1988. *Producing Jazz: The Experience of an Independent Record Company*. Temple University Press.

Kubernik, Harvey, and Kenneth Kubernik. 2011. *A Perfect Haze: The Illustrated History of the Monterey International Pop Festival*. Santa Monica Press.

Morton, John Fass. 2008. *Backstory in Blue: Ellington at Newport '56*. Rutgers University Press.

Mueller, Darren. 2014. 'Quest for the Moment: The Audio Production of Ellington at Newport'. *Jazz Perspectives* 8 (1): 3–23.

Mueller, Darren. 2024. *At the Vanguard of Vinyl: A Cultural History of the Long-Playing Record in Jazz*. Duke University Press.

Nicholson, Stuart. 1990. *Jazz: The Modern Resurgence*. Simon & Schuster.

Nicholson, Stuart. 1998. *Jazz-Rock: A History*. Canongate.

Nicholson, Stuart. 2001. 'Europeans Cut In with a New Jazz Sound and Beat'. *New York Times*, June 3. https://www.nytimes.com/2001/06/03/arts/music-europeans-cut-in-with-a-new-jazz-sound-and-beat.html.

Nicholson, Stuart. 2011. 'Review of Miles Davis *Tutu*: Deluxe Edition'. *Jazzwise*, July 28, 2011. https://www.jazzwise.com/review/article/miles-davis-tutu-deluxe-edition.

Rasula, Jed. 1995. 'The Media of Memory: The Seductive Menace of Records in Jazz History'. In *Jazz Among the Discourses*, edited by Krin Gabbard. Duke University Press.

Szwed, John. 2002. *So What: The Life of Miles Davis.* Simon & Schuster.

Tingen, Paul. 2001. *Miles Beyond: The Electric Explorations of Miles Davis, 1967–1991.* Billboard Books.

Wenner, Jann. 1967. 'Editorial.' *Rolling Stone* 1 (1), November 9, 1967.

Williams, Katherine. 2017. 'Duke Ellington's Newport Up! Liveness, Artefacts and the Seductive Menace of Jazz Revisited.' In *New Jazz Conceptions*, edited by R. Fagge and N. Pillai, 121–139. Routledge.

5

Resurrecting Miles in *Dingo* (1991)

Michel Legrand, Billy Cross and Miles Davis

Will L. Finch

Stepping down from a Boeing-707 on a dusty airstrip in the Australian outback is international jazz star Billy Cross. Fresh from entertaining fans in Japan, he addresses a perplexed crowd of assembled residents: "I've been through a lot of interesting places, but I don't think I've ever had the pleasure of visiting . . . Poona Flat. My name is Billy Cross. If you don't mind, we'd like to play something for you". Standing at the front of the audience is John Anderson, a young, barefoot white boy. He looks on as the band begins to play, transfixed by Cross, shirtless under a loose-fitting, black-and-white patterned jacket and bringing to his lips a red trumpet (Figure 5.1). Anderson shuts his eyes as Cross begins a solo chorus and moves the trumpeter from the runway and into his imagination (Figure 5.2). In his chiaroscuro fantasy, Anderson fixates on the sound and image of his miraculous encounter, savouring the spontaneity and improvisational flare of this, the moment of his musical awakening.

This is one telling of the hook to *Dingo* (1991, 109 minutes), a Franco-Australian film directed by Rolf de Heer ([1991] 2005) and written by Marc Rosenberg (1992). The character of Cross was Miles Davis' first and only extended acting role on film. Davis also co-composed and played for the film's soundtrack (released by Warner Brothers in 1991 with additional music not heard in the film) (Davis and Legrand 1991). Davis' contributions to *Dingo* are a significant example of the artist's later commitment to diverse creative collaborations that transgressed the boundaries of different media and fields of cultural production. The film demonstrated his appetite for ventures within the mainstream and his careful negotiation of white-dominated culture industries. As he put it, "You could be a great musician, an innovative and important artist, but nobody cared if you didn't make the white

Will L. Finch, *Resurrecting Miles in* Dingo *(1991)* In: *Rethinking Miles Davis*. Edited by: Roger Fagge, Nicolas Pillai, and Tim Wall, Oxford University Press. © Oxford University Press 2026. DOI: 10.1093/9780190085834.003.0005

Figure 5.1 Billy Cross (Miles Davis) and his band perform 'Concert on the Runway' beneath the wing of his tour plane.

Figure 5.2 A close-up profile of Billy Cross (Miles Davis) in the imagination of the young John 'Dingo' Anderson.

people who were in control some money" (Davis and Troupe 1989, 205). "Popularity didn't make my music any less worthy, or great" (206).

Simultaneously, Davis' departures beyond the vanguard and prestige of 'venerable' jazz practice are underpinned by the recognition that jazz *was* a popular music and that mass popularity was compatible with so-called artistic integrity: "I never thought that the music called 'jazz' was ever meant to reach just a small group of people . . . it should reach as many people as it could, like so-called popular music, and why not?" (Davis and Troupe 1989, 205). Despite the film's potential to help us better understand Davis' self-assured and productive relationship with mainstream and/or popular cinema—or perhaps because of this potential—*Dingo* has featured primarily as a footnote in jazz scholarship and is rarely interrogated as a serious part of Davis' output and cultural legacy. In fact, the paucity of scholarship focused on *Dingo* is likely a result not only of its associations with commercial cinema but also of its failure to achieve the kind of mass popularity which might otherwise have drawn attention.

Phil Freeman's (2005, 174) consideration of the film suggests Davis took the role as he found the idea of portraying the kind of "magical N*gro" played by Dexter Gordon in *'Round Midnight* (1986) "flattering". Whilst the comparison to *'Round Midnight* is pertinent, this conclusion precludes a more critical appraisal of the film and risks characterising Davis' appearance in *Dingo*, perhaps alongside his other television and film appearances, as an inconsequential vanity project. Krin Gabbard's chapter on Davis' representation in and on film mentions *Dingo* in passing and as an example of the musician's rare work as an actor (2007, 261). George Cole's (2006) book on Davis' last decade gives a fuller account of the film's synopsis and production history based on a valuable interview with de Heer (de Heer n.d.). *Dingo* is not, however, fully integrated into the book's wider, discography-based account of Davis' post-1980s output. Cole recognises the film as "an interesting view of another side to Miles' artistic talents" (2006, 481) but stops short of exploring the features of such a view and their implications. Other studies that cover Davis' later years also offer short, biographically focused accounts of the film, though they too avoid a more critical exploration of its potential significance (Tingen 2001, 244; Szwed 2002, 389; Carr 1999, 520; Cook 2005, 306).

This chapter aims toward such an exploration, suggesting that *Dingo* ought not be overlooked as a mere novelty nor as a postlapsarian appendix to Davis' earlier successes—a final step "on the path of the sellout", as Stanley Crouch (1990) notoriously described Davis' trajectory after *In a Silent Way* and *Bitches Brew*. The film is an important example of Davis' creative labour beyond the purely musical (itself an impossible category) and can help unpick how the diverse ideas about Davis' persona and cultural capital were shaped and mediatised. As discussed by Nicolas Pillai (2018, 269–270) and further demonstrated by the contributions in this collected edition, Davis' work on television and film, in music videos and magazine advertisements, his fashion-conscious image and repeated reinvention offered "powerful opportunities for meaning and agency in the media ecology of the 1980s" and beyond. By treating *Dingo* as one such opportunity, I aim to test and refine the boundaries of the artist's varied signification. I contend a more sympathetic and contextualised appraisal of *Dingo* can expand our understanding of Davis' work and his establishment as a figure "omnipresent in the popular imagination[s]" of the 21st century, as Gabbard (2007, 261) has described him.

In what follows, I begin by further describing *Dingo*'s plot and its reception. Here I draw specific attention to similarities between Cross and Davis' biographies which have shaped impressions of the film and Davis' performance in it. Whilst these similarities should not be overlooked, especially as they pertain to the film's reception, I contrast them with more salient differences to expose within *Dingo* a productive and multifaceted dialogue between fiction and reality, between Davis' celebrity persona and the character he plays in *Dingo*. It is around this dialogue that I build my analysis of the film, specifically its soundtrack. I consider how *Dingo*'s soundtrack incorporates, supplants and negates Davis' varied musical practice for its own filmic purposes. I focus in particular on the agency of Michel Legrand (1932–2019), a French composer and pianist who collaborated with Davis on *Dingo*'s soundtrack. Legrand's prior associations with Davis and his experience as a film, classical, jazz and popular music composer were crucial to the production of *Dingo*'s musical materials; his musical practice strongly shapes *Dingo*'s soundtrack and, therefore, the Cross/Davis dialogue at the heart of its reception and my analysis. Legrand's shaping in this regard is fundamental to the film's function as a means by which we might reflect and rethink Davis' cultural legacy and signification today.

Davis and Cross

Dingo tells the story of the adult John 'Dingo' Anderson (played by Colin Friels), who, inspired by his runway encounter with Billy Cross, is now a budding jazz trumpeter. Anderson has creative aspirations beyond his employment as a handyman and dingo trapper—the latter inspiring his nickname.

He is not satisfied 'woodshedding' in the outback nor with experiments blending his virtuosic jazz trumpet stylings with his skiffle band, Dingo and the Dusters. Leaving behind his family and troubled marriage—the film's unsettling B plot—and spurred on by dreamy visions of performing alongside Cross, he saves $3,000 without the knowledge of his wife (Helen Buday) and travels to Paris. There he finds a languid Cross, no longer interested in playing trumpet or performing live. The two are soon involved in a minor car accident outside Paris' premier jazz club. So arises the opportunity for Anderson to goad Cross into retaking the stage. "What you afraid of?", he asks. "Nothing", replies Cross. In the club, Cross secures Anderson a chance to sit in with the band and to test his chops in Paris' funk-fusion-jazz scene. Seemingly spurred on by Anderson's performance, Cross unexpectedly takes to the stage and so fulfils the Australian's fantasy of performing alongside his idol.

Despite a significant investment of $5.3 million (*Cinema Papers* 1990, 72) and the allure of Davis' celebrity, the film was difficult to distribute.[1] Rosenberg notes the film opened in Paris in 1991 (Stanley 1993), with a fuller, though still limited Australian release beginning on January 30,1992, where it drew a total box office of just $132,500 (AUD).[2] As de Heer recounts on his website, a major US release was delayed by Davis' death on September 28, 1991, and over fears the film might become an unintentional tribute to the star ('*Dingo*: Overview,' n.d.). A second attempt at a US release, tied to *Dingo*'s eligibility for the Academy Awards, was thwarted, so de Heer continues, by an error in paperwork. A third and final attempt was reportedly stopped after trailer reels were delivered unplayable from the laboratory. *Dingo* did receive a two-week run at Cinema Village, New York, in 1991, but not until 1993 was the film distributed more widely in the US, though still to only select theatres (Stanley 1993).

Those critics who did see the film during this patchy distribution responded with mixed, often tepid reviews. For many, the film was a curious and adventurous, if not particularly successful, take on rural isolation (a recurrent theme in Australian cinema), human ambition and the timelessness of dreams (see Macdonald 1992; Younis 1992). Praise for *Dingo*'s

[1] In 2005 Umbrella Entertainment released a standard definition version on DVD which is now easily available. This version of the film was consulted for my research.

[2] Australian release and box office data, confirmed by Motion Pictures Distributers Association of Australia via personal communication. *Dingo*'s sparse distribution made confirming the full extent of its cinematic release difficult and a task beyond the scope of my research here.

filmography, emotional sentiment and music (Dixon 1992) were offset by disappointment over the plot's contrivance (Williams 1992) and uneven pacing (Jillett 1992). Stephen Holden for the *New York Times* saw the film as in two halves: a "pungent portrait of Australian rural life" contrasted with a glimpse of "Parisian jazz life as a millionaire's dream world" (Holden 1994). Another regular feature in reviews was Friels' portrayal of the wistful Anderson—"strong" and "utterly charming" by some accounts (Holden 1994), "mildly engaging" by others (Byrnes 1992). However, more space is frequently given to discussions of Billy Cross and the man who played him.

This is perhaps unsurprising given the role is Davis' only major acting performance and one of his last outputs. That Davis plays a celebrity jazz trumpeter who looks and sounds something like Miles Davis (both in voice and trumpet) was seized upon by critics naturally respondent to the sliding signifiers of a celebrity persona crossing (mass) media boundaries. Holden (1994) described Cross as "an eccentric variation of [Davis'] famously reclusive enigmatic self"; the *Sydney Morning Herald* suggests the film could be subtitled "Miles Davis in Meekatharra" (Jurman 1992); and one synopsis in the *Los Angeles Times* simply replaces Cross' name with Davis' (Thomas 1993).

These responses are evidence of Davis' celebrity and 'transmedia intertextuality'; they are hallmarks of his place within the "ever-expanding supersystem of entertainment" described by Marsha Kinder in 1991 (1). As Michael Quinn explored a year earlier, within this super-system, star personas and the fictional characters they play frequently blend together, seeping between media and fictions to feed desires "for an aesthetics of familiarity, recognition, and fulfilment" (1990, 160). This is not a phenomenon unique to the culture industries of the late 20th century nor to scholarship concurrent with *Dingo*'s release (see Dyer 1998; Holland 1979). Nevertheless, the proliferation of mutable media encounters made a celebrity actor's attempt to embody a fictional character—the paradoxical negation and extension of self at the heart of such performance—increasingly conditioned by awareness of the actor's biography and/or prior performative acts. By the 1990s, Davis' persona, variously defined by his culturally and socially bound performances, was fluid and compound. Moreover, it was increasingly accessible to his audiences thorough diverse media, including television, magazines, radio, film, and his 1989 autobiography (see DeVeaux 1992). As Lee Barron has suggested, the adaptability of celebrity personae became increasingly necessary to maintain public notability within the media landscapes and markets of the late 20th and 21st century (2018, 65–66). *Dingo* represents one part of Davis' negotiation of this landscape; in addition to the project's creative potential it is also an appeal to the kind of diversification necessary to maintain celebrity. It is a text invariably seen through the lens of Davis' persona, itself modulated through a feedback loop of interpretation and representation, performance and perception.

As part of this feedback loop, *Dingo* has sometimes been understood as an oblique biopic in which Davis is merely playing "a version of himself", as one 2015 UK re-review put it (Buckmaster 2015). Davis was not originally considered for the role, nor was the script rewritten after his casting; de Herr (2016) described him as "the last cab off the rank" after considering others to take the part, including Yaphet Kotto and Sammy Davis Jr. Rosenberg described his motivations when writing the script as having little to do with jazz, which he chose as "a free-form source of expression and inspiration" that complemented his real motivation to "explore the theme of the unfulfilled dream" (Stanley 1993). Nevertheless, connections between Cross and Davis appeared so intentional that Leonard Feather (1991), interviewing Legrand for the *Los Angeles Times*, reported that the film's script was "written with Miles in mind".[3] Whilst this myth is not supported by the record, it is not hard to understand its origins within the film's materials and the transmedial contexts outlined above.

For example, when Anderson travels to meet Cross in Paris, the star is retired from public performance and has given up the trumpet—a narrative trajectory not uncommon in musical biopics but one that might be mapped onto Davis' own hiatus between 1976 and 1980. Such a conclusion is strengthened by Cross' performance on the electric keyboard, an instrument Davis also played as part of his return to music making (Szwed 2002, 347–348). A further point of contact revolves around the fact that both musicians suffered strokes. That *Dingo*'s depiction of Cross' stroke was roughly synchronous with Davis' death seemed to only heighten the film's reception as an allegory for Davis' life, especially his ill health and creative interruption during the "silent years" (Carr 1999). I will return to the possible significance of this biographical coincidence at the end of this chapter. For now, it is important to note that beyond these similarities, Cross and Davis' biographies and characters remain distinct. In attending to their differences, we can

[3] Although Feather does not clarify, he may be inferring that Rosenberg was influenced by Davis' biography while preparing the script.

expose the critical tension between Davis and Cross indicative of the cultural dialogics of Davis' performance and reception (Tomlinson 1991).

Perhaps the most obvious difference between the two is that Cross is cloistered in Paris with his French wife, Angie (Bernadette Lafont), and not Manhattan, where Davis spent much of his hiatus.[4] Other, less obvious though more important differences rest at the heart of *Dingo*'s narrative. Whilst Davis' stroke in 1982 happened after he had returned to music making, Cross' was apparently induced by his self-identified artistic decline. As he says in the film, "After playing the same old shit for forty years my soul pulled a switch on me. I was becoming a jazz museum piece. I caused the stroke myself". As Davis' output and autobiography make clear, becoming a "jazz museum piece" was not an inevitability for him, as it seemingly was for Cross. Contrary to an older generation of jazz musicians and critics who were, according to Davis, "too lazy to try something different", Davis was perceptive to the necessity of change within his creative practice (Davis and Troupe 1989, 394). Cross seemingly gained this perspective only following the stroke which marked the start of his artistic decline and then reclusive experimentation. As he describes to Anderson, "I was able to sleep four-hour shifts, integrate my dreams with my music. And now it's like a new start. Everything is fresh". Perhaps the most striking difference between Davis and Cross' stories and characters, however, is that it is Anderson who gives Cross the push needed to return to the stage and so fulfils the role of white saviour and disciple-cum-master. Anderson's pivotal status in Cross' return to public performance confirms that *Dingo* is a story that Davis never lived.[5]

As suggested above, these important differences are often overlooked in favour of identifying similarities between Davis and Cross' stories and characters. Such an approach can misinterpret or devalue Davis' on-screen performance as nothing more than a re-performance of his own experiences. Whilst many reviewers tied Davis' acting abilities to the ease he supposedly had in playing a character so like himself, they nevertheless often comment on his engaging on-screen performance: "[A]n impressive actor with a regal

[4] De Heer recalls the script was originally set in Australia and the US, following the success of *Crocodile Dundee*'s (1986) Outback/US encounter. Rosenberg chose Paris over the US to draw upon understandings of the city as a "colour-blind" escape for American jazz musicians (de Heer 2021).

[5] The temptation to see Anderson as an analogue to those who helped Davis recuperate further demonstrates how such comparisons can be reductive. In addition to Davis' nephew, Vincent Wilburn, Davis' recuperation was helped by many figures, including Dorothy Mae, Chaka Khan, and Cicely Tyson (Carr 1999, 352–354).

screen presence" (Dixon 1992); "[Y]ou can't take your eyes off him.... His presence is both regal and spectral" (Byrnes 1992); "[H]e has an intense, hypnotic presence and his performance is oddly gentle and humorous" (Williams 1992), to give three examples from a notably 'gazing' Australian press. For John Stanley (1993) of the *San Francisco Chronicle*, *Dingo* offers fans "a new side to the entertainer they may never have suspected ... a powerful dramatic actor.... Davis brings a world-weary quality to Cross". Perhaps the most compelling, though naturally partisan, account comes from de Heer himself. Although initially cautious about the problems he might face working with a notoriously particular man and largely untested dramatic actor, de Heer recounts:

> He turned out to be a wonderfully instinctive actor. When he wasn't "in the moment" as his character, he forgot the dialogue.... [T]his made it impossible for him to be bad. Most of the time he was "in the moment", and very good....
>
> When we were shooting Miles' first major dialogue scene in the music room in Paris, I turned to his manager, Gordon Meltzer, and said: "This is fantastic!" Gordon said: "You don't know the half of it. I've never seen Miles like this, he has never been this co-operative with anybody doing anything. There's something very special going on here". ('*Dingo*: Production Notes', n.d.)

As this account suggests, there may be much to gain by setting aside the coincidental similarities between Cross and Davis and appraising *Dingo* on its own terms. However, such dislocation is perhaps impossible or at least inadvisable when attempting to further contextualise *Dingo* as part of Davis' cultural legacy and artistic practice. As Pillai has suggested, the instinctive, almost inevitable mapping of Cross onto Davis reveals in *Dingo* an impossibly distorted vision of Davis, "a divergent history of failure" through which "we may better apprehend Miles' success" (2018, 270). Whilst any superficial mapping might flatten our understanding, a more considered attempt draws into relief those moments of tension and correlation between Cross' and Davis' music, character and celebrity which expose the signification and agency imbedded into the film. In other words, as an imaginary counterpart in dialogue with Davis, Cross serves as a provocation to rethink Davis as actor, as transmedia celebrity, as musician whose legacy stretches deeply into the cultural imaginary.

For the remainder of this chapter, I focus on the ways in which *Dingo*'s soundtrack takes a central role in this dialogue, grappling with the provocative *sound* of Cross and its interrelationship with Davis' own music. As part of this dialogue, I consider the agency of Legrand, whose shaping of *Dingo*'s music is vital to contextualising and understanding this interrelationship and, it follows, understanding *Dingo* as a document that reflects and inscribes Davis' persona and cultural legacy.

Legrand and Davis

Dingo's musical soundtrack makes regular allusions to and deviations from Davis' musical output that strongly contribute to the Cross/Davis dialogue outlined above. Although Davis is credited as co-composer, the music in *Dingo*, and thus the music of Cross and Davis, is refracted through Legrand's musical practice and experience. I begin by describing the professional and musical contexts that led to Legrand's contribution to *Dingo*'s score and which played a role in shaping Davis' mainstream representation. Not only are these contexts important to a critical assessment of *Dingo* as part of Davis' output and as a popular-music document more widely, but Legrand and Davis' earlier association is worthy of further attention as part of this collection's wider rethinking of Davis.

Many accounts of Legrand's early musical experience tend to contrast his training in European art-music with his encounters with North American jazz. As a student at the Paris Conservatoire from the age of 11 (Legrand and Lerouge 2013, 32),[6] Legrand studied under the "benevolent tyranny", as he described it, of Nadia Boulanger (42).[7] When asked to play at a dinner party hosted by Boulanger (for André Malraux and Jean Cocteau, no less), Legrand recalls in one telling anecdote, "my rebellious character began to assert itself, I started a piece by Duke Ellington. [Boulanger] stared at me with machine-gun eyes but, in front of her guests, did not dare open fire" (40). This anecdote, like all those from Legrand's collaborative autobiography, seeks to frame his experience in certain ways. In this instance, it reinforces the close relationship Legrand had with Boulanger (his "musical mother")

[6] Other accounts suggest Legrand entered the conservatories at age 10 in 1942. See, for example, Anderson (2019).

[7] All translations in this chapter are my own unless otherwise stated. I have opted for the most literal translation available to me.

and European artistic traditions. It also demonstrates Legrand's "rebellious" predilection for jazz, which, as the story goes, was later confirmed in 1948, when he first encountered bebop whilst watching Dizzy Gillespie at the Salle Pleyel, age 16.[8] This encounter began, so Legrand and many biographies have since reported, his exploration of contemporary jazz, which played counterpart to his art music training throughout his career.

Focus on Legrand's education in European art-music with interjections from Ellington, Gillespie and later Davis has obscured another side to his early musical career and practice which is vital to interpreting his association with Davis and their collaboration in *Dingo*. Legrand was the son of Raymond Legrand and Marcelle Der Mikaëlian, the sister of Jacques Hélian. His father and uncle were bandleaders who, like their colleagues Ray Ventura and Fred Adison, popularised and shaped jazz for white French audiences in the early and mid-20th century (Powrie 2013, 155). Raymond rose to prominence during the German occupation of France, when his orchestra filled gaps in the popular jazz and light-music market left by Ventura and Paul Misraki's exile to South America. During the early 1940s, his orchestra appeared between Nazi propaganda radio programs (Sprout 2013, 13) and in films like Richard Pottier's *Mademoiselle Swing* (1942) (Burch and Sellier 2013, 143–144). Raymond's collaboration with the Vichy government saw his conviction by *le comité d'épuration* and his position in the French musical mainstream taken by Legrand's uncle, Hélian. Hélian later gained popularity with the song 'Fleur de Paris' (1944), which became a regular feature on French radio at the time and an anthem of liberation still performed as part of Bastille Day celebrations (Rearick 1997, 271).

Legrand's integration within these networks of popular cultural production were important to his earliest experiences as a professional musician. As he recalls, his first work deposited with the French music distribution and royalty collection association SACEM was an arrangement for Hélian's orchestra. Moreover, the arrangement was one of Legrand's own compositions written for the vaudeville and operetta writers Bertal-Maubon, who, it so happened, shared offices with Legrand's mother when she worked for Ventura's publishing company in the 1930s (Legrand and Lerouge 2013, 17).[9] By 1947, despite his earlier conviction, Legrand's father was able to find

[8] Some accounts place the Gillespie concert in 1947, in contrast to the date provided in (Legrand and Lerouge 2013, 120). According to Ken Vail's (2003, 57) itinerary of Gillespie's concerts at the time, Gillespie did not perform at the Salle Pleyel in 1947 but did in 1948.

[9] Legrand gives the title 'Il y a des filles', though I have been unable to trace this composition further.

work with Decca's Belgian licensee, Fonior. There he employed his son to arrange and direct music for Édith Piaf, who was signed to Decca. It was his father too who Legrand cites as giving him his first contacts within the film industry. This privileged access to the networks and contracts made Legrand well-placed to continue the family's prominent place in the French musical mainstream, something he first achieved with his hit album *I Love Paris* (1954).

Replete with luscious strings and *Parisien* accordions, Legrand's 'light' orchestral-jazz album comprised an instrumental selection of Broadway songs and chanson. It was an unexpected success for Columbia in the US and described by Robert Kotlowitz for the North American music and audio-equipment magazine *High Fidelity* as probably "[t]he single best record in the Music Between category received for review in the past year" (1955, 58). 'Music Between' was a category introduced to *High Fidelity*'s readership by Kotlowitz's predecessor in 1951, as "the most popular type of non-popular music" (Merritt 1951, 3) or "that great body of music lying between the master-works of the concert repertory, and the daily out-pouring of Hollywood and Broadway" (63).[10] The magazine's review and categorisation of Legrand's album is evidence not only of *I Love Paris*' popularity but also of its place within the ambiguous genres of 'light' and 'easy-listening' music. It was Legrand's association with this market segment, established by the success of *I Love Paris*, that gave Columbia the confidence to invest in Legrand's next album, *Legrand Jazz* (1958), where he first collaborated with Davis.

Apparently granted carte blanche by Columbia, *Legrand Jazz* was an ambitious project which sought to "bring together the stars [*le gratin*] of the new American [jazz] generation" (Legrand and Lerouge 2013, 124). Following their meeting whilst Davis was in Europe in 1957, Legrand had the trumpeter at the top of his list for the album.[11] Legrand got his wish, and Davis recorded tracks alongside Paul Chambers, Herbie Mann, Phil Woods, Kenny Dennis, John Coltrane and Bill Evans, amongst others. *Legrand Jazz* was well received (five stars from *Downbeat*'s Dom Cerulli) though regrettably has received little attention in jazz studies, perhaps owing to its 'light' associations.

[10] The magazine's coverage of music 'between' represented for readers both a welcome addition to its flagship focus on European instrumental art music and a tolerable precursor to later coverage of, "if you will pardon the expression, *stinking jazz!!*", to quote one reader (*High Fidelity* 1953, 15, emphasis in original).

[11] By his own account, Legrand attended the Club Saint-Germain to see Davis perform on three consecutive nights and was introduced as "le petit jeune" behind *I Love Paris* (Legrand and Lerouge 2013, 124).

It remains, however, an inventive album featuring tightly structured, virtuosic and often unexpected ensembles alongside solo choruses for the album's headliners. Of the tracks Davis features on, ''Round Midnight' and 'Wild Man Blues' best demonstrate the album's imagination, flare and broad appeal. Accompanying the distinctive solo performances of the assembled jazz vanguard, Legrand's arrangements exhibit a musical versatility, and at times self-indulgence, that he would later deploy in *Dingo*. His musical experience from within and 'between' diverse fields of musical production is easily recognisable; romantic harp flourishes, dissonant clusters of saxophone and vibraphone, abrupt tempo and meter changes and dynamic modernist harmonies from bebop, cool jazz and French impressionism in particular, all contribute to *Legrand Jazz*'s idiosyncratic sound.

For the story of Legrand and Davis, and *Dingo*, the album demonstrates two important things. First, the album marks Legrand's involvement in the development of Davis' more mainstream reputation and representation, especially as conditioned by the aesthetics of the Franco-American exchange. As John Szwed has explained, the album was a way for Columbia to solidify and expand Davis' existing successes, and it was an opportunity for Davis to broaden his international audience by collaborating with a rising star in an allied but more mainstream market (2002, 163). Second, *Legrand Jazz* represented for Legrand a significant development of his own jazz practice. He said of it, "I owe a lot to this album: it gave me credibility, legitimacy as a 'jazz man.' For me, it's much more than just a record. It's an act of birth" (Legrand and Lerouge 2013, 130). Not only this, but alongside *le gratin* of US jazz, especially Davis, whose name appears second largest on the album's cover, Legrand further established his own international reputation, which was cemented a decade later with an Academy Award for his score to *The Thomas Crown Affair* (1968).

Despite not working closely together again until *Dingo*, a further notable instance of Davis and Legrand's association came in 1962, when Legrand composed the score to Joseph Losey's film *Eva*, starring Jeanne Moreau. No doubt inspired by the success of Davis' soundtrack to *Ascenseur pour l'échafaud* (1958), Losey had originally attempted to secure Davis to compose the score for his own blend of *la nouvelle vague*'s existential cool and Michelangelo Antonioni's Italian ennui (Caute 1994, 157). Losey had used Davis' music whilst shooting the film, but when the trumpeter was not available, Losey employed Legrand. Legrand may well have seemed the ideal candidate because of his established association with *la nouvelle vague* and his work with Davis on *Legrand Jazz*.[12] The resultant score was undoubtedly inspired by Losey's temp track and Legrand's own musical dialogue with Davis. Losey later recalled, perhaps in awareness of the hermeneutic and ethical complications of intertextual and appropriative practices, "When I finally did not get Miles Davis . . . he [Legrand] was able to see the film with a complete score virtually. I'm not suggesting that Michael Legrand copied [Davis but he] managed . . . to produce an equivalent that was fantastic" (Losey and Ciment 1985, 215–216).

Taking as an example *Eva*'s opening music, which underscores misty scenes of Venetian gondolas, Legrand's lamenting trumpet melody over brass chords, punctuated by vibraphone and woodwind stabs, echoes Davis' work on *Birth of the Cool* (1950), whilst its shifting harmonic centres and sequential melody evoke 'Milestones' (1958) and 'So What' (1959). Legrand here also relies and builds upon Davis' earlier contribution—in collaboration with French jazz musicians—to *Ascenseur pour l'échafaud*'s "postwar transatlantic attitude of removal and disengagement otherwise known as 'cool'" (Perchard 2015, 120). In *Eva*, then, Legrand refracted Davis' contemporary cool significance through his own musical lenses. Thus *Eva* (and *Legrand Jazz*) offer, alongside *Ascenseur*, examples of Davis' creative diversification and transatlantic cultural exchanges and his continued integration into the musical and cultural vernacular (Gabbard 2004).

As this survey has shown, Legrand's experience working across different fields of cultural production and in dialogue with Davis and Davis' sound provided him with a set of professional and aesthetic proficiencies that made his subsequent collaboration with Davis in *Dingo* perhaps inevitable. As the story goes, when de Heer approached him to take the role of Cross and to supply music for *Dingo*, Davis accepted on the condition that Legrand would work with him on the score. For de Heer this was an astute choice, though one that came with a necessary budget increase; Legrand was an experienced film composer whose knowledge of the film industry and Davis' music would prove vital to the creation of *Dingo*'s soundtrack ('*Dingo*: Production Notes', n.d.). Though I have found no account of this decision from Davis' perspective, it seems possible that in addition to the practical benefits of working with Legrand, Davis sought to build upon the wider significance

[12] Legrand provided scores for Jean-Luc Goddard, Agnès Varda and Jacques Demy. Demy and Legrand's association in particular demonstrate how, in midcentury France, "boundaries between art music and jazz, even self-consciously 'arty' jazz and popular song were increasingly permeable" (Stilwell 2003, 126).

of their existing association. In other words, he perhaps saw once again the means by which and through which he might further cultivate a commercial and creative dialogue that engaged new and existing audiences across media boundaries. What is more, Legrand's agency in *Dingo*'s soundtrack constitutes a vital connection as well as a fissure between Cross and Davis. The music Cross performs is, like the life he led, a distorted image of Davis' own; it is a musical glimpse of an imagined history by which we are forced to rethink and confront Davis' musical output through the lens of Legrand's musical experiences.

Legrand, Cross and Davis

Although Davis is listed as co-composer of *Dingo*'s soundtrack, the score's arrangement and composition were seemingly undertaken largely by Legrand, with little initial input from Davis. By Legrand's account, work began on the majority of *Dingo*'s soundtrack only three weeks before filming was due to start. The score was required in advance to provide for on-set miming, with a later session arranged for additional material to be recorded after primary photography was complete (Legrand and Lerouge 2013, 134). As such, the majority of the score was produced with reference to only "the script, a few pages of [de Heer's] notes and a one hour tape of Australian bush sounds" ('*Dingo*: Production Notes', n.d.). After confirming his commitment to the project, Legrand arrived in the US at Davis' request. Once there, he found Davis seemingly uninterested in discussing the film or its score; rather Legrand recalled the two were to "drink great wines, talk about music, [their] lives, swim in the Pacific" at Davis' Malibu villa (Legrand and Lerouge 2013, 133–134). After the third day, Legrand returned their attention to the production calendar, telling Davis, "[I]t's Saturday, we have to be in the studio on Wednesday" (134).[13] When Davis did take out his trumpet, he did so without enthusiasm and, according to Legrand, threatened to pull out of the project altogether. With the necessity to produce the music quickly, Legrand suggested he write and record it himself, so Davis could play over the tracks later. Davis' collaboration with Marcus Miller on *Tutu* (1986), in which Davis is "essentially soloing over pre-prepared music" (Cole 2006, 243),

[13] The days vary by Legrand's own telling; see, for instance, Williams (2018).

occurred to Legrand as a suitable model, although one which precluded the kind of live in-studio interaction that Legrand had hoped for. Davis agreed so readily that Legrand suspected this arrangement had been Davis' motive for requesting him as collaborator all along. Legrand worked fast—four days, by his account—to produce the score before assembling musicians to record it at Crystal Studios, Los Angeles, in March 1990. In addition to session musicians, Legrand hired Davis' then quintet (John Bigham, Ricky Wellman, Foley and Kenny Garrett), along with Chuck Findlay to play the role of Anderson's trumpet throughout the film.

Legrand identified Findlay's high-octane LA session sound as a fitting counterpart to Cross (and, by association, Davis). The distinction between Cross/Davis' and Findlay's trumpet sounds allows for clear differentiation of Anderson's trumpet from Cross' in the score. As a result, *Dingo* emphasises Davis' earlier sonority and style, more specifically his work in the 1950s. It is notable, for example, that Anderson's trumpet remains unmuted in the film, while Cross' is almost always muted, naturally, with harmon mute. Legrand recounted that he sought a median between Davis' contemporary output and the "lyrical Miles of the Gil Evans years, which [he] so wanted to resurrect"—Legrand's choice of word here indicates a particular way of framing his contribution to *Dingo* which I give more attention to below (Legrand and Lerouge 2013, 135). Whilst allusion to this 'lyrical', muted Davis dominates Cross' performances in *Dingo*, the film's depiction of Cross performing in more explicitly fusion genres and with electronic instruments constitutes a vital part of the film's narrative.

As described above, when Anderson first finds Cross in Paris, Cross has all but given up the trumpet. In one of the film's most arresting scenes, Cross stands in his music room, behind an electric piano and playing discrete chords and phrases, like a recitative accompaniment to their conversation. Seeing Anderson spot a trumpet in the room, Cross asks him to play a C. Cross deftly samples the note before continuing his conversation and self-accompaniment, now with the sound of Anderson's trumpet rather than electric piano. Seemingly put out by Cross' abandonment of the analogue trumpet, or defensive about the quality of his tone now repeating on him, he pushes Cross, asking, "Don't you play trumpet anymore?" Cross, replies, "I am playing trumpet", and, when asked again, replies, "I don't play trumpet". Whether a joke worthy of René Magritte or, as Andrys Onsman and Robert Burke (2018, 53–54) have explored, a compelling example of the complex ontologies and aesthetics of computer-aided jazz practice and improvisation, the scene takes an important place within the Dingo–Cross dialogue I am interested in.

Embracing digital technologies was, for Davis, vital to his evolving musical practice. If there was a moment in which the images of Davis and Cross aligned closest in *Dingo*, it is perhaps here. It is notable too that this alignment happens when Davis, rather than Legrand, is primarily in control of Cross' music—save for postproduction adjustments. On the one hand, this scene paints Cross as a provocative enigma, the recluse who, through Anderson's prodding, will eventually re-emerge on the stage to take up the trumpet again. On the other hand, behind the piano is the Cross who, since (or perhaps whilst) recovering from his stroke, has sought new ways to not only better enable his music making but also reassess the inevitability of his self-identified trend into jazz obscurity. These two readings are not exhaustive or mutually exclusive, but when mapping each onto Davis, the role *Dingo* might serve in rethinking Davis' cultural legacy becomes clearer. A central part of my thinking here, which I address further in my conclusion, concerns the narratives of ageing, ill health, artistic 'lateness' and the 'promise' of renewal that permeate the Davis/Cross dialogue in *Dingo*. In other words, through its depiction of Cross' lateness, *Dingo* offers speculative fictions which draw into relief the reception and presentation of Davis' own lateness.

As already described, at the film's denouement Anderson and Cross find themselves in a jazz club. Cross fixes Anderson a chance to sit in with Caesar's Band, where he takes a few choruses over their funk-jazz groove in a tune titled for the soundtrack album The Jam Session. Anderson uses the opportunity to properly showcase for the first time not only his virtuosic abilities and fizzing tone but also the half-valved glissandi that serve as his trademark 'dingo howl' throughout the film. As he finishes his solo with a flurry of impressive-sounding, alternative-fingered trills, Cross unexpectedly takes to the stage, muted and reserved with his bell pointed characteristically toward the floor. Together, and alongside Caesar (played by Onzy Matthews in the film and Nolan Shaheed on the soundtrack), the three trumpeters trade bars and solo alongside and over each other as the track builds to its end.

Like all of *Dingo*'s music, the track is conditioned by its mainstream presentation in the film and Legrand's own musical sensibilities and professional experience. However, whilst Legrand's experience arranging alongside Davis' sound in the 1950s filtered into self-assured orchestral big-band arrangements and tightly arranged material elsewhere in *Dingo*, it is possible that Legrand had paid less attention to Davis' later work. 'The Jam Session'

Example 5.1 Melody from 'The Jam Session', in *Dingo*, as played by Caesar (top), with Anderson's response (bottom) b.17–24.

offers ample space for Cross (Davis), Dingo (Findley) and Caesar (Shaheed) to improvise over the groove, which seems to be shaped primarily by the recording artists' experience and proficiency performing in the style, rather than precise orchestration featured elsewhere in the score. Indeed, Legrand's own musical style is less identifiable here, save for the melody, which was presumably one of the few strictly notated parts from the recording session (Example 5.1). Cross' muted performance in a handful of solo choruses do brush against Davis' work on tracks like 'Splatch' (*Tutu*) and 'Jilli' and 'Jo-Jo' (*Amandla*, 1989). Yet the protean digital-analogue textures of *Aura* (1989) and sophisticated sampling of 'Black Satin' (*On the Corner*, 1972) are, unsurprisingly, all but missing in Caesar's Band's sound and Cross' solo. This brief analysis is not intended as a denunciation of the scene, nor of Davis and Legrand's work in it. Rather, in 'The Jam Session' we get another striking glimpse of Davis' distortion in Cross. It is a vision of what some of Davis' post-1970s critics perhaps hoped for Davis' later output: competent yet restrained jazz-funk-fusion, without the 'noise'. These moments, in which the Cross/Davis dialogue surfaces in *Dingo*'s music, are also recognisable when Legrand sways toward the 'lyrical Miles', Davis' post-bebop, cool and modal soundworlds that characterise Cross' other musical appearances in *Dingo*.

Example 5.2 Top: Opening riff from 'Concert on the Runway', b.1–8, in *Dingo*. Bottom: A section head from 'Milestones', b.1–8.

This is no clearer than in the film's opening hook, described above, and in the music which accompanies it, titled 'Concert on the Runway'.

Poona Flat's miraculous encounter with Cross is the dramatic impetus of the film and remains one of its more enduring sequences, in part due to its surprising visuals, but also because of its music. This is also the only performance in which we see Cross at the height of his international performance career and perhaps at his most confident: "The Japanese were crazy about us", Cross tells Anderson later in the film when he recalls the tour. The music which Cross and his band perform is clear in its resemblance to Davis' 1958 track 'Milestones'. Legrand's opening melody to the track, soon revealed to be just a riff beneath the true melody, immediately signals the head of 'Milestones'. The first phrase of both tracks, played over a Gm7 vamp, share similarities in rhythm and in the prominence they give to the 9th of Gm7 at their apex (Example 5.2). The 'Milestones' effect is solidified 32 bars later, when the whole band shift one tone higher to Am7, matching the shift in 'Milestones' during its B section (Example 5.3).

There are important differences, however. Legrand's riff starts on the 5th rather than the 7th as in 'Milestones', and the omission of the C pedal from the A section of 'Milestones' streamlines Legrand's harmony. More prominent is the blistering 300 bmp tempo Legrand chooses for the track, which

Example 5.3 Top: B section from 'Concert on the Runway', b.48–56, in *Dingo*. Bottom: B section from 'Milestones', b.17–24. The top line of the lower two systems shows a transcription of Davis' performance, the bottom a simplified version of the B section melody.

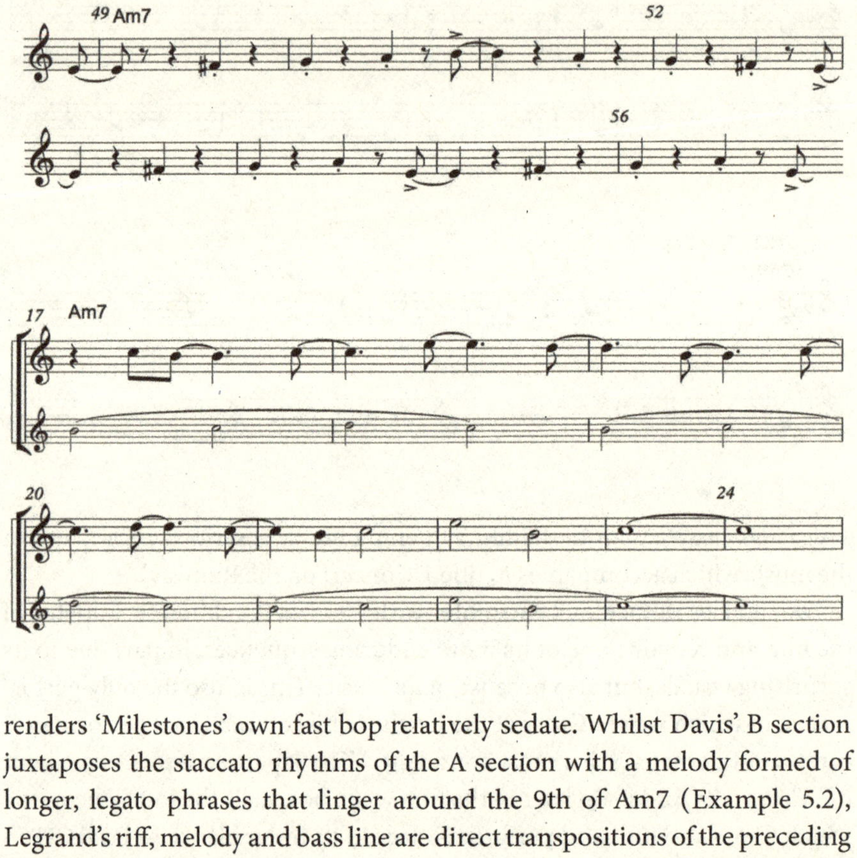

renders 'Milestones' own fast bop relatively sedate. Whilst Davis' B section juxtaposes the staccato rhythms of the A section with a melody formed of longer, legato phrases that linger around the 9th of Am7 (Example 5.2), Legrand's riff, melody and bass line are direct transpositions of the preceding A section, again exaggerating and reducing Davis' source material into something altogether different. These distinctions indicate, first, the cinematic functions of Legrand's score, which in the scene strives to elevate and elongate the energy of 'Milestones' opening 16 bars for the hook of *Dingo*. Second, they expose the differences in Davis' refraction through Cross' music. Legrand's musical framework conjures here productive ruptures in the Davis/Cross dialogue which further reveal a speculative fiction where Davis had returned to 'Milestones' throughout the 1960s, reworking it and leveraging its nostalgic value for new fans in far-flung markets.[14]

[14] This reading finds a connection back to Davis' own output through a 1964 return to 'So What'

Legrand is not the sole author of Cross' reflection of Davis' earlier musical outputs in the film. Later in 'Concert on the Runway', Cross' solo choruses give Davis more space and echo moments in *Legrand Jazz* where the ensemble sections make way for the headliners. Cross' solo serves as an example in which we might clearly sense Davis' most concerted contribution to *Dingo*'s score. As Legrand described it, with the music prepared and already recorded, and in a more intimate setting with only Legrand and the sound engineer, Davis arrived in the recording studio a different man from the one that met Legrand on arrival. "Five days earlier he was discouraged and lazy like a lizard; now, I found the flame of Miles Davis from 1958" (Legrand and Lerouge 2013, 135). By this account, Davis' 'resurrection' might seem well underway. Indeed, as Davis reportedly said of working with Legrand, or at least as presented in a series of decontextualised quotes appearing on de Heer's website, "I tried to rediscover the sound, the ambience of my cool period, the style of 'Kind of Blue,' 'Sketches of Spain' and 'Milestones'" ('*Dingo*: Production Notes', n.d.).

However, like the similarities between Davis and Cross' biographies, the relationship of 'Concert on the Runway' to 'Milestones' is, in most respects, superficial. It is Legrand's retelling of Davis' proto-modal stylings, moulded into an extended big-band arrangement, and rendered unrecognisably and extravagantly new at times, for instance when echoey voices sing mysteriously, "Once you get back to me, never leave, never leave, never leave". As if to solidify Legrand's and the film's stamp on this new 'Milestones', in place of a fade-out Legrand offers a triumphant coda that might have served well as a replacement for Morton Stevens' *Hawaii Five-O* theme. The alterity of this creative reimagining of 'Milestones' is only heightened by the fact that this pivotal scene takes place, so an opening caption and Cross later tell us, in 1969, a decade after 'Milestones'. By that time Davis had long since remodelled his music and fashion once again for *In a Silent Way* (1969) and *Bitches Brew* (1970). As Pillai notes, in this respect *Dingo*'s alternative reality is one in which "the late Columbia and Warner albums had never happened" (2018, 270). 'Concert on the Runway' is a track that Davis could not have recorded without Legrand, and certainly not in 1969. It firmly establishes Legrand's musical voice—conditioned by his associations with music

recorded live in Tokyo (*Miles in Tokyo*, 1969), which showcases many of the differences between the First and Second Great Quintets, but where Davis doubles the original tempo of his 1959 hit.

'between'—within the Cross/Davis dialogue played out in *Dingo* and its reception.

Another notable example of Legrand's refraction of Davis' 1950s output comes later in *Dingo*. After a frustrating rehearsal with Dingo and the Dusters, Anderson returns home to clean his trumpet. Inspecting his valves, he listens to Cross' album *Billy Cross, Live*. For this moment, Legrand provides a track which adopts materials from 'All Blues' and rearranges them for a contemporary big band. Were it not for the lacklustre applause edited onto the end, the resultant track might not have sounded out of place at the 1991 Montreux Jazz Festival, where Quincy Jones revisited many of Gil Evans' arrangements with Davis for a modern big band sound. It is the next track on *Billy Cross, Live*, however, where we see Legrand's most concerted effort to 'resurrect' Davis in Cross.

Titled 'The Dream', the track features *Dingo*'s de facto theme, which is heard five times throughout the film (Example 5.4). Its first appearance comes as residents of Poona Flat rush outside at the sound of Cross' approaching jet plane; Anderson and the audience, however, hear only Cross' solo muted trumpet emerging from the ether. This is Cross' calling card; over a minute of spacious trumpet solo, rich with rubato and a quietness in the vein of 'Blue in Green', 'Chez le photographe du motel' from *Ascenseur pour l'échafaud*, or 'Django' from *Legrand Jazz*. Whilst I suggest these as likely touchstones for Legrand's evocation of one of Davis' most dominant cultural significations, it is for me a theme that closely revisits Davis and Evans' version of George Gershwin's marketplace calls on 'Fishermen, Strawberry and Devil Crab'. The theme's descending phrases grow longer throughout the track and rise sequentially in pitch before being joined by accompanying strings and piano. In other renditions in the film, the theme merges into a brisk waltz.

In all its forms, however, it serves as a reminder of Cross' place at the heart of Anderson's musical ambitions. As the film scholar Bruno Starrs has suggested, the first hearing of the theme, inaudible to the gathering crowd in Poona Flat, gives *Dingo*'s audience a glimpse of Anderson's internal

Example 5.4 'The Dream', opening phrase, b.1–4, in *Dingo*.

perspective (2010, 32). Oblivious to the jet's whirring engines, Anderson anticipates and experiences a direct line of musical communication between Cross and himself. De Heer utilises a particular form of intersubject focalisation here, giving access to an internalised experience shared between Cross and Anderson and repeated throughout the film as an indicator of their connection. Moreover, the theme gives voice to Anderson's compulsion to idolise and seek out Cross in the future, a trajectory which de Heer further establishes in the opening hook, by replaying the dream theme as Cross, recognising something in Anderson, says, "You ever tried music, John? You should try one day.... You seemed tuned into us.... If you ever come to Paris, look me up".

On its third appearance, whilst Anderson cleans his trumpet, he 'tunes in' again to Cross, beginning to play along with him before imagining that Cross is performing live on-stage for him. During the theme's fourth appearance, Anderson is performing on stage in Australia when he closes his eyes to tune out his own band; this time, as the dream emerges in his mind, he joins Cross on stage in a premonition of his looming performance alongside Cross in Paris. The final playing of the theme accompanies Anderson, who, having fulfilled his dreams in the jazz club, heads home to a surprise party held by his family and friends—the remarkable resolution of that unnerving B plot. For this final rendition, Davis dubbed over himself on the track, interjecting and weaving amongst his existing performance. Although this detail is easily missed whilst watching *Dingo*—and as such I tread carefully—it opens an interpretation that, following his encounter with Anderson and re-emergence into public life, Cross was able to reconnect with the version of himself who had reached out to Anderson in 1969 in Australia. In other words, in revisiting the music he used to form a connection to Anderson, Cross enters back into dialogue with the self he had previously condemned. Notably, by de Heer's account, the decision for Davis to record with himself like this was his own:

> The first session was disastrous, Miles was clearly not well, and he was unhappy with his playing, struggling.... [T]he following night was our last chance at it. Miles arrived, Michel [Legrand] was full of care and concern for him but Miles shrugged it off—let's play. Twelve minutes later, two numbers were down.... But Miles wasn't finished ... he wanted another track on this one, and [to] play his first one back. Into record, and Miles started playing the counter melody.... [I]t was almost shocking in its beauty, so

> unexpected, so breath taking. I'll never forget those three minutes. When it was over, and Michel and I were still recovering, Miles packed up his trumpet and left. ('*Dingo*: Production Notes', n.d.)

Thus the final recording sessions, in September 1990, followed a trajectory similar to Legrand and Davis' initial recordings in March, in which Davis was, by Legrand's account, transformed from listless and unwilling to perform to a professional with a creative drive to excel. This account of Davis' dramatic shift in demeanour is a clear example of his ongoing negotiation of his ill health, especially in the 1990s. In this light, Legrand's purported desire to 'resurrect' Davis in *Dingo* is all the more conspicuous.

Resurrection

Throughout my analysis and discussion, I have attempted to integrate Legrand's musical practice and experience within *Dingo*'s representation of Cross and Davis. More specifically, I have explored ways in which *Dingo* can be understood as a dialogue between Davis and Cross that is conditioned by Legrand's refraction of Davis' music in *Dingo*'s score. Underpinning this refraction, both in my analysis and in *Dingo*'s reception, are the topics of Davis' and Cross' ill health and, more broadly, the narratives of decline and lateness. In conclusion, I argue here for the importance of these topics to understanding *Dingo* as a provocation to rethink Davis' legacy and cultural signification.

As the final chapter of Cole's (2006, 437–444) history of Davis' last decade makes clear, by the end of the 1980s Davis' reception was replete, though not overwhelmed, with the tropes of lateness, retirement and decline, and the desire or necessity for a metaphorical and artistic resurrection were perhaps not uncommon amongst critics and musicians. The notion that Miles had little new to say artistically or that what new things he did have to say were no longer interesting are explored throughout the chapter and by the other contributions in this volume, as are the rejections of such ideas. As Joseph Straus has identified in relation to art music, the myriad ideas which surround musical lateness have as much do to with an artist's negotiation of mortality or declining artistic reputations as they are expressions and experiences of disability and/or aging (2008; see also Stras 2009; Lubet 2011; McKay 2019; Straus 2011). Indeed, Davis' supposed musical decline was closely though often tacitly linked to stories of his ill health and progressing age. This link is itself driven by the hegemonic social and cultural contexts that prioritise youth and able bodies as the most social and creatively productive (Twigg 2015). During the production of *Dingo*, as de Heer's account suggests, Davis' health at times represented a barrier to his performance and involvement in the film. Another example from the director's production notes gives some indication of these obstacles, which were multiple and varied and derived as much from the stigmatisation and concern over Davis' bodily difference, illness and ageing as from any impairment itself: "One day in France there was a major hubbub. . . . [T]hey had found a syringe in Miles' caravan . . . and were wondering what to do about it. The explanation was simple. . . . Miles is a diabetic and required insulin injections. . . . Because he didn't look 65, you tended to forget how hard he found some things" ('*Dingo*: Production Notes', n.d.). In addition to his stroke in 1982, which temporarily paralysed his right hand, Davis had diabetes, arthritis, sickle cell anaemia and bouts of pneumonia for several years as he got older. Moreover, his hair loss, changing physical appearance, regular hospital visits and perceived frailty contributed to a focus on his physical decline that included false rumours that he was experiencing the effects of an HIV infection (Cole 2006, 317).

In light of these conditions, and its proximate release to Davis' death, *Dingo*, as I have suggested, served for many as a curious eulogy to Davis' earlier successes, recalling at times the sound of his early Columbia recordings and, at other times, collapsing his post-1970s output into a short, sedate funk-jazz jam tailored to *Dingo*'s mainstream cinematic audience. *Dingo* is protentional in this regard, once again promising an image against which we can draw into relief Davis' life and work.

As Walter van de Leur has written, Davis' ill health and death were key factors in the reception of his performance on *Live at Montreux*, recorded in July 1991; although the concert was not Davis' last performance, this "famous last concert" was repeatedly received as a final, heroic vision of a performer resolute but in decline (2019, 61). The fact that Davis revisits earlier material at the concert was "welcomed almost with a sense of relief [and] understood as a musical pilgrimage to his earlier now-uncontested successes, a form of penance to right his noisy wrong turns since *Bitches Brew*" (61). Of course, Davis' performance at Montreux was no such thing; not only was it what he was being paid to do, but it was also an act of remembrance for Gil Evans rather than a self-reflective tribute to the most highly regarded aspects of his own cultural legacy.

Although Legrand signals his commitment to balance Davis' later work alongside his earlier sounds, in his use of the term *ressusciter* when retrospectively describing his work on *Dingo* he inevitably contributes to a similar narrative. *Dingo*, in this interpretation, is the documentation of another kind of pilgrimage, where Legrand, the master of ceremonies, strives to (re-) present Davis' earlier, 'lyrical' successes. The word *ressusciter*, which I have translated as 'resurrection' throughout, holds all the mystic and mythic overtones of the English word. Indeed, Legrand's usage here is aligned with the kind of public revival and memorialisation at the heart of *Dingo*'s refraction of Davis' music, ill health and ageing. However, whilst the Montreux concert showcased Davis performing material from his own past, *Dingo* and Cross were vessels for something necessarily *new*, a cinematic fiction rendered partially mimetic through its reception as such. Unlike work purposively conceived as speculative fiction, *Dingo* was not a departure from reality, as it never subscribed to any reality; it was also never *intended* as a means to turn a wry light on the historiographical method nor to creatively unpick received truths though a series of 'What-ifs' (Oziewicz 2017). Instead, its connection to Davis' reality was placed upon it. Although the 'What-ifs' may have been retrospectively asked and answered by critics and audiences keen to point out similarities between Cross and Davis, this does not detract from their potential significance, not least as examples of questions audiences and critics *wanted* to ask about Davis, and what they thought the answers might be. Indeed, condensed in *Dingo* and its reception and in the dialogue (through Legrand) between Davis and Cross is a set of enigmatic questions about Davis' output, life and legacy: How should we summarise Davis' work in a feature-length film? Which of Davis' works would we include?

I have seized upon Legrand's use of the word 'resurrection' so willingly throughout this chapter not because of the glimpse it may give of Legrand's intentions but because it serves so keenly as a motivating idea redolent of the discourses surrounding Davis' later output and the 'rethinking' of this collection. Of course, it is interesting that Legrand framed his work on *Dingo* in such a way, but more interesting in Legrand's use of the term is *Dingo*'s most remarkable provocation: the *possibility*, first, that Davis was dead and, second, that he needed resurrection. At the time Legrand was working with Davis on the score, nether were, of course, true, and only the first had transpired by the time Legrand came to write his biography.

References

Anderson, John. 2019. 'Michel Legrand, Pianist and Film Composer, Dies at 86'. *New York Times*, January 26. https://web.archive.org/web/20190126160832/https://www.nytimes.com/2019/01/26/obituaries/michel-legrand-dead.html.

Barron, Lee. 2018. 'Postmodern Theories of Celebrity'. In *Routledge Handbook of Celebrity Studies*, edited by Anthony Elliott. Routledge. https://doi.org/10.4324/9781315776774.

Buckmaster, Luke. 2015. '*Dingo* Rewatched—Rolf de Heer Curio Featuring a Magnetic Miles Davis'. *The Guardian*, March 20. https://www.theguardian.com/film/2015/mar/20/dingo-rewatched-rolf-de-heer-curio-featuring-a-magnetic-miles-davis.

Burch, Noël, and Geneviève Sellier. 2013. *The Battle of the Sexes in French Cinema, 1930–1956*. Translated by Peter Graham. Duke University Press.

Byrnes, Paul. 1992. 'A Sweetly Corny Yarn'. *Sydney Morning Herald*, February 13.

Carr, Ian. 1999. *Miles Davis: The Definitive Biography*. Thunder's Mouth Press.

Caute, David. 1994. *Joseph Losey: A Revenge on Life*. Oxford University Press.

Cinema Papers. 1990. 'Production Surveys'. May. https://archivesonline.uow.edu.au/nodes/view/5088#idx39927.

Cole, George. 2006. *The Last Miles: The Music of Miles Davis, 1980–1991*. Popular Music History. Equinox.

Cook, Richard. 2005. *It's About That Time: Miles Davis on and off Record*. Atlantic.

Crouch, Stanley. 1990. 'Play the Right Thing'. *New Republic*, February 12.

Davis, Miles, and Michel Legrand. 1991. *Dingo: Selections from the Motion Picture Soundtrack*. Warner Bros. Records. CD.

Davis, Miles, and Quincy Troupe. 1989. *Miles: The Autobiography*. Simon and Schuster.

de Heer, Rolf dir. (1991) 2005. *Dingo*. Umbrella Entertainment. DVD.

de Heer, Rolf. 2016. 'Interview: Rolf de Heer on Miles Davis and 'Dingo' (1991)'. *Pelican Magazine*, March 14. https://pelicanmagazine.com.au/2016/03/14/interview-words-rolf-de-heer/.

de Heer, Rolf. 2021. '*Dingo* and *All That Jazz*'. FilmInk, February 2. https://www.filmink.com.au/rolf-de-heer-dingo-and-all-that-jazz/.

de Heer, Rolf. n.d. 'Interview: Rolf de Heer Interviewed by George Cole'. *The Last Miles*. https://www.thelastmiles.com/interviews-rolf-de-heer/.

DeVeaux, Scott. 1992. *Review of Miles: The Autobiography*, by Miles Davis and Quincy Troupe. *American Music* 10 (1): 89–94. https://doi.org/10/bfgjdb.

'*Dingo*: Overview'. n.d. Vertigo Productions. http://www.vertigoproductions.com.au/dingo_overview.php.

'*Dingo*: Production Notes'. n.d. Vertigo Productions. http://www.vertigoproductions.com.au/dingo_production_notes.php.

Dixon, Norm. 1992. 'Miles Lifts Charming Outback Fairytale'. *Green Left Weekly*, February 5. https://www.greenleft.org.au/content/miles-lifts-charming-outback-fairytale.

Dyer, Richard. 1998. *Stars*. BFI.

Feather, Leonard. 1991. '"Dingo": Sweet Swan Song of Legrand Jazz from Davis'. *Los Angeles Times*, December 8.

Freeman, Phil. 2005. *Running the Voodoo Down: The Electric Music of Miles Davis*. Backbeat Books.

Gabbard, Krin. 2004. 'Miles from Home: Miles Davis and the Movies'. *Jazz Research Journal* 1 (1): 28–42.

Gabbard, Krin. 2007. 'White Face, Black Noise: Miles Davis and the Soundtrack'. In *Beyond the Soundtrack: Representing Music in Cinema*, edited by Daniel Goldmark, Lawrence Kramer and Richard Leppert. University of California Press.

High Fidelity. 1953. 'Readers' Forum'. August.

Holden, Stephen. 1994. 'Jazz Finds a Lonely Follower in the Australian Desert'. *New York Times*, November 11.

Holland, Peter. 1979. *The Ornament of Action: Text and Performance in Restoration Comedy.* Cambridge University Press.

Jillett, Neil. 1992. 'The Man Who Captured Miles Davis on Film'. *The Age*, February 2.

Jurman, Elizabeth. 1992. 'Today's People: Legends'. *Sydney Morning Herald*, January 15.

Kinder, Marsha. 1991. *Playing with Power in Movies, Television, and Video Games: From Muppet Babies to Teenage Mutant Ninja Turtles.* University of California Press.

Kotlowitz, Robert. 1955. 'Building Your Record Library'. *High Fidelity*, May.

Legrand, Michel, and Stéphane Lerouge. 2013. *Rien n'est grave dans les aigus.* Cherche midi.

Losey, Joseph, and Michel Ciment. 1985. *Conversations with Losey.* Methuen.

Lubet, Alex. 2011. 'Let's Face the Music and Dance: Jazz and Physical Disability'. In *Music, Disability, and Society.* Temple University Press.

Macdonald, Dougal. 1992. 'Script's Shortcomings Lessen Movie's Impact'. *Canberra Times*, February 19.

McKay, George. 2019. 'Jazz and Disability'. In *The Routledge Companion to Jazz Studies*, edited by Nicholas Gebhardt, Nichole Rustin-Paschal and Tony Whyton. Routledge Music Companions. Routledge.

Merritt, Edward. 1951. 'The Music Between'. *High Fidelity*, Fall.

Onsman, Andrys, and Robert Burke. 2018. *Experimentation in Improvised Jazz: Chasing Ideas.* Routledge.

Oziewicz, Marek. 2017. 'Speculative Fiction'. In *Oxford Research Encyclopedia of Literature*, edited by Paula Rabinowitz. Oxford University Press. https://oxfordre.com/literature/view/10.1093/acrefore/9780190201098.001.0001/acrefore-9780190201098-e-78.

Perchard, Tom. 2015. *After Django: Making Jazz in Postwar France.* University of Michigan Press.

Pillai, Nicolas. 2018. 'A Star Named Miles: Tracking Jazz Musicians Across Media'. In *Jazz@100*, edited by Wolfram Knauer. Darmstadt Studies in Jazz Research, vol. 15. Jazzinstitut Darmstadt.

Powrie, Phil. 2013. 'The French Musical: Swing and Big Bands in the Cinema of the 1940s and 1950s'. *Screen* 54 (2): 152–173. https://doi.org/10/ggwz48.

Quinn, Michael L. 1990. 'Celebrity and the Semiotics of Acting'. *New Theatre Quarterly* 6 (22): 154–161. https://doi.org/10/b55dxb.

Rearick, Charles. 1997. *The French in Love and War: Popular Culture in the Era of the World Wars.* Yale University Press.

Rosenberg, Marc. 1992. Dingo *(Motion Picture).* Currency Press.

Sprout, Leslie A. 2013. *The Musical Legacy of Wartime France.* University of California Press.

Stanley, John. 1993. '"Dingo" Jazz Great Davis Hit High Note Down Under'. *San Francisco Chronicle*, October 10.

Starrs, D. Bruno. 2010. 'The Aural Point of View in the Early Films of Rolf de Heer'. *Quarterly Review of Film and Video* 28 (1): 28–40. https://doi.org/10/bdkb59.

Stilwell, Robynn J. 2003. 'Le Demy-Monde: The Bewitched, Betwixt and Between French Musical'. In *Popular Music in France from Chanson to Techno: Culture, Identity, and Society*, edited by Hugh Dauncey and Steve Cannon. Ashgate Popular and Folk Music Series. Ashgate.

Stras, Laurie. 2009. 'Sing a Song of Difference: Connie Boswell and a Discourse of Disability in Jazz'. *Popular Music* 28 (3): 297–322. https://doi.org/10/fm4nr6.

Straus, Joseph N. 2008. 'Disability and "Late Style" in Music'. *Journal of Musicology* 25 (1): 3–45. https://doi.org/10/fwcpp8.

Straus, Joseph N. 2011. *Extraordinary Measures: Disability in Music.* Oxford University Press.

Szwed, John. 2002. *So What: The Life of Miles Davis.* William Heinemann.

Thomas, Kevin. 1993. 'Miles Davis—as Actor—Jazzes Up "Dingo"'. *Los Angeles Times*, February 22. https://www.latimes.com/archives/la-xpm-1993-02-22-ca-327-story.html.

Tingen, Paul. 2001. *Miles Beyond: The Electric Explorations of Miles Davis, 1967–1991.* Billboard Books.

Tomlinson, Gary. 1991. 'Cultural Dialogics and Jazz: A White Historian Signifies'. *Black Music Research Journal* 11 (2): 229–264. https://doi.org/10/cjr4q4.

Twigg, Julia, ed. 2015. *Routledge Handbook of Cultural Gerontology*. Routledge International Handbooks. Routledge, Taylor & Francis Group.

Vail, Ken. 2003. *Dizzy Gillespie: The Bebop Years, 1937–1952*. Scarecrow Press.

van de Leur, Walter. 2019. 'Swan Songs: Jazz, Death, and Famous Last Concerts'. In *The Routledge Companion to Jazz Studies*, edited by Nicholas Gebhardt, Nichole Rustin-Paschal and Tony Whyton. Routledge Music Companions. Routledge.

Williams, Evan. 1992. 'Hypnotic High Notes in Uneven Composition'. *Weekend Australian*, February 1.

Williams, Richard. 2018. 'Soundtrack Legend Michel Legrand: "I've Been an Adventurer!"' *The Guardian*, September 4. http://www.theguardian.com/music/2018/sep/04/michel-legrand-interview-film-soundtrack-legend-composer.

Younis, Raymond. 1992. 'Dingo'. *Cinema Papers*, April. https://archivesonline.uow.edu.au/nodes/view/5096#idx40564.

6

Fashioning Miles Davis

Dressing and Undressing Television Stardom

Nicolas Pillai

Miles Davis wore clothes well. Indeed, so iconographic is he that, when considering one or another musical style that he explored, one tends to associate its sound with his clothes in that era. In this chapter, I analyse a significant but largely ignored aspect of Davis' career in the 1980s—his appearances on television—through close readings of the clothes that he wore. Dressing is, for all of us, an intentional act that begins the day. I will argue that for Miles Davis it was also an iterative and highly imaginative part of his music-making process, as well as a means of signalling his ownership of star identity and engagement with new audiences. For Davis, the building of a 'look', the choice of which garments to wear together, which fabrics and patterns to combine, the shaping of a silhouette, was a method for thinking through creative possibilities. The reuse of garments in new contexts was a playful exercise in which drape, volume and texture constituted a sartorial repertoire.

In essence, then, I propose that Davis' calculated use of clothing to disrupt those elements of his persona which threatened to become stable has not been adequately treated in the existing scholarship. Further, I suggest that the critical turn against Davis' music in the 1980s was premised on prejudicial conceptions of the jazz body, its display and decorum. As redress, I interrogate the assumption that Davis' outfits were reactive to his music, arguing instead that they were constituent to his musical development, and then present two close analyses of this embodied subversion mediated through television: Davis' acting role in *Miami Vice* and his music video for the album *Tutu*. But I open with a consideration of the intimacy of clothing—specifically, a T-shirt seen on a cop show.

Nicolas Pillai, *Fashioning Miles Davis* In: *Rethinking Miles Davis*. Edited by: Roger Fagge, Nicolas Pillai, and Tim Wall, Oxford University Press. © Oxford University Press 2026. DOI: 10.1093/9780190085834.003.0006

Dolphin Music

In an episode of HBO's *Homicide: Life on the Street* ('Son of a Gun', February 10, 1993), series regular Crosetti (Jon Polito) sits at the hospital bedside of his comatose squad buddy Chris, shot in the line of duty. Chris' wife, Eva (Edie Falco), is there too, in what appears to be a familiar scene from this kind of television programme. The sudden incursion of tragedy has interrupted the procedure of the police procedural: daily duties, squad room and household, are pushed aside in a new routine of hospital vigils and sleepless nights. Crosetti, a nervy Italian American, is still wearing his work clothes: a crumpled brown suit, tie askew.

Earlier in the episode we have seen Crosetti break down while at work, so worried is he over Chris' condition. Speaking to fellow cops at a crime scene, he relates how they had become friends: "When Chris worked under me, we found that we both liked jazz, the modern composers like Gato Barbieri and David Sanborn. Keith Jarrett in the early recordings. And Chris says that it's like dolphin music 'cause it puts him in this water state where it's like floating. And communication happens without any words. [*long pause*] Anyway, up in heaven God listens to jazz, you know?" Helplessly, Crosetti beats his fist into the side of a squad car, then announces, "I think I broke my hand", as the scene breaks for adverts. Polito's performance is affecting in this moment: deflecting his inarticulate grief with the anecdote, braced against the car as if he has been winded. But it is also very funny, Polito's mannered delivery of "Keith Jarrett in the early recordings" skewering the stereotypical jazz aficionado, always in thrall to the past.

The episode ends in the hospital, late at night. When Eva leaves to use the bathroom, Crosetti carefully places one set of headphones on the coma victim and another set on his own head. Laboriously, comically, Crosetti strips his office shirt to reveal underneath a black T-shirt bearing the celebrated 1989 Jeff Sedlik photograph of Miles Davis with finger to lips, sometimes called 'Silence' (Figure 6.1). Crosetti takes Chris' hand and listens pensively to 'Something I Dreamed Last Night' from the album *Steamin' with Miles Davis*, recorded in 1956. It's a communicative non-communication, this stout hardheaded dolphin calling out and hearing nothing back. As the image fades to black, the tape continues playing over the producer credits before segueing into *Homicide*'s weekly closing score.

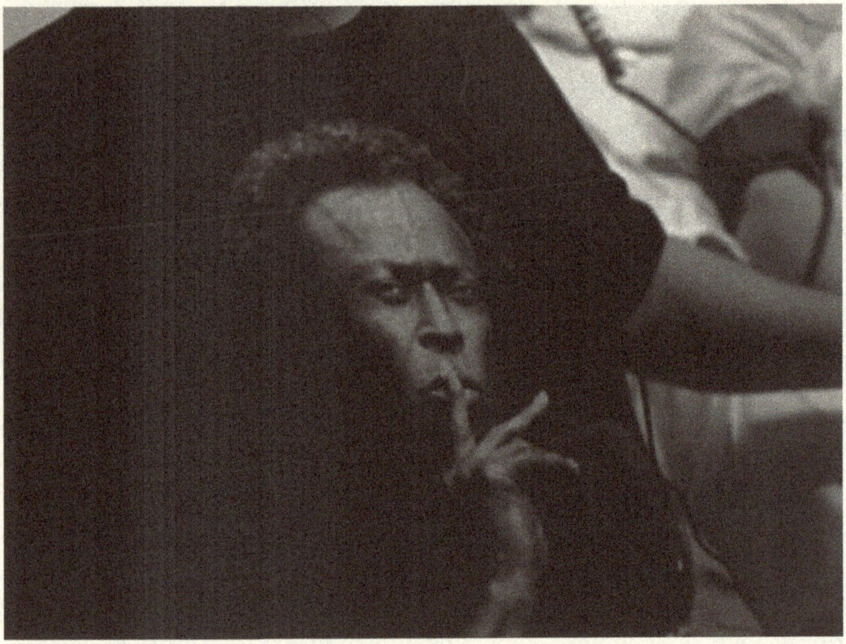

Figure 6.1 A Miles Davis T-shirt in *Homicide: Life on the Street.*

It may seem perverse to begin a chapter on Miles Davis by describing the emotional life of two fictional white policemen. After all, Davis expressed his aversion to law enforcement many times, and with good reason. But my assertion here is that this moment from *Homicide* meaningfully dramatises the totemic power of Miles Davis, where tenderness is enabled by the literal inhabiting of blackness. The concealed T-shirt shows us how personal, hidden away and treasured the connection to Davis can be for those who love his music. Crosetti's sartorial testament to friendship—the T-shirt as undergarment—is not at all stylish. Yet it delicately shows us that the relationship between these two policemen has been a kind of marriage, as Crosetti's disrobing mimics getting ready for bed. Chris' coma recalls the earlier mentions of 'floating' and 'communication without any words', but through shot composition and sound effects we are aware of the mediation of technologies (the mechanism of music playback, the mechanism of life support). It is a scene that proposes a kind of time travel, a dual continuity that Davis might symbolise. Crosetti and Chris' shared history, represented by a song from the past ("Something I Dreamed Last Night" in 1956), has been silenced by a bullet, a punctuation emphasised by Davis' raised finger in the Sedlik image from 1989.[1]

We Want Miles (in Suits)

In a discussion of black youth style on television in the 1980s, Herman Gray (1995) draws a comparison between "the pose of the rapper, the stance of the jazz musician, the celebration rituals of the athlete, and the popular dances of black youth". Taking the specific example of the jazz body, Gray observes, "As Miles Davis and many of his critics and admirers recount in his autobiography, for musicians and listeners alike, the body, dress, and general style of many musicians, especially during the 1950s and 1960s, served as a crucial means of expressing black passion, defiance, and authority" (155). So too Eric Lott has argued that bebop musicians had expressed social resistance through "styles of dress, music, drugs and speech homologous with the structures of their experience" and that with "secrecy, exaggeration, and wit, self-images were formed, alliances made, strategies of differentiation concocted" (1998, 460). To build upon Gray's suggestion that "the body, dress, and general style" were important to Davis throughout his career, we might turn first to his autobiography. In the case of tailoring, Davis describes expensive clothes as status symbols—"I have always got my suits made when I had the money" (Davis and Troupe 1990, 68)—but also as visible markers of cultural currency, specifically of 'hipness' in the jazz world (100–101). In the latter case, Davis recounts an anecdote in which he anxiously changed the way he dressed so that he might gain the approval of Dexter Gordon.

As fashions evolved, so too did Davis' style and the way he related his clothes to the playing of music:

> I was changing my attitude about a lot of things, like the look of my wardrobe. . . . Plus, everyone was starting to dress a little looser at concerts, at least the rock musicians were, and that might have affected me. Everybody was into blackness, you know, the black consciousness movement, and so a lot of African and Indian fabrics were being worn. . . . I had moved away

[1] We might recall here Stuart Hall describing his lifelong devotion to the trumpeter's sound: "Miles Davis put his finger on my soul and it never went away" (Desert Island Discs, BBC Radio 4, February 13, 2000).

> from the cool Brooks Brothers look and into this other thing, which for me was more what was happening with the times. I found I could move around on stage much better. I wanted to move on stage, play in different places, because there are areas on stage where the music and the sound are much better than other places. I was starting to explore for those places. (Davis and Troupe 1990, 300)

Evidently, Davis' continued engagement with fashion was both politically inflected and practically informed by changes in his music making. In the passage above, Davis pinpoints a few motivations working in tandem: establishing equivalency and connection to rock musicians, accessing contemporary constructions of blackness, sloughing off the past by moving away from a previous mode of dress, increasing mobility onstage (which has a double meaning, since 'to play in different places' is to move beyond genre).

Interestingly, Miles Davis' agency in these decisions is downplayed by Ian Carr (1999, 234) and reassigned to singer-songwriter Betty Davis (born Betty Mabry, Davis' second wife). In an interview, Betty modifies this narrative:

Michael Stradford: Would you say you helped him figure out his new style?

Betty Davis: I really didn't. He'd just come to the stores with me when I shopped.... It was just his taste at the time.... He knew how he wanted to look before he got dressed. I didn't voice my opinion, because it was the way he wanted to look.... I would pick out things like scarves, belts and shirts for him. But his jackets and trousers he'd pick out for himself. (Stradford 2020, 116–117)

With Betty's eye for accessories, Miles was putting pieces together in front of a mirror in the spirit of creative experimentation. Indeed, Betty asserts, "The clothes were before the music" (Stradford 2020, 116), which reverses a common understanding that Miles was dressing to illustrate his new sound. This testimony suggests rather that the act of trying on, of dressing up, of looking at oneself and feeling one's look, had become part of Miles' approach to new sounds and methods of working. It may, then, be useful to draw upon Carol Tulloch's (2016, 91, 128) analysis of the style of Billie Holiday, particularly the notion of collage, where the act of dressing and accessorising can "inform an alternative understanding of the subject" and implement style as "a technology of self-telling". Like the bebop musicians he revered, Davis was using the process of dressing as a process of thought, as a means of expressing agency, difference and defiance. I will return to this idea in my textual analysis of television texts, with particular attention to details of outfitting and the permeation between clothing (garments worn day-to-day) and costume (those garments that 'perform' onstage or onscreen).

Davis' fiercest critics in later years saw his new style of dress as a manifestation of the degradation of not just his musical style but also his moral compass. When Stanley Crouch (1990, 30) bemoans the fall from the "exquisite dress" of the 1950s, by which he means Brooks Brothers suits, to the "expensive bad taste of rock 'n' roll" in the 1970s and 1980s—Andrea Aranov, Issey Miyake and Kohshin Satoh—he is positing the latter garments as externalisations of corruption, resulting in "terrible performances and terrible recordings". Strikingly, Crouch associates what he perceives to be a decline in musical and fashion standards with popular culture forms such as film or television: "Davis' music became progressively trendy and dismal, as did his attire; at one point in the early 1970s, with his wraparound dark glasses and his puffed shoulders, the erstwhile master of cool looked like an extra from a science-fiction B-movie" (35). At times, as in this quotation, Crouch's concerns can seem laughably fogeyish. At others, his moral outrage is convincing and stirring. I do not mean to patronise this impassioned and famous essay; indeed, its anger at Davis' abuse of women, egotism and macho posturing have aged well. At his core, Crouch is deeply suspicious of a tendency he recognises as early as the Columbia years to present as "a star, a large influence, a matinee idol" (32), which he suggests degrades Davis and black culture more generally through "obnoxious, vulgar, and anti-social behaviour" (35). Crouch links Davis to black political and cultural figures he reductively associates with violence, vulgarity, obscenity and immorality: Eldridge Cleaver, Huey Newton, the Black Panthers, Richard Pryor, Eddie Murphy, Spike Lee, Ice-T and Public Enemy.

To understand Crouch's rhetorical strategies, we might compare them to the way that Jeffrey Sconce has theorised 'trash' cinema, which includes exploitation flicks, gory horror and—yes—science fiction B-movies. Sconce pinpoints approaches to film style as the dividing factor between the academy and para-cinematic audiences: "One could say that while academic attention to excess often foregrounds aesthetic strategies within the text as a closed formal system, paracinematic attention to excess, an excess that often manifests itself as a film's failure to conform to historically delimited codes of verisimilitude, calls attention to the text as a cultural and sociological document and thus dissolves the boundaries of the diegesis into profilmic and extratextual realms" (1995, 387). Crouch's concern is to locate value within a canon defined by a sense of loss, similar to the cop in *Homicide* who prized "the early recordings". Miles Davis will never again reach the "heroic intimacy" (Crouch 1990, 34) of *My Funny Valentine*, the 1965 album identifiable by the preppy outfit Davis models on its cover. What comes later is trash because, stylistically, it does not conform to the closed formal musicological system which Crouch uses to interpret and evaluate the Davis oeuvre.

Crouch's rejection of extratextual elements that formed Miles Davis' stardom—clothes, television, advertising and celebrity—replicate historically dismissive attitudes toward the feminine and the queer. In a description of a TV interview between Davis and Prince, Crouch dismisses the latter as "the Minneapolis vulgarian and borderline drag queen"; the 1948–1950 *Birth of the Cool* nonet recordings are "little more than primers for television writing"; the "academic temptation of Western music" is judged to be "effete"; and—in a phrase picked up elsewhere in this volume by Roger Fagge—Crouch invokes fetishism and male prostitution when he calls Davis a "licker of moneyed boots . . . willing now to pimp himself" (1990, 30–34). Crouch concludes by deploring Davis' self-exclusion from "aristocracies of culture", an elitist comment which summarises his critique. Comparing Davis unfavourably to the "elegant and exigent Afro-American authenticity of the likes of Ellington", Crouch bemoans a surrender to the "youth culture vulgarity that vandalises the sweep and substance of Afro-American life" (37). Implicitly, the tailored suit becomes emblematic of a prelapsarian age in which "the suited man is dependable, the dandy is not" (Bruzzi 1997, 69). To draw upon M. W. Barnes' definition of vulgarity, Davis has become "the person who can be expected to exhibit refinement behaving like one who cannot be" (1980, 75).

In a study of changes in Englishmen's outerwear between 1688 and 1832, David Kuchta (1996) observes that the introduction of the three-piece suit, defined by its "essentially modern uniformity and darkness" was an insistence on sobriety after an era of excess. With clean lines and unadorned fabric, "political legitimacy was expressed in masculinist attitudes toward consumption and luxury" (54–55). "Both by making masculinity a prerequisite to political legitimacy and by claiming masculinity as their own, aristocratic men used the label of effeminacy to directly exclude from power all other men—lower- and middle-class men, as well as men with alternative sexual practices—and to indirectly yet doubly exclude all women from power (by associating femininity with luxury and masculinity with legitimacy)" (63). This association of effeminacy with luxurious fabrics or soft draping informs not just Crouch's critique but also that of the jazz writer Francis Davis, whose disappointment in Miles found "something pathetic about the sight of a sixty-three-year-old man in clogs, parachute pants and Jheri curls shaking his fanny to a younger generation's beat" (1996, 42). Wynton Marsalis seconded this criticism, hyperbolically deploring black male role models who "go out with a dress on, a skirt, panties" (quoted in Zabor and Garbarini 1994, 121–122).[2] The authors of these words seek to divorce jazz from a history observed by Monica L. Miller, who points out that "in the early twentieth century, it was principally within the gay and lesbian community and the entertainment industry that black dandyism flourished; later, the art world too became an arena in which dandyism presented a challenge to notions of blackness from within and without the heterogeneous black community" (2009, 222).

I am not interested here in rehearsing speculation over Davis' sexual preferences or in engaging with the patent absurdity of Marsalis' assertion that "Miles has really a bisexuality in his sound" (quoted in Dunkel 2016, 47). Rather, I wish to contextualise the overdetermined heterosexuality of Crouch and Marsalis as forms of moral panic, in which "policy and moral debates explicitly target popular music, music video, and dance in relation to social, cultural, and moral debates about increased violence against women, increased homophobia and gay bashing, and increased teen pregnancy" (Gray 1995, 155).[3] As Mario Dunkel has argued, the narration of jazz history has been severely limited by the perceived necessity to legitimate jazz, thus closing off narratives that "productively integrate critical views on sexuality and gender" (2016, 48).

If, as Lara Pellegrinelli has argued, jazz has from its very conception been "symbolically gendered" (2008, 34), then we might begin to have an inkling of why Davis' rejection of men's suits was so troubling to Crouch, Francis Davis and Marsalis. It is my contention that Davis was consciously

[2] Miles Davis's assertion that these new clothes allowed him to "move around on stage much better" (Davis and Troupe 1990, 300) gets short shrift from Crouch (1990, 30), who despairs when the 1980s Davis "walks about the stage, touches foreheads with the saxophonist as they play a duet, bends over and remains in that ridiculous position for long stretches as he blows at the floor". For its lack of nobility, Crouch hated the crouch.

[3] As John Gennari (2006, 355) notes, Crouch had "promulgated a dress code for jazz masculinity" and, in 1982, had outed Cecil Taylor as gay by "suggesting that this sexual orientation explained why Taylor couldn't swing".

using "clothing's distancing, disruptive potential" (Bruzzi 1997, 34) as part of a larger challenge to orthodoxies of jazz tradition. Through wearing loose and luxurious cuts of sensuous fabric, and through participation in cultural forms such as television, Davis presented an affront to those for whom narrow categorisation and classification were bound up in an elitist sense of the music's value, and for whom these hierarchies of style and genre were inherently binary and heterosexualist.

At stake in the condemnation of Miles Davis' clothing, and more widely the commercialisation of black music, is an anxiety around demasculinisation and loss of power. Evidently this is played out in language that implies that Miles' decline, his "corruption", to use Crouch's loaded word, betrays the straightness of the jazz canon, which found its purest visual expression in clean silhouettes of dark suits. Writing of historical suspicions toward fashion, John Harvey describes clothes as "treacherous companions, perhaps the more so because they touch us so closely, because they touch our skin" (2014, 4), and this intimacy may help to explain the sense of betrayal and loss that underpins Crouch's argument. The vulgar eclecticism of Miles' clothing in the 1970s and the 1980s, his experimentation with fabric and accessories, is thus seen as an undesirable queering of the music, a fear that the mack might fall yet further and become the hustler.

It is instructive to compare these fears with Kodwo Eshun's (1998, 7) description of Miles Davis' clothes as an advanced performativity, a conscious engagement with posthuman sound: "The sleeve for '75's *Dark Magus* shows Miles wearing bug-green fly shades, adapting to the audiomenagerie by becoming insectile himself. Superfly shades access the tsetse fly's magnified vision. Sight becomes compounded, triggering the reticulated hearing electronic jazz demands". One wonders if Eshun is deliberately rebuffing Crouch's (1990, 35) association of "dark wraparound sunglasses" with science fiction here. For Afrofuturist readings of black culture, fashion as a technology of self-telling is one way of realising the alternate and subversive. Sunglasses, or 'shades' (a term that invokes the classical world), trigger an act of self-transformation, Ovidian metamorphosis that permits heightened senses of seeing and hearing, compounded into methods of appreciation which we might call watching and listening. Unlike Davis' detractors, Eshun is happy to accept that fashioning oneself might inform the production and consumption of jazz.

In the textual analyses that make up the rest of this chapter, I model attentive watching and listening (rather than merely seeing and hearing) of encounters between Miles Davis and the televisual forms of narrative drama and music video. By taking such artefacts of popular culture seriously I hope to answer the following questions:

- How does television create meaning when it shows us the clothing of Miles Davis?
- Can the close analysis of Miles Davis' clothed body inflect our understanding of his star persona?
- What can this type of analysis add to our understanding of Miles Davis' later work?

I will begin by considering what happens when the collaging of one's look, the "technology of self-telling", is bounded by the demands of fictional narrative.

A Male Sort of Madame

In 1985, Miles Davis acted in an episode of the hit NBC crime show *Miami Vice* ('Junk Love', November 8). In one sense, this was not remarkable. Throughout the 1980s, Davis would make numerous appearances on television: advertising brands such as Gap, Van Liquor, Honda motorcycles and TDK cassette tapes; as a guest on David Letterman's and Dick Cavett's chat shows; in music videos for his albums *Decoy* and *Tutu*; and of course in international broadcasts of concerts.[4] This broad transmedia reach has been recorded by Davis' biographers: John Szwed (2002, 359, 374) discusses the chat show spots, Ian Carr (1999, 469, 482–483) charts Davis' growing celebrity and George Cole (2005, 479–482) provides "Miles on Video" listings. However, the scarcity of academic writing on these subjects suggests that this form of celebrity sits uneasily for jazz scholars; as Mark Laver has observed, "the notion of an opposition between music (and jazz in particular) and commerce has proven remarkably durable, both in jazz musicians' own understanding of their relationship to the culture industries and in the way that relationship is represented in the popular media" (2015, 40). While not directly relevant to this study, it is encouraging to see sophisticated writing

[4] Off-screen, Davis also soundtracked one episode of NBC's *Alfred Hitchcock Presents* ("Prisoners", December 8, 1985).

on jazz and television emerging in the past 10 years, such as Doctor (2016), Gebhardt (2016), Borshuk (2018) and Solis (2018).[5]

My own understanding of television's role in Davis' career builds on Herman Gray's (1995, 159) account of the medium as a contested site of cultural politics: "Indeed, television, especially music television and advertising, is the common place where different and differently interested claims on blackness (ethnic, racial, corporate capitalist, suburban middle-class, nationalist, assimilationist, urban poor) meet, each borrowing from the others, each using the others for its own ends, each making meanings of the others in often different, conflicting ways". If we accept Gray's thesis, then one must view Davis' appearances on television as interventions into this contestation. As we have seen, Davis' reminiscences framed his changes in personal style as a political act; television appearances are thus interactions with a key site of discourse. Given Gray's privileging of music television and advertising in the quotation above, even the choice to appear on *Miami Vice* is interesting. Famously, the show had its inception in an executive memo that simply read, "MTV Cops".[6] The resulting production became a television phenomenon, as much for its striking visual style as its glamorous locale and charismatic stars. Overseen by film director Michael Mann, the show deployed aspects of his postmodern aesthetic to great effect. As well as the smooth metallic surfaces favoured by Mann and the synthesised soundtrack of Jan Hammer, *Miami Vice* became synonymous with clothing, a pastel-shaded catwalk of loose-fitting suits over T-shirts, gold chains and boat shoes. The two lead characters, detectives Sonny Crockett and Ricardo Tubbs, were played by Don Johnson (white, from Missouri) and Philip Michael Thomas (black, of Afro-American and Native American heritage).

Television scholars have found *Miami Vice* to be an exemplary postmodern text (see Feuer 1995, 102–104). This reconceptualisation of a staple television genre (the cop show) placed excessive emphasis on formal innovation that invoked the editing and texture of music video, "moving from a framework that approached broadcasting primarily as a form of word-based rhetoric and transmission . . . to a visually based mythology, framework, and

[5] My engagements with the topic can be found at Pillai 2016a, 2018a, 2023. Early thoughts on Miles Davis and television were presented at the 2017 Darmstadt Jazzforum, later published as Pillai 2018b.

[6] Sue Turnbull notes, "Following the MTV impulse, *Miami Vice* was one of the first television shows to use recorded pop music and embed this into a soundtrack that also included up to thirty minutes of original electronic music composed by Jan Hammer" (2014, 81).

aesthetic based on extreme consciousness of style" (Caldwell 1995, 4). For John Fiske, the appeal of the programme lay in the way that narrative could be productively subsumed into style: "However hard the narrative fights to close each episode with a resolution in which sense, control, and masculine closure are all achieved, the style, the music, the look, the interruptions of the narrative remain open, active, disruptive and linger on as the pleasures of *Miami Vice*" (1987, 262). Caldwell's and Fiske's theoretical emphases on the visual are useful for my argument that clothing is an active maker of meaning in Miles Davis' appearance in *Miami Vice*. But it may be worth registering here that television studies has afforded perhaps too much importance to this programme *precisely because* it smoothly intersects with postmodern theory. I would argue that style and look have always been active makers of meaning in the production of television as a textured and designed medium.

Cast as brothel keeper and people trafficker Ivory Jones, Davis has five long scenes in the 45-minute episode, playing out the pimp fantasy that Robin D. G. Kelley (2001, 7) identifies in the Miles persona as "the mack, that despicable character we find so compelling and attractive". In his account of the experience, however, Davis demonstrated some equivocation. On the one hand, he writes, "I didn't like so much that I had to play a pimp, although I did it. I didn't like the idea of reinforcing some stereotypical view that a lot of people have of black men. I was mostly playing a businessman in that part, a male sort of madame. So in my mind I wasn't playing a pimp, but a kind of businessman and so that's why I played the role" (Davis and Troupe 1990, 366). But, as though revelling in the contradiction, Davis also writes, "I knew how to play a pimp because I knew a little about that from the old days" (365). That year Davis had also acted the pimp for Anthony Barboza's camera, as the photographer shot sleeve art for the Columbia album *You're Under Arrest*. The gatefold depicts two of Barboza's images (unused shots feature in Barboza and Maxwell 2013) front and back, the interior showcasing Davis' paintings of women dancers. In the photographs, Davis is depicted wearing two different jackets, which Barboza recalls the musician had bought specially (113): one embroidered with a phoenix, the other a marching-band jerkin with patterned African masks and glass diamond studs—a white version of the jerkin will feature in the *Tutu Medley* video, discussed later. The look is completed by a black fedora hat, black leather pants and, bizarrely, a toy machine gun.

Set against a blood-red background, Davis appears as a parody of a gangster, glowering out at us. Barboza would recall of the various photographs,

"The one that they finally used was not my favourite, because I wanted him to be more sinister, there's another shot that I like more because he's looking at you at a glance. They picked one where he's looking straight ahead" (Stradford 2020, 112). Somewhat fancifully, Barry Maxwell reads these images as a presentiment of death, suggesting that the lines of the gun and trumpet frame "a proleptic death mask" (quoted in Barboza and Maxwell 2013, 98). As discussed in this book's introduction, the tendency to view an artist's 'late' work through the lens of their death can be reductive. While *You're Under Arrest* contains soundscapes of state oppression and nuclear apocalypse (Cole 2005, 164), to read Davis' cover image so funereally ignores evident kitsch qualities. In these photographs, Davis is having fun dressing up.

Having playfully inhabited the stereotype of the black pimp on the cover of *You're Under Arrest*, the role in *Miami Vice* offered Davis another opportunity to explore alternate masculinities. Where the album cover is a butch fantasy, the pimp character in *Miami Vice*—"a male sort of madame"—is more nuanced. In the episode's pre-credits sequence, Tubbs is undercover in a brothel, while his cop partner Crockett waits outside for the sting to go down. As scantily clad women strut past, Tubbs is more interested in a catalogue of female sex workers offered by the proprietor, Ivory Jones. They leer together over the relative merits of the photographs, erotic potential located in the sharing of this pornographic document rather than the actual women in the lobby. At one point Tubbs reaches over the counter to finger the chain Jones wears around his neck. Jones tells Tubbs the chain is Nigerian, and Tubbs quips back, "So am I" (Figure 6.2). It is a scene of seduction.

This baiting of Jones by Tubbs (who contextual knowledge of the series tells us is resolutely heterosexual) is taken through to its thematic conclusion as the episode progresses and Jones is "turned" by the police force. The trope is familiar from crime films such as *The Narrow Margin* (1952, dir. Richard Fleischer) and *The Big Heat* (1953, dir. Fritz Lang) in which a gangster's moll is "turned" for information and suffers grim consequences; like the characters played by Marie Windsor and Gloria Grahame in those films, Ivory Jones will die on his undercover assignment and, in doing so, achieve redemption. Seeking to infiltrate the network of drug smuggler Juan Carlos Silva (Jose Perez), Jones takes Crockett and Tubbs to an auction for the yacht *Lauderdale Lady*. Jones salaciously describes Silva's sexual appetites with a wink to Crockett, and as the auction progresses Crockett becomes paranoid

Figure 6.2 Tubbs (Philip Michael Hall) reaches out to Ivory Jones (Miles Davis) in *Miami Vice.*

that Silva is attracted to him: "Sure he's not into guys?" By forcing up the auction price, the detectives describe their strategy as "sticking it to" Silva. The episode will conclude with the revelation that Silva has maintained an incestuous relationship with his daughter for many years. At a narrative level, this unpleasant melodrama is engaging with ownership (of women, yachts, children) and uncomfortably positioning the queer-coded Jones as mediator between the swaggering heterosexuality of Crockett-Tubbs and the perversity of Silva.

Beyond narrative, the episode offers richness through costuming and performance. In that pre-credits scene with Tubbs, Davis is dressed elegantly, in a silk-satin cornflower blue drop-shoulder haori-style jacket, which complements the fashion aesthetic of the show—"pastel-clad undercover cops wearing designer shades" (Turnbull 2014, 81)—but is distinct from that aesthetic. Physically, Davis appears small and vulnerable on-screen, especially against the show's vigorous leads. He does not wear braids; his pate is on show, this physical sign of aging complicating audience reaction to his character. So, while Jones is despicable—Lieutenant Castillo (Edward James

Olmos) tells Crockett and Tubbs, "Ivory arranged passports for Vietnamese women during the war. Married them to military men, five thousand dollars apiece. And he brought them in to work the brothels"—Miles Davis' physical vulnerability, and his incorporation of that into his performance, is endearing. Add to this the charisma Davis brings to his acting, within a limited range. He cleverly underplays dialogue in a manner that serves his character, especially compelling for viewers used to Johnson's strident line deliveries. In the scene where Castillo convinces Jones to work for the police, Davis subtly links dialogue and gesture, hesitating as he lifts a piece of jewellery and delivers the line, "I was lucky . . . to get out of there alive".[7]

While Davis' contribution to *Miami Vice* might seem extraordinary or bizarre to jazz aficionados, in fact the use of musicians as actors in network television was commonplace. Indeed, the pleasure of tuning into a favourite show and seeing a musician out of context has always been part of the US TV tradition; in the crime genre alone, one thinks of Jo Jones in *Route 66* ('Goodnight Sweet Blues', 6 October 1961, CBS), Johnny Cash in *Columbo* ('Swan Song', 3 March 1974, NBC) or Isaac Hayes in *The Rockford Files* ('The Hammer of C Block', 1 July 1977; 'Second Chance', 14 October 1977, both NBC). As Jonathan Nichols-Pethick has noted in relation to *Miami Vice*, these were "special events for the series, opening up opportunities for new fans, including older viewers, to find the show by following a favorite performer to it" (2012, 39–40). Across its five-year run, *Miami Vice* included guest appearances by stars diverse as Frank Zappa, Sheena Easton, James Brown, Leonard Cohen, Barbra Streisand, Little Richard, Phil Collins and Willie Nelson. What seems noteworthy about Davis' guest role in *Miami Vice* is the absence of any explicit acknowledgement, diegetic or otherwise, of his jazz career save for a repeated line about possessing "good timing".

We might usefully contrast Davis' appearance in *Miami Vice* with a much smaller cameo one year later, in an episode of Michael Mann's 1960s period piece *Crime Story* titled 'The War' (7 October 1986, NBC). Davis has no dialogue in his one scene and is portrayed on stage in a smoky nightclub playing an acoustic version of *Tutu*'s 'Tomaas'. Curiously for this 1960s-set scene, Davis is dressed in a long sequined jacket and balloon pants—his 1980s concert look—while his band and everyone else in the club are in

[7] Davis proudly records Cicely Tyson's praise of his performance in his autobiography (Davis and Troupe 1990, 366).

period-appropriate suits. Narratively, the moment follows a conventional pattern in which "black people validate the white artist's achievement" (Gabbard 1996, 86), in this case a crooked lawyer sitting in with the Davis band. At one level, the discontinuity of Davis' outfit and the choice of song in *Crime Story* can be explained away as canny marketing for the new Warner Bros. album. But the discontinuity is also very characteristic of Davis' star persona at this time (think of the dual chronology in *Homicide* or the scenes from *Dingo* discussed by Will L. Finch in chapter 5), in which the past is invoked only to be rejected. In a re-creation of a 1960s nightclub Davis, surrounded by men in suits, wears clothes from the future.

Davis' television appearances have tended to be written about cursorily, but they offer a compelling instance of a star in dialogue with his mediated identity. Earlier in this chapter I connected Davis to the practice of dandyism, suggesting that his stardom provocatively engages with the gendering of jazz. The fact that *Miami Vice* regularly privileged "the pleasures of style, look, and appearance that our culture has traditionally associated with the feminine" (Fiske 1987, 221) provided an appropriate contextual framework for this provocation, and for Davis' portrayal of Ivory Jones to queer the pimp archetype. These are stances which productively challenge homogenising approaches to jazz history, as in the *Crime Story* cameo. Reflecting on the experience of appearing in *Miami Vice*, Davis would write, "When I did that role, someone asked me how I felt about acting and I told them, 'You're acting all the time when you're black.' And it's true. Black people are acting out roles every day in this country just to keep on getting by. If white people really knew what was going on in most black people's minds it would scare them to death. Blacks don't have the power to say these things, so they put on masks and do great acting jobs just to get through the fucking day" (Davis and Troupe 1990, 365). The wearing of clothes, donning screen 'masks', was an opportunity for Davis to undertake a process of questioning via his star persona. The experimentation with clothing that he so enjoyed translated well to the 'trying on' of acting roles, and all the better if this was in television shows that were youth-oriented, promoted black stars such as Philip Michael Thomas and were "alert to the politics of race and class, not to mention gender" (Turnbull 2014, 83). In his final scenes as Ivory Jones, Davis will wear a black suit cut very loose over a patterned shirt and gold slippers. This restyling of a garment, the severely masculine suit, into something luxurious and casual exemplifies the way clothes perform meaning for Davis' star persona in television contexts.

Music Video Miles

Tutu Medley (1986, dir. Spike Lee) is a very unusual music video. Its subject is an old man, alone, roaming a loft apartment. It breaks with one very important characteristic of its form, that "music videos, almost without exception, do not make so much as a single incision in the sound or structure of the song" they showcase (Berland 1993, 25). Instead, this music video mashes four songs together, spliced as a medley—'Splatch', 'Tutu', 'Tomaas' and 'Portia'—so that rather than supporting the release of a single, this video conveys the variety of an album. When Davis acted as guest presenter for the VH1 *Video Hits 1: New Visions Disk Jockey Show* in 1987, he recalled this bricolage approach to the *Tutu* video:

> I told Tommy LiPuma, the producer, I said, "Tommy, on the video I know a way you can get four songs, because I used to listen to this particular piece—it's a play—you got all this music that sounds like Stravinsky, and all of a sudden the actor goes to the window, and they lift the window up and marching band comes right through, so the music, like Stravinsky, all at once you hear ttt-ttt-ttt-ttt-ttt". So I told Tommy LiPuma, "All you have to do is play one minute of each composition". So we played one minute and we got four compositions. And then I told him, "Put them all together", so he put them all together like a collage. So that's where you get four tunes.

Davis describes a dramatic concept through spatial relations, an opened window that changes the acoustic landscape. As we will see, this is an important structuring dynamic in the *Tutu Medley* video which extends the experimentation and iconoclasm of the *Tutu* album rather than merely illustrating or merchandising it.

Of course, showcasing four tunes should also be understood strategically, as an expression of the new 'personality' of the Warner Bros. contract discussed by Tim Wall in chapter 3, and perhaps even as indicative of certain failures of that strategy: George Cole tells us that Warner hoped—unsuccessfully, as it shook out—that songs from *Tutu* would find their way onto smooth jazz radio station playlists (2005, 204). One context, then, for understanding *Tutu Medley* is as part of the corporate ambition to rebrand Miles Davis from Columbia jazzman into Warner hitmaker. Another is that personal manipulation of one's own star persona which Krin Gabbard (2009, 184), analysing the Davis and Troupe autobiography, has described as "the

Figure 6.3 Miles Davis and Spike Lee on the set of *Tutu Medley*.

image he [Davis] wished to project at the end of his life". These mediating forces are integral to our understanding of jazz's cultural persistence. As Jeremy A. Smith observes, "[I]f jazz scholars can accept music's material circulation as a necessary aspect of a recording's social life, then marketing can be understood not as a corrupting force but rather as an influence on jazz's dissemination" (2010, 32).

After the fruitful collaboration with Marcus Miller on the album, the video was an opportunity for Davis to work with film director Spike Lee. The son of a jazz musician, Lee had been fêted in the press heralding a New Black Cinema and would release his first feature, *She's Gotta Have It* (1986), in the same year as *Tutu Medley*. Interviewed on set, Lee described the collaborative nature of his relationship with Davis as based in mutual respect: "He's not going to do nothing he doesn't like, the stature that he has. I'm not going to impose something on him. I know everything has to be cleared with him, man that's fine with me. We've had no problems at all" (Figure 6.3).[8]

Over the course of the four-and-a-half-minute medley, we see Davis run through eight costume changes. This modelling of different looks provides

[8] This moment is reproduced in Mike Gibb's 2001 documentary *The Miles Davis Story*. Davis's respect for Spike Lee's father, the jazz bassist and composer Bill Lee, prompted him to tell Spike on their first meeting, "I love your father's work so I'm not going to curse you out" (quoted in Gross 2019). Spike Lee would later read *Miles: The Autobiography* to inspire his screenplay for *Mo' Better Blues* and distributed the book to cast members (Lee and Jones 1990, 41, 116).

the music video with one important structuring element, while the gradual exploration of location provides another. Below I distinguish the various costumes or 'looks' that Davis wears throughout the music video. While a variety of styles is displayed, certain themes emerge. Davis favours loose fabric that moves, often with statement shoulders and sleeves. There is a commitment to layering throughout, with certain garments being repurposed for new looks. This layering creates texture, while the repurposing creates a building sense of collage. The sense of 'medley' aimed for in the editing together of four songs is mirrored by the collaging of Davis' clothes.

Miles Davis *Tutu Medley* Lookbook

1. Black shirt with short cuffed sleeves. The sleeves are 'grown-on', without seams, to provide a softer shape. A long waistcoat with pockets is decorated with horizontal black and grey stripes. The look is accessorised with a gold bangle, two neck chains and a pinkie ring. Davis wears sunglasses.
2. A gold lamé jacket with contrasting plain silver-white lapel and matching trousers. The jacket shoulders are very structured, but the rest of the jacket has a lot of drape and a lot of fabric in the sleeves, which are gathered into a wide cuff. The jacket is cinched in with a wide belt.
3. A very similarly cut long jacket and belt combo, but this time made from blue shot silk, with lapels folded back and no cuffs on the sleeves.
4. A short-sleeved satin bomber jacket with appliqué motif on the back, worn with pegged trousers and slippers. Very fitted to the waist with a sash.
5. Boxy red-orange-black jacket in a shiny translucent material, giving the effect of fire. Trousers in a shiny animal print, Cuban-heel boots. The trousers are ballooned and voluminous, pegged at the heel. The jacket sleeves have a jagged-edge black cuff. Davis wears sunglasses.
6. A marching band jacket in white, finished with gold and white embroidery and silver diamond-shaped studs. Worn open, over a black T-shirt. The jacket has no lapel, an unusual raised collar and elaborate beadwork on the sleeve hem and the back. The back is an intricate design of two African masks. Worn with balloon pants.

7. A shiny plummy-purple duster coat with standaway patch pockets. Over the coat (or perhaps built onto it) is a waistcoat. Under the coat, another waistcoat, long and white with a cutaway at the hips. Pegged silver-grey trousers and tall Cuban-heeled boots (see Figure 6.3).
8. An oversize duster with a raincoat collar, perhaps in PVC. Under the coat, a long dark waistcoat worn open and a short jacket with shag bustle detail. Shiny lamé trousers. Davis wears sunglasses.

I hope my descriptions convey that a huge part of my enjoyment of this video is in the evolving looks, my awareness of their colours and fabrics, the details of their accessorising. It is not outlandish to say that these costume changes constitute a narrative, a sort of clothing story which unfolds over what loosely seems to be a day. The video begins on the street, looking up at images of Davis on a billboard; then to Davis moving around a shadowy loft apartment at night; in daylight, we see Davis painting and playing his trumpet within the apartment; finally playing on the rooftop at night. As the shot listing demonstrates, this diurnal progression is somewhat complicated by Lee's shot composition and editing, while dynamic camera movements invest the video with energy, creating a framework for the reading of certain iconographic aspects of the Davis persona.

Tutu Medley is made up of 36 shots. For a music video, this is surprisingly few. In the descriptions, I attempt to capture the content of these shots, their transitions and patterning, as well as their relationship to the music played and the clothes worn.

Tutu Medley Shot Listing

SHOT 1: A handheld camera proceeds jerkily along a New York street. The cameraman might be in a car. We are approaching a scaffolded marquee on which we see, digitally overlaid, a video insert of Miles Davis bringing his trumpet to his lips in close-up. On the marquee, three reproductions of one Irving Penn portrait on the scaffolding.[9] Bottom right of frame, the title *MILES DAVIS TUTU MEDLEY*.

[9] George Cole writes, "Warner Bros' marketing department went into overdrive when it came to promoting *Tutu*. . . . There were 12-inch singles including remixes of 'Full Nelson,' huge poster campaigns in cities such as New York, and the airwaves were saturated with the sound of *Tutu*" (2005, 263).

SHOT 2: Jump cut, passing by the Penn billboard.

SHOT 3: Almost upside down, the camera spins under the billboard and pans left to view the sky.

SHOT 4: Jump cut, the camera spinning under the billboard and toward the blank sky.

SHOT 5: Against a blank wall in mid-shot, Miles Davis stands hands on hips. He seems to acknowledge someone off-screen right, as though taking a cue.

SHOT 6: Jump cut, Davis is leaning forward to paint on glass positioned in front of the camera's lens.

SHOT 7: Jump cut, Davis extends the brush stroke.

SHOT 8: Jump cut, Davis leans back to survey his work, a series of brush strokes which bisect the frame.

SHOT 9: Jump cut, Davis is elaborating on the figure, now a swirling cross.

SHOT 10: Jump cut, Davis has filled the frame with further abstract shapes.

SHOT 11: Jump cut, Davis is nowhere to be seen. We view the painting as a finished piece and the shot is held for a second longer than those that have preceded it.

SHOT 12: The camera is positioned at the end of a long corridor lit by pink neon. It proceeds swiftly toward the figure at the end of the corridor, Davis with his back turned. As the camera draws nearer, Davis spins on his heel and walks forward, playing his trumpet. The camera retreats along the corridor as Davis strides forward confidently, trumpet to his lips.

SHOT 13: The camera is behind Davis as he proceeds down the corridor, in silhouette.

SHOT 14: Positioned low at a corner, the camera is passed by Davis against a backdrop of wall art.

SHOT 15: In long shot, Davis comes into a room. One wall is white plastered, another is exposed brick with an Exit sign hanging sideways, uselessly pointing at the floor. Davis walks closer to the camera, looks ahead of himself, then proceeds off-screen left.

SHOT 16: The camera is at floor level. To left of frame, a grilled radiator in extreme close-up, its perspectival line drawing attention to a wall on which two human figures are painted. On the ground a box cage on which art materials rest. At extreme right, Davis enters, his shadow falling over the paintings. With one hand behind his back, he crosses the room and makes a delicate adjustment with his paint brush to one of the painted figures. He dips his brush onto a palette resting on the cage.

SHOT 17: A different perspective on the apartment which has a radiator in the background next to some pipe-like structure in different colours. It may be functional or sculpture. Davis blows his trumpet, crouching as he does so. Natural light is falling in through a skylight onto the back wall. Straightening, Davis moves up off-screen. We see his feet take a precise step forward, then back, then forward again in heeled boots.

SHOT 18: A canvas showing six dancing figures, with natural light falling across the centre of the image. As with shot 11, the shot is held like a punctuating point.

SHOT 19: Same opening composition as shot 12, but the camera remains static. In extreme long shot, Davis crosses from right to left at the end of the corridor. He then walks backward, retracing his steps.

SHOT 20: Same composition as shot 16, Davis working at his wall painting, then turning toward camera. He stomps his right leg in time with the music.

SHOT 21: Mid-shot of Davis, playing his trumpet. Behind him, we see through large loft windows onto a city skyline. The camera dollies left, and surprisingly, Davis moves with it through some unseen mechanism.

SHOT 22: A long shot of the loft space, with pillar in foreground left of frame. The camera slowly tracks right to reveal Davis in extreme long shot playing his trumpet in front of the windows. He is surrounded by various sculptures.

SHOT 23: As in shot 21, the camera and Davis track left, passing three windows. A dissolve . . .

SHOT 24: . . . into the same composition, but with Davis now side-on, twisting as though on an office chair.

SHOT 25: Cut to Davis twisting left and looking off-screen right as he plays. Dissolve to . . .

SHOT 26: . . . Davis gesturing with his left hand, stretching the fingers as though fatigued. The dolly mechanism now begins to track Davis rightward. He pivots 180 degrees on his seat, turning his back to us, then another 180 to face us again and point off-screen right, as if to a member of the crew.

SHOT 27: Extreme long shot of the apartment, similar to shot 22. Davis stands stock still, head turned away, bent at the waist amid sculpture.

SHOT 28: A shot up through the skylight. Davis is seen through the glass, from below, playing his trumpet. The camera tracks forward, moving under a ceiling beam.

SHOT 29: Match shot of a beam, from which the camera cranes down toward Davis standing on a large piece of diaphanous fabric. The pink fabric is backlit, spider-webbing out from Davis' feet. Strewn about him are paintings on sketchbook paper, in the same style as the paintings we have seen before.

SHOT 30: Close-up on Davis, holding up a sketch, looking into the camera.

SHOT 31: As in shot 29, the camera cranes down on Davis playing amid the fabric and sketches.

SHOT 32: Mid-shot of Davis cross-legged on the floor, looking into camera. He brandishes a sketch and then tosses it like a playing card. The camera is craning up and backward so that the shot opens out on him surrounded by the sketches on the floor. He brandishes two more, tossing them. A third seems to hold his attention. He brandishes it too but refrains from throwing it. The camera rises, past a ceiling beam, up into the high ceiling toward the skylight. A dissolve to . . .

SHOT 33: . . . a track across from the skyline, past the pitched skylight, over the rooftop toward Davis standing in front of five large sheets. On four are printed the silhouette icon used in Columbia publicity. On a fifth, Davis' shadow is projected by floor lighting.

SHOT 34: A very low handheld shot captures Davis playing trumpet while rocking on his heels. His pose combined with the ground-level camera resembles shots from hip-hop videos of the time.

SHOT 35: Another low angle, this time in murky lighting.

SHOT 36: With Davis playing in front of the five sheets, the camera pulls back swiftly and shakily. Davis' shadow is cast clearly on the blank sheets. As the final musical phrase plays, Davis moves from standing straight into a crouch, as though in supplication.

As this shot breakdown conveys, Lee's visual style is sometimes frenetic, sometimes measured, always intricate. Earlier, I stressed the importance of watching and listening as an interpretive act, based in close textual observation. This is particularly important in music video, where the nature of the form is so dependent on the tension between sound and vision. Thus when Charles P. Linscott describes shots 1–4 as "all four tracks play simultaneously in a nearly indiscernible cacophony that nevertheless serves as a sort of sonic 'establishing shot' for the whole piece" (2020, 148), one notes an interest in sound only; as we see from the shot breakdown, this elides the process trickery which places the moving image of Davis on the billboard, a frame within a frame, and the jump cuts in shots 2 and 4 which draw attention to the process of editing. Lee's bombastic aesthetic draws here on Nouvelle Vague technique, foregrounding those cuts between shots which narrative cinema traditionally seeks to make invisible. So while Linscott reads the audio track as preparing the audience for "deconstruction, sampling, synthesis, and noise" (148), I would add that these opening visuals foreground video editing processes and their ability to manipulate time.

A particularly striking effect is achieved in the sequence where Davis is seen moving back and forth before a window that frames the New York skyline (look 6; shots 21, 23–26). After the shadowy sequences that preceded it, these shots are brilliantly lit, enhancing the spectacle of Davis' white jacket. Camera movement is very distinctive, with Davis seeming to move in tandem with the camera through some shared dollying mechanism—an early version, perhaps, of a trick developed in Lee's later feature films, "placing the camera and actors on a moving dolly to create a strange otherworldly feeling of movement" (Pizzello 2002, 107).[10] The shots track left and then right, forward and then back, and variations on this kind of motion are seen in shots 12 and 34–36 (with the camera moving in close only to retreat) and in Davis' own movement, walking back on himself in shots 17 and 19. These idiosyncratic manoeuvres bond Davis' body to Lee's camera in an unconventional occupation of the space of performance.

Peter Wollen has argued that the music video collapses distinctions between television and video art, the culmination of a trend in which the

[10] In *Mo' Better Blues*, the camera movement is featured when the jazz musician protagonist Bleek (Denzel Washington) rehearses in his loft apartment. Pizzello notes versions of this shot in *Jungle Fever*, *Malcolm X*, and *Clockers*. One might take this repeated trick to be Lee paying homage to the drunk sequence in Martin Scorsese's *Mean Streets*, achieved by fixing an Arriflex body brace to Harvey Keitel's torso as he moved (see Christie and Thompson 2003, 47).

traditional fashion catwalk has been supplemented by music, lighting, dance and embryonic narrative (1986, 170). This may help us understand the idiosyncratic inhabitation of space in Lee's video, as successive shots seemingly unfold a floorplan of the loft apartment. Is it a home, a catwalk, a gig space, a gallery? As Michael Heller reminds us, in a discussion of musicians' lofts in New York between the 1960s and the 1980s, these spaces found multipurpose applications for experimental music communities: "The majority of these spaces were also musician's homes, a factor that allowed them to operate with minimal overhead costs (though also with some sacrifice of privacy). In various contexts, lofts also acted as rehearsal halls, classrooms, art galleries, living quarters, and meeting spaces. Their most visible role, however, was as public performance venues, especially for younger members of the jazz avant-garde" (2017, 18). Similarly, Sharon Zukin emphasises the openness of lofts and the ways in which they presented social aspiration: "The sheer physical layout of most lofts, uninterrupted by few doors or walls, opens every area and every social function to all comers. . . . Living in a loft is a little like living in a showcase" (1982, 68–69). Resembling the dancing women inside the *You're Under Arrest* LP gatefold, Davis' painted figures in *Tutu Medley* are also reminiscent of croquis, those fashion designer sketches which often elongate limbs. We might see the loft in *Tutu Medley* as a kind of blank canvas, not just because Davis paints on its walls but because it allows Lee to showcase constituent elements of the Davis persona: the face on billboards, the painter, the fashion plate, the lone genius. And while the loft is not presented as a space of public performance in the way that Heller means (we do not see Marcus Miller or any on-screen audience), we, as television viewers, are involved in this showcasing. In shots 6–10, Davis seems to be painting onto our television screens, enmeshing us in his artistry.

If, as I have suggested, Davis' various costumes constitute a clothing story, what story is being told? We see a man who dresses unconventionally, defined by his celebrity first and foremost (the billboards, shots 1–4), his bohemian tendencies secondly (the painting, shots 5–10) and by his musicianship third (shot 12 onward). I do not mean to suggest that Lee is downplaying Davis as a musician, rather that he is careful to contextualise Davis' music making within discourses of commerce and artistry. The sense of idiosyncratic movement in the video—stepping forward, then back, from one song to another—is visualised through costume change, sometimes returning to already-seen outfits, as in shot 20, sometimes recycling styles, as in the white version of *You're Under Arrest*'s marching band jacket. In shot 32, as in

Barboza's album cover for *You're Under Arrest*, Davis looks directly down the camera lens; at other times, his eyes are screened by sunglasses. Clothes are worn to display their spectacle but are also part of the work, be that painting or playing trumpet.

Lee's feature film output attests to the importance of clothing in his storytelling. One need think only of Bugging Out (Giancarlo Esposito) fretting over his soiled Air Jordans in *Do the Right Thing* to see that, in Lee, Davis had found a director who prized fashion's contribution to black aesthetic modes. In the short *Horn of Plenty* (1986) and his features *Mo' Better Blues* (1990) and *Crooklyn* (1994), Lee drew on painful autobiography to depict dandyish, disreputable jazz musicians who fail their lovers and families. Yet in *Tutu Medley*, the stardom of Miles Davis provides a framework for Lee to imagine a more hopeful vision of jazz masculinity. Television, that medium so defined by daily routine, encourages him to depict the variety of Davis—his many moods, interests, clothes—across the space of one day, in which the progress of time is tricksy and ludic. With each new combination of clothing, Davis collages himself anew. Lee's video resonates with that central tension in late Miles Davis, between past and future.

In *Tutu Medley*, the ageing Miles Davis is celebrated as a playful yet authoritative artist, whose multifaceted practice extends into the collaging of clothes as a form of self-exploration. At a formal level, this persona finds an analogy in Lee's visual style, with editing and transitions producing their own form of collage. As Carol Vernallis has observed, music video time is "moment by moment, riddled with its own ellipses" (2004, 14) and this is certainly true of *Tutu Medley*, where Davis can seem to change costume midstride (from look 2 to 3, shots 13–15). Throughout, movement—of body, of camera, between costumes—is unpredictable, suggesting a "subversive repetition" that Judith Butler sees as one way to unsettle the repetitive mechanism of "power regimes of heterosexism and phallogocentrism" (1990, 32). In the final shots on the rooftop, Lee makes his most explicit engagement with Davis' iconographic past, reproducing four large-scale boards of the "little ink-sketched silhouette of a man in profile, playing a trumpet" that appeared on five LP covers in the 1960s, which Richard Williams describes as "Columbia's art department recognising the marketing value of his [Davis'] stance as the symbol of inner freedom, of improvisation, of the creative individual rather than the interpretive group" (2009, 102). On the rooftop, Lee has positioned a fifth board, left blank, onto which Davis' shadow falls. The message is clear: this is the same man, but he is a new man.

Shades of Miles

In this chapter, I have reframed the critical discourse around late Miles as a form of moral panic, based in societal fears of effeminacy and bodily display. In the detailed textual analysis, I have sought to understand how certain televisual processes of narrative drama and music video construct alternative readings of the Miles Davis star persona in the mid-1980s. These processes mediate and interpret the act of clothing in ways I take to be far more significant than credited. By contextualising Davis' clothed body within formal and stylistic frameworks, I have produced textual readings which show how collage, queerness, movement and iconographic play inflect the presentation of the star persona. I have posited that Davis used these frameworks with intention and creativity but that their importance has been neglected in a critical discourse which overdetermines the legitimacy and moral imperative of jazz.

It seems, then, appropriate to end with a striptease. In a *Vogue* magazine profile of Irving Penn, the photographer recalled his *Tutu* photoshoot:

> Once Davis had finished primping, he stepped in front of the camera. . . . "'I bet you want me to take this shirt off?' He said. 'Yep,' I replied. 'I bet you want me to take all these gold chains off, too?' 'Yep,' I said again. Then, for about half an hour, we went to work. At the end, I said, 'Thank you very much.' He got up, came over to me, and kissed me on the mouth. I didn't know what to say. We shook hands, and he left. Later, I got the chance to know his music, and it struck me as being a visual art of a most profound kind. How terrible I couldn't share that with him then". (Fielden 2009)

Penn describes the growing intimacy between subject and photographer and the itemisation of component parts of a 'look' (shirt, gold chains) as Davis disrobes. It's a little like that opening scene of *Miami Vice*, even down to the jewellery detail. But Penn shares an intimacy more profound than did Tubbs, and the *Vogue* piece concludes: "Penn rested a finger across his mouth, as he often does when thinking. 'This is one of the heartbreaks of the profession', he added. 'I have only the kiss to remember.'"

In this chapter, I have shown how, as in Penn's studio, Miles Davis used his body and clothing to construct variations on his star persona. This was a crucial aspect of his creative process; indeed, he referred to the trying-on of clothes as "rehearsing" (Stradford 2020, 195). My aim has been to show the care with which Davis approached the work of dressing and how televisual frames presented that work. While I have chosen to focus on narrative drama and music video, my argument could equally have been made with reference to appearances on chat shows or in advertising, and my hope is that this chapter contributes to the growing scholarship on jazz mediation. As others in this book have shown, to understand the music of Miles Davis we must also understand the complex world in which he made it. When that music affects us, it does so as part of a larger social discourse and cultural politics.

If, as Szwed (2002, 183–205) has argued, Davis created meaning through his phrasing, his use of the microphone, his stage persona, his clothing, then we must also make room for his use of television, and for television's uses of him. To do so is not to concede appreciation of the music but rather to acknowledge the extent of its sensuousness. In the 21st century, one can enjoy the prosthetic experience of sipping a Sony-licensed Miles Davis beer while sporting Miles Davis headphones. But it goes deeper than that: Penn's kiss, the finger on Stuart Hall's soul, Crosetti in *Homicide* hiding the T-shirt under his work clothes. These intimacies are meaningful because they are material, because each in some way invokes the body and breath of Miles Davis. We wear him close.

Acknowledgments

I would like to thank Wolfram Knauer for his invitation to the Darmstadt Jazzforum in 2017, which started my work on Miles Davis and television. In writing this chapter, I was supported by Dominic Pillai and Sean McTiernan, who generously shared resources. Dunk Murphy gave useful comments on an early draft. Róisín Muldoon's enthusiasm for late Miles was a constant encouragement, and her dressmaking expertise provided the vocabulary of garment construction.

References

Barboza, Anthony, and Barry Maxwell. 2013. 'Photographing Miles Davis'. *Nka: Journal of Contemporary African Art* 32: 96–113.

Barnes, M. W. 1980. 'Vulgarity'. *Ethics* 91: 72–83.

Berland, Jody. 1993. 'Sound, Image and Social Space: Music Video and Media Reconstruction'. In *Sound and Vision: The Music Video Reader*, edited by Simon Frith, Andrew Goodwin and Lawrence Grossberg. Routledge.

Borshuk, Michael. 2018. 'The Sound of Jazz as Essential Image: Television, Performance, and the Modern Jazz Canon'. *Jazz Research Journal* 12 (1): 12–35.

Bruzzi, Stella. 1997. *Undressing Cinema: Clothing and Identity in the Movies*. Routledge.

Butler, Judith. 1990. *Gender Trouble: Feminism and the Subversion of Identity*. Routledge.

Caldwell, John Thornton. 1995. *Televisuality: Style, Crisis, and Authority in American Television*. Rutgers University Press.

Carr, Ian. 1999. *Miles Davis: The Definitive Biography*. Harper Collins.

Christie, Ian, and David Thompson, eds. *Scorsese on Scorsese*. Faber and Faber, 2003.

Cole, George. 2005. *The Last Miles: The Music of Miles Davis 1980–1991*. Equinox.

Crouch, Stanley. 1990. 'Play the Right Thing'. *New Republic* 202 (February 12): 30–37.

Davis, Francis. 1996. *Bebop and Nothingness*. Schirmer.

Davis, Miles, and Quincy Troupe. 1990. Miles: The Autobiography. Picador.

Dibb, Mike, dir. 2001. *The Miles Davis Story*. Dibb Directions/Channel 4 Television.

Doctor, Jenny. 2016. 'Jazz Is Where You Find It: Encountering Jazz on BBC Television, 1946–66'. In *Watching Jazz: Encounters with Jazz Performance on Screen*, edited by Björn Heile, Peter Elsdon and Jenny Doctor. Oxford University Press.

Dunkel, Mario. 2016. 'Sexuality, Eroticism, and the Construction of the Jazz Tradition'. In *Gender and Identity in Jazz*, edited by Wolfram Knauer. Wolke Verlag.

Eshun, Kodwo. 1998. *More Brilliant Than the Sun: Adventures in Sonic Fiction*. Quartet.

Feuer, Jane. 1995. *Seeing Through the Eighties: Television and Reaganism*. Duke University Press.

Fielden, Jay. 2009. 'Remembering Irving Penn: The Stranger Behind the Camera'. *Vogue*, October 27. https://www.vogue.com/article/vd-remembering-irving-penn-the-stranger-behind-the-camera.

Fiske, John. 1987. *Television Culture*. Routledge.

Gabbard, Krin. 1996. Jammin' at the Margins: Jazz and the American Cinema. University of Chicago Press.

Gabbard, Krin. 2009. 'How Many Miles? Alternate Takes on the Jazz Life'. In *Thriving on a Riff: Jazz and Blues Influences in African American Literature and Film*, edited by Graham Lock and David Murray. Oxford University Press.

Gebhardt, Nicholas. 2016. 'Screening the Event: Watching Miles Davis' My Funny Valentine'. In *Watching Jazz: Encounters with Jazz Performance on Screen*, edited by Björn Heile, Peter Elsdon and Jenny Doctor. Oxford University Press.

Gennari, John. 2006. *Blowin' Hot and Cool: Jazz and Its Critics*. University of Chicago Press.

George, Nelson. 1986. 'Rhythm & Blues'. *Billboard*, October 11, 30.

Gray, Herman. 1995. *Watching Race: Television and the Struggle for Blackness*. University of Minneapolis Press.

Gross, Terry, host. 2019. 'Spike Lee on Gentrification, Jazz and How He Got His Start in Film'. *Fresh Air*, February 15. https://www.npr.org/2019/02/15/694696224/spike-lee-on-gentrification-jazz-and-how-he-got-his-start-in-film?t=1625578488695.

Harvey, John. 2014. *Clothes: The Art of Living*. Routledge.

Heller, Michael. 2017. *Loft Jazz: Improvising New York in the 1970s*. University of California Press.

Kelley, Robin D. G. 'Miles Davis: A Jazz Genius in the Guise of a Hustler'. *New York Times*, May 13, 2001, 7.

Kuchta, David. 1996. 'The Making of the Self-Made Man: Class, Clothing, and English Masculinity, 1688–1832'. In *The Sex of Things: Gender and Consumption in Historical Perspective*, edited by Victoria de Grazia and Ellen Furlough. University of California Press.

Laver, Mark. 2015. *Jazz Sells: Music, Marketing and Meaning*. Routledge.

Lee, Spike, and Lisa Jones. 1990. *Mo' Better Blues*. Fireside.

Linscott, Charles P. 2020. 'Secret Histories and Visual Riffs, or, Miles Davis, Alice Coltrane, and Flying Lotus Go to the Movies'. *JCMS: Journal of Cinema and Media Studies* 59 (2): 145–150.

Lott, Eric. 1998. 'Double V, Double-Time: Bebop's Politics of Style'. In *The Jazz Cadence of American Culture*, edited by Robert G. O'Meally. Columbia University Press.

Lyons, James. 2010. *Miami Vice*. Wiley-Blackwell.

Miller, Monica L. 2009. *Slaves to Fashion: Black Dandyism and the Styling of Black Diasporic Identity*. Duke University Press.

Nichols-Pethick, Jonathan. 2012. *TV Cops: The Contemporary American Television Police Drama*. Routledge.

Pellegrinelli, Lara. 2008. 'Separated at 'Birth': Singing and the History of Jazz'. In *Big Ears: Listening for Gender in Jazz Studies*, edited by Nichole Rustin and Sherrie Tucker. Duke University Press.

Pillai, Nicolas. 2016a. *Jazz as Visual Language: Film, Television and the Dissonant Image*. I. B. Tauris.

Pillai, Nicolas. 2016b. 'Watching Men Play: The Erotics of the Hollywood Jazz Film'. In *Gender and Identity in Jazz*, edited by Wolfram Knauer. Darmstadt Studies in Jazz 14. Wolke Verlag Hofheim.

Pillai, Nicolas. 2018a. 'Editorial'. *Jazz Research Journal* 12 (1): 5–11.

Pillai, Nicolas. 2018b. 'A Star Named Miles: Tracking Jazz Musicians Across Media'. In *Jazz @ 100: An Alternative to a Story of Heroes*, edited by Wolfram Knauer. Darmstadt Studies in Jazz 15. Wolke Verlag Hofheim.

Pillai, Nicolas. 2023. 'Reinstating Televisual Histories of Jazz'. In *Jazz and American Culture*, edited by Michael Borshuk. Cambridge University Press

Piper, Helen. 2015. *The TV Detective: Voices of Dissent in Contemporary Television*. I. B. Tauris.

Pizzello, Stephen. 2002. 'Between 'Rock' and a Hard Place'. In *Spike Lee: Interviews*, edited by Cynthia Fuchs. University Press of Mississippi.

Sconce, Jeffrey. 1995. "Trashing' the Academy: Taste, Excess, and an Emerging Politics of Cinematic Style'. *Screen* 36 (4): 371–393.

Smith, Jeremy A. 2010. 'Sell It Black: Race and Marketing in Miles Davis's Early Fusion Jazz'. *Jazz Perspectives* 4 (1): 7–33.

Solis, Gabriel. 2018. 'Hip Nostalgia: Jazz and the Politics of Representation in Three Dramedies'. *Jazz Research Journal* 12 (1): 138–162.

Stradford, Michael. 2020. *MilesStyle*. Primedia eLaunch.

Szwed, John. 2002. *So What: The Life of Miles Davis*. William Heinemann.

Tulloch, Carol. 2016. *The Birth of Cool: Style Narratives of the African Diaspora*. Bloomsbury.

Turnbull, Sue 2014. *The TV Crime Drama*. Edinburgh University Press.

Vernallis, Carol. 2004. *Experiencing Music Video: Aesthetics and Cultural Context*. Columbia University Press.

Wollen, Peter. 1986. 'Ways of Thinking About Music Video (and Post-Modernism)'. *Critical Enquiry* 28 (1–2): 167–170.

Williams, Richard. 2009. *The Blue Moment: Miles Davis's* Kind of Blue *and the Remaking of Modern Music*. Faber and Faber.

Zabor, Rafi, and Vic Garbarini. 1994. 'Wynton vs. Herbie: The Purist and the Crossbreeder Duke It Out'. In *The Jazz Musician*, edited by Mark Rowland and Tony Scherman. St. Martin's Press.

Zukin, Sharon. 1982. *Loft Living: Culture and Capital in Urban Change*. Johns Hopkins University Press.

7

My One Miles Davis LP

A Photo Essay on the Personal Resonance of Miles Davis' Recorded Music

William Ellis and Tim Wall

The portraits in this photo essay are part of a wider collaborative project between William Ellis, a professional photographer specialising in images of jazz performance, and Tim Wall, a popular-music studies academic whose work ranges across jazz and other forms of popular music. In the project, we ask musicians, fans and others working in the cultural industries: "if you had to choose just one Miles Davis LP, what would it be?"

This chapter brings together some of those musicians and their chosen record. The project seeks to capture the inspirational qualities of jazz recordings and the impact they have on people's lives. Each portrait features the subject holding a recording that is of fundamental importance to them. The photograph is accompanied by a short interview that explores the meaning and value of the selected album.[1]

The 15-year collaboration between William and Tim has focused on a continuing discussion about how we represent jazz culture through the visual image and the possibilities of reimagining jazz portraiture that captures new ways of seeing our relationship with recorded music and its place in forming our cultural identity. In 2010, William commenced the project as a response to conversations with musicians about their relationship with the work of other artists encountered via recordings. These conversations had focused on the albums that had profoundly moved the subjects. Once we started working together, we expanded the range of portrait subjects and music covered, embracing fandom in the British northern soul scene for *One 45* and global reggae for *One Love*. The project now includes over 350 people in a

[1] The interviews next to each portrait were edited for clarity and concision from longer audio recordings.

William Ellis and Tim Wall, *My One Miles Davis LP* In: *Rethinking Miles Davis*. Edited by: Roger Fagge, Nicolas Pillai, and Tim Wall, Oxford University Press. © Oxford University Press 2026. DOI: 10.1093/9780190085834.003.0007

spectrum of occupations and music genres, including music fans, artists, academics, broadcasters, musicians, writers, photographers. All images and interviews in the wider project can be found at http://onelp.org.

Conversations about music are transient, usually committed only to memory, and so we aim to locate that moment in an evocative portrait and record those exchanges for posterity. In the interviews our subjects excavate layers of memory, influence, being and uniqueness. *One LP* has come to represent a journey into another's soul: the album that each artist selects is a part of them, their past, present and future. William was eager to find a format that would adequately document his interactions with the artists, and Tim to seek to understand what they revealed about the way we represent our enthusiasm for music in the visual image and spoken word. The *One LP* series is the outcome of these engagements.

The portraits in this photo essay cover a range of musicians who chose a Miles Davis album as their 'one LP' and include many who worked with Davis. Dave Liebman played live and recorded with Davis in 1973 and 1974, and both Mike Stern and Marcus Miller were with Davis from 1981 to 1983, the latter producing Davis through a series of Warner Bros. records from 1986's *Tutu*[2] onward. Others have expressed their commitment to Davis' music in their own recordings, most notably Eddie Henderson's 2002 *So What*,[3] which explores many of the compositions associated with Davis' recording career, and Joe Lovano's 2006 *Streams of Expression*,[4] which features three songs arranged by Gil Evans for the 'Birth of the Cool" Nonet usually attributed to Davis. Unsurprisingly, Davis' music looms large in the musical life of the trumpeters who sat for One LP portraits. Terence Blanchard's trumpet playing owes much to Davis' approach and London-based trumpeter Dick Pearce, whose muted, economical style echoes much of the Davis sound. Playing Davis' music was a formative influence for both Henry Lowther and Laura Jurd, British trumpeters from different generations, and they have memorably played Davis' music in live settings. Theo Croker even celebrated the Davis centenary with *Miles Davis Mixtape* a live interpretation of these influences at London's Royal Festival Hall. Norma Winstone

[2] *Tutu*, Warner Bros. Records, 9 25490-2. Recorded at Le Gonks West, West Hollywood, February 6, 1986; Capitol Tower, Los Angeles, February 10, 12, 13, 1986; Clinton Recording Studios, New York City, March 12–25, 1986. Released September 29, 1986.

[3] Eddie Henderson, *So What*, Eighty-Eight's, CK 87172. Recorded March 13, 14, 2002. Released 2002.

[4] Joe Lovano Ensemble, *Streams of Expression*, Blue Note, 0946 3 41092 2 2. Recorded Avatar, New York City, December 13–14, 2005. Released August 1, 2006.

clearly found inspiration in the trumpeter's recordings, as did pianists Fred Hersch, Steve Kuhn and George Cables and London-based drummer Rod Youngs. It is also very interesting to see that Fairport Convention member, Ric Sanders, chose a Miles Davis record as his One LP, rather than one from a fellow folk rock musician.

It is perhaps not surprising that three of the musicians we featured chose Davis' 1959 *Kind of Blue*,[5] although the modal jazz of the recording is often some distance from the music for which they themselves are well known. *Kind of Blue* is famously one of the best-selling commercial jazz recordings of all time and often features in lists of jazz all-time-great records. The records that lead up to that seminal album are also well represented. Kuhn chose the Prestige-released *Cookin' with The Miles Davis Quintet*[6] from 1957. It is the Columbia releases which feature most, with Lovano selecting *'Round About Midnight*, Jurd choosing 1957's *Miles Ahead*[7] and Lowther and Miller, 1958's *Milestones*.[8] However, Davis' early 1960s output is very well served by Liebman's preference going to 1960's *Sketches of Spain*,[9] Hersch spotlighting *In Person Friday Night at the Blackhawk, San Francisco*,[10] from 1961, Blanchard selecting 1964's *Four & More*,[11] Pearce 1965's *E.S.P.*,[12] and Cables goes for *My Funny Valentine*,[13] also released in 1965. Three of those featured go for the trumpeter's recordings from the late 1960s and early 1970s, with Croker selecting Miles Smiles,[14] Youngs opting for *Water Babies*,[15] released in 1968, and Sanders *On the Corner*,[16] released in 1972.

[5] *Kind of Blue*, Columbia, CS 8163. Recorded at Columbia 30th Street Studio, New York City, March 2 and April 22, 1959. Released August 17, 1959.

[6] The Miles Davis Quintet, *Cookin' with The Miles Davis Quintet*, Prestige, 7094. Recorded Van Gelder Studio, Hackensack, NJ, October 26, 1956. Released July 1957.

[7] *Miles Ahead*, Columbia, CL-1041. Recorded May 6, 10, 23, 27 and August 22, 1957, at Columbia 30th Street Studio, New York City. Released in US October 21, 1957.

[8] *Milestones*, Columbia, CL 1193. Produced by George Avakian and recorded February 4 and March 4, 1958, at Columbia 30th Street Studios, New York City. Released September 2, 1958.

[9] *Sketches of Spain*, Columbia, CL 1480. Recorded Columbia 30th Street Studio, New York City, November 15, 20, 1959, and March 10, 1960. Released July 18, 1960.

[10] *In Person Friday Night at the Blackhawk, San Francisco*, Columbia, CS 8469. Recorded at The Blackhawk Restaurant, San Francisco, California, April 21, 1961. Released September 1961.

[11] *Four & More Recorded Live in Concert*, Columbia, CS 9253. Recorded Philharmonic Hall, New York City, February 12, 1964. Released January 17, 1966.

[12] *E.S.P.*, Columbia, CS 9150. Recorded Columbia, Hollywood, January 20–22, 1965. Released August 16, 1965.

[13] *My Funny Valentine*, Columbia, CL 2306. Recorded live at Philharmonic Hall, New York City, February 12, 1964. Released February 23, 1965.

[14] *Miles Smiles*, Columbia, CL 2601. Recorded at Columbia 30th Street Studio, New York City, October 24–25, 1966. Released February 16, 1967.

[15] *Water Babies*, Columbia, PC 34396. Recorded Columbia 30th Street and Columbia 52nd Street, New York City, June 7, 13, 23, 1967, November 11–12, 1968. Released November 1976.

[16] *On the Corner*, Columbia, KC 31906. Recorded at Columbia 52nd Street, New York City, June 1, June 6 and July 7, 1972. Released October 11, 1972.

Reimagining the Jazz Photographic Portrait Through the One Miles Davis LP

As this photo essay shows, our practice-based research focuses on alternative ways in which we can document jazz through photography. We seek to present musicians and their relationship to recorded music in new relationships, and in doing so we are re-engineering the dominant ways of documenting jazz and jazz musicians, emphasising their agency, giving voice to the way they relate to records and repositioning our gaze when we look.

We take Berger's statement in *Ways of Seeing* that "the relation between what we see and what we know is never settled" (1972, 7), and we seek to 'unsettle' what we see in and know about jazz through portrait photography. We invite you to ask questions about the way that jazz photography has established a formal relationship between an objectified musician and a romanticised representation of jazz culture. These are core questions about the way the documents of jazz culture invite us to interpret jazz of the past and present, the way that musicians articulate that relationship of past and present and the way that our gaze as the onlooker meets their gaze as the subject and object of the photograph.

Geoff Dyer (1996, xi–xii) dedicates his 1996 collection of articles, *But Beautiful: A Book About Jazz*, to John Berger and opens the book with 'A Note on Photographs', in which he explicitly talks about an image created by the celebrated jazz photographer Milt Hinton, and he later cites the work of Carole Reiff. This was noteworthy in 1996 and remains pertinent today because photographs as documents of jazz culture continue to evade our critical attention. Because of its brevity, Dyer's points in *But Beautiful* make a relatively modest contribution to our understanding of jazz photography. Nevertheless, in linking theorist Berger to jazz photographers Hinton and Reiff, Dyer offers a first attempt to bring together cultural criticism with the images created through photographic practice.

There have, of course, been some important histories of jazz photography. Most notable are Alan Ainsworth's (2017a, 2017b, 2019) studies of early New Orleans band photography, 'testimonial advertising' in *Down Beat* and Detroit and Los Angeles postwar photographer Bob Douglas along with Benjamin Cawthra's (2011) broader exploration of photograph's engagement with jazz.

It remains remarkable that so little has been done to critique and build upon Dyer's 'first attempt', especially as our collective understanding of jazz photography has increased so much in the past 25 years. Put another way, while we now understand so much more about some jazz photographs, the domains of jazz studies and visual communication have provided very little insight into the dominant modes of that photography, how these modes fit within jazz culture and how we can understand these images as a document of jazz. Additionally, while jazz studies as a field has become increasingly successful at integrating the cultural study of jazz with creative performance practice, it has not yet started to embrace the possibility of integrating the cultural study of jazz and jazz creative performance practice with the creative practice of those who document jazz culture. This project is an exploration of how that could be done.

Our Manifesto

We aim to move from existing documents of jazz to new ways of documenting jazz, from seeing jazz to new ways of seeing jazz. In creating the images, Ellis was guided by our joint manifesto:

- *Photography should be a reflexive process to document jazz through its creators.* The images were produced by emphasising the human relationships between photographer and photographed and being aware of the mediating and editing functions of the photographer and exhibition curator.
- *Image and words are equals in documenting jazz.* We exhibit a single shot from each photographic session, but also words derived from an interview with the subject that explains their choice of LP.
- *We should move beyond the rhetoric, affect and art of photographic image-making.* We aim to create personal, direct and context-appropriate images which avoid the mythologies of jazz and their photographic tropes.
- *We will give voice to musicians.* We will treat the photographed as agents, not objects and capture their words as a way of explaining their images.
- *We will construct jazz as a lived experience.* That construction will be determined by the individual subject and the places where we encounter them, avoiding any romanticised essentialism that dominates jazz photography.

In articulating his approach to the photographer process, Ellis emphasises a commitment to producing a body of work that is "completely personal", that "captures the 'personality' of the person by bring the photograph out of a personal relationship", that generates "a unique and intimate interaction between photographer and musician". He describes the process as an "opening of the heart" and talks about encouraging his photographic subjects to "revisit their inspirations", "to see them go back in time to reconnect and re-view the album that meant so much to them".

Thinking Through the Cultural Study of Jazz, Jazz Performance Practice and the Photographic Documentation of Jazz Culture

Dyer's 'Note on Photographs' is no more than that: a few speculative comments before the page numbering starts. Nevertheless, the fact that Dyer's tentative juxtaposition of some cultural theory of photography with the work of some photographers is still worth noting nearly 25 years after its publication just reveals how few attempts there have been to theorise jazz photography and to inform photographic practice with cultural theory.

As we have already indicated, a range of important contributions has extended our knowledge and understanding of the powerful imagery created within an international jazz culture, especially in the jazz photography of the late 1950s and early 1960s. Interest in this photography increased in the 1980s—as part of what was then called the 'jazz renaissance' (Nicholson 1990), ideas linked to 'neoclassical jazz' (Gennari 2006)—and subsequently through a range of major studies. We are thinking here, among other instances, of the London exhibition of Herman Leonard's work in 1988, the art book publications of his photographs (Leonard 2010; Leonard et al. 2006) and the book-length study by Helen Pinson (2010); the New York exhibition *The Sound I Saw: The Jazz Photographs of Roy DeCarava* in The Studio Museum in Harlem in 1983, Maren Stange's (1996) critical evaluation of his work and the career retrospective art book publication (DeCarava 2001); and the Michael Cuscuan–curated publication of Francis Wolff's Blue Note photographs (Wolff et al. 2000). It is notable that, although William Claxton's 1950s and 1960s jazz photography became available in book form beginning in the late 1990s, his images did not achieve the ubiquity of those produced by DeCarava, Hinton, Leonard, Reiff and Wolff (see, for instance,

Claxton and Namekata 1992; Claxton and Chitolina 1999; Claxton and Berendt 2005).

Too often these publications emphasise celebration over investigation, the poetic over the analytical, and they end up adding more to the mythologising of jazz culture than they do to understanding it. Dyer, for instance, asserts that photography can be as sensitive to sound as it is to light: "[G]ood photographs are there to be listened to as well as looked at; the better the photograph the more there is to hear. The best jazz photographs are those saturated in the sound of their subject" (1996, xi). For the author, images created by celebrated jazz photographers Hinton and Reiff are successful in "depicting what has just *been* said, and *what is about to be said*" (xi–xii, original emphasis). Such a perspective fits with Dyer's approach to create a literary "imaginative criticism" (ix), but it also drives him to try to capture in words some cultural 'essence" of jazz that he believes is found in certain forms of photography and writing. Dyer's book is certainly more about how literary forms could articulate certain romantic views of jazz than it is about how jazz has been romanticised through certain forms of photography and literature. And in dedicating his book to Berger, Dyer draws more on Berger's commitment to overtly literary writing than he does on the latter's critical engagement with images as a process of cultural production and consumption, which have been transformed by photography.

In doing so, *But Beautiful* ignores the main thrust of Berger's work to explicitly interrogate the socially constructed ideological meanings embedded in images and the cultural processes through which they were created. In particular, it disregards Berger's debt to Walter Benjamin's seminal essay, 'The Work of Art in the Age of Mechanical Reproduction' (1936). This is strange, because elsewhere Dyer has explicitly celebrated Berger's importance as a development of Benjamin's ideas, and in relation to others—like the French cultural analyst Roland Barthes and American public intellectual Susan Sontag—who have similarly probed the cultural place and representational power of the photographic image (see, for instance, Dyer 1986, 2017). We also read Dyer's 'A Note on Photographs' as an intertextual reference to Sontag's highly influential 1964 essay 'Notes on "Camp."' Barthes' and Sontag's work has become, of course, a touchstone for theoretically informed writing on photography, perhaps to the point of becoming an academic rote, but collectively this writing does represent the groundwork for a developed engagement with jazz photography. In particular, they all contain important

LAURA JURD

Miles Ahead (1957)

Miles Davis is obviously a musician who made so many different-sounding records across his lifetime—which is something that's very inspiring to me—someone who's constantly moving and evolving, so it's very hard to pick one particular album as being, like, a favourite, but I have picked one just to talk about, one that is very close to my heart and one that perhaps grew on me. Like, when I first listened to it, I thought, ah this is different.

You've got this large ensemble environment and Miles is playing a lot of the melody and improvising in between sections, and he plays such simple things so amazingly. I think, you know, it's a two-way thing. Gill Evans has carved these spaces which he knows Miles is going to fill in this magic way.

I actually played this music once, which felt very bizarre. It's like being inside. It almost feels like you're an intruder, being inside something so familiar, you know, being inside something that's so familiar. I played the [Miles] part and it felt really mad because I didn't want to copy. I know all the notes he plays very well, but I didn't want to do that. I wanted to bring something of myself to it, but also, it's important to bring the essence of him somehow.

So much about how he plays on that is very inspiring to me, like how to fit into the context in a really complementary exciting way.

Laura Jurd was born in Medstead, Hampshire, England, in 1990 and emerged as a prestigious prize-winning young British trumpet player in her 20s.

Portrait taken at Band on the Wall, Manchester, England, 26 May 2024.

MILESTONES....MILES DAVIS

MARCUS MILLER

Milestones (1958)

> Miles at his height in the fifties, before jazz took another turn. This album, along with the other Miles of this period, was really at the height of the elegant era of jazz. Then it went somewhere else that was equally amazing.
>
> But I really love how the combination of soulfulness and intelligence that these guys played with—'Trane and Red Garland, Paul Chambers, Philly Joe, Cannonball, and Miles—just an unbelievable group and this record is just—Philly Joe, Paul Chambers—they're just killin' on this record.

Marcus Miller was born in New York City in 1959 and established himself as a multi-instrumentalist, composer, and record producer. He played bass with Miles Davis from to and was the primary composer and producer of Davis's *Tutu* (1986), *Music from Siesta* (1987) and *Amandla* (1989) albums.

Portrait taken at Band on the Wall, Manchester, England, November 2011.

MILES DAVIS
Kind of Blue

NORMA WINSTONE

Kind of Blue (1959)

I'm sure loads of people chose this one. I had to choose it because it had a profound effect on me. I don't know how many other albums I'd bought before then, but I think the first one that I ever bought, and I saved up for when I was at school, was *Ella and Louis* with the Oscar Peterson Trio. And I was also very affected by Dave Brubeck's quartet with Paul Desmond, and I found that I was listening to the solos, I was learning the solos, I didn't realize they were improvised because Paul Desmond was so clear in the way he played, and you could actually copy it.

But I think I joined a club, and we saved up so much a week and then this guy would come round and he'd say "Well this album's new . . . and this one's new . . . and I can order it for you", and he said "There's a new one by Miles Davis, John Coltrane, *Kind of Blue*", and I thought, "Oh have to have that!"

Norma Winstone was born in London in 1941 and became one of Britain's leading jazz singers, contributing to a body of innovative European jazz.

Portrait taken at Jazz Midland Hotel, Manchester, England, 26 July 2018.

STEREO
COLUMBIA
MILES

DAVID LIEBMAN

Sketches of Spain (1960)

> Miles Davis in collaboration with Gil Evans, and the reason that I love it so much is because it goes beyond music, beyond idiom, beyond style, and even beyond Spain even though it's dedicated to the culture of Spain in a certain way.
>
> There's just a feeling on that record between the writing and the way Miles plays that's just the universal cry of blues, of joy, of humanity and everything. . . . I mean I get a feeling from that record beyond category and beyond vernacular. . . . It's not even jazz; it's art at its highest level.
>
> I've recorded *Sketches of Spain* and played it many times and it's a very challenging piece of music. Miles just handles it with such grace and so much class the way he plays the music that . . . if it was only that it would have been a great piece, but the writing is great and Gil Evens . . . I mean they surpassed themselves on that record for me.

David Liebman was born in Brooklyn, New York, in 1946 and became a jazz saxophonist and flautist of international renown, playing with Miles Davis between 1970 and 1974.

Portrait taken at Jazz Standard, New York City, 5 October 2018.

RIC SANDERS

On the Corner (1972)

The album that I've chosen comes from one of his most far-out periods. I think 'far-out' is a good term to use! *On the Corner* wasn't particularly well received. The world wasn't ready for it, it was ahead of its time. I think it's still ahead of its time. It's supposed to be one of his most 'difficult' albums, but I loved it from day one, and I've listened to it most days since!

It predates a lot of techniques now used in recording. He used drum and bass loops and dub techniques. It's a mixture of live playing and editing, which Miles and his producer Teo Macero were much into at the time, recording long, long jams which they would edit into kind of suites, you know.

It's got some fabulous musicians on it, obviously Miles himself playing electric trumpet. Chick Corea and Herbie Hancock playing keyboards, John McLaughlin on guitar, Dave Liebman on saxophone, and the great Michael Henderson playing bass, to name but a few. These were long groove pieces. I remember when the album came out on vinyl it had track names, but as the side went through the needle just carried on with no change. That was pretty hip, I thought! The cover art was by a hip artist and friend of Miles called Corky McCoy. I still think *On the Corner* is waiting for the world to catch up, you know!

Ric Sanders was born in Birmingham, England, in 1952, taking up the violin in British jazz-rock, folk, and folk-rock bands, including Soft Machine and Fairport Convention.

Portrait taken at Camp and Furnace, Liverpool, 27 February 2016.

JOE LOVANO

'Round About Midnight (1957)

Well, I would have to say *'Round About Midnight.*

I grew up listening to this recording as a kid, and the poetic expression, the ensemble playing between John Coltrane and Miles Davis, Red Garland, Paul Chambers, and Philly Joe Jones, just captured my attention from an early age.

And, of course, their solos within each tune were just so masterful, you know. But yet, as a quintet, there was a real ensemble sound that gave me a lot of direction through the years.

Joe Lovano was born in Cleveland, Ohio, in 1952 and came to hold a dominant position as a multi-instrumentalist, best known for his tenor saxophone playing across jazz styles.

Portrait taken at Birdland, New York City, 21 September 2014.

CBS
Miles Davis / E.S.P.

DICK PEARCE

ESP (1965)

> Well, the most important album that I've ever listened to is *ESP*, which was with Wayne Shorter, Herbie Hancock, Ron Carter, and Tony Williams. And the first time I heard this album I didn't like it, but I bought it anyway, and I took it home and listened to it a few times.
>
> And then one day—I still didn't like it—and then one day I was working in a music shop, I had only just left school, and I had some music going around in my head all day and I couldn't think what it was, and it suddenly dawned on me on the way home—on the bus—it's *ESP*, it's that album, And that's been my favourite album of all time since. And that's it, really.

Dick Pearce was born in London in 1951 and became an important trumpet and flugelhorn player in British jazz from the 1970s onwards.

Portrait taken in Llandudno, Wales, 25 July 2015.

TERENCE BLANCHARD

Four & More (1964)

It's Miles Davis *Four and More.* I remember the first time I heard it as a kid. Listening to that live performance blew me away because I had been listening to a very different style of trumpet playing and improvisation.

Those guys just kept me in a tailspin trying to figure out what they were doing, where they were going, and I remember I was trying to get a handle on what jazz was so I would play each track. And this was back in the days of albums, so you're trying to find that spot on the record with the needle! So I used to play 'em over and over and over again.

I would play, you know, like, 'Four'. I would listen to Miles play, then I would only listen to Herbie, go back then, only listen to Ron, go back, only listen to Tony. I kept doing, man, until in my mind, the whole album, man, that album had such an impact on my life because it was so forward thinking in the realms of this music. To think that it still stands the test of time today speaks volumes about how important it is.

Terence Blanchard was born in New Orleans, Louisiana, in 1962, becoming one of the leading jazz trumpeters and composers for film and television of his generation.

Portrait taken at Old Fruit Market, Glasgow, 30 June 2011.

MILES AHEAD MILES DAVIS + 19
GIL EVANS

STEVE KUHN

Cookin' with The Miles Davis Quintet (1957)

> In the, I guess it was in the fifties, Miles Davis had a quintet that included Philly Joe Jones, Paul Chambers, Red Garland, and John Coltrane. They made several LPs for Prestige, and any of them are my favourites. The cohesion in that band, the swing, it just had a great influence on me. So, I just loved that quintet.
>
> Miles had some other great bands, and he influenced the music quite a bit, but this particular quintet captured my heart.

Steve Kuhn was born New York City in 1938, making a name for himself as a versatile jazz pianist, composer, and educator. He has led trios with a number of Miles Davis alumni.

Portrait taken at Birdland, New York City, 2 May 2013.

MILES DAVIS
Kind of Blue

MIKE STERN

Kind of Blue (1959)

Kind of Blue has obviously captured a lot of people's hearts. It's a huge success in terms of getting out there and people hearing the music, and for good reason. It just has an amazing balance of a lot of space and a lot information too. Man, 'Trane and Cannonball play their asses off on it! And of course, Bill Evans and Wynton Kelly are both on the record, and Jimmy Cobb.

I loved getting the chance to play with him—and actually this whole band—this particular band [Four Generations of Miles], with Sonny Fortune and Buster Williams, who are phenomenal musicians and really great people too. And of course, Jimmy.

But this record just really knocked me out. It's really hard to pick your favourite record, but this is certainly one of the greatest records ever, I think, and for obvious reasons.

And Miles of course just played his heart out all the time, he just played from the heart, and everybody on that record did.

So they gave amazing performances, amazing, amazing, beautiful record.

Mike Stern was born in Boston in 1953, establishing himself as a major jazz guitarist of the fusion era. Mike played with Miles Davis from 1981 to 1983 and then again in 1985.

Portrait taken at Band on the Wall, Manchester, England, March 2011.

MILES DAVIS
Kind of Blue

EDDIE HENDERSON

Kind of Blue (1959)

Well, that record is the world-famous *Kind of Blue*, which was the most-sold jazz record in history. The reason it's dear to my heart is because Miles Davis was staying at my parents' house when he made that album. I was in high school, and my stepfather was his doctor. And I was playing trumpet and going to the conservatory, and Miles gave my stepfather the test pressing—you know, with no grooves on one side—and so I became enthralled with Miles Davis.

And then just the music on there is just so classic, you know, with Coltrane on it, you know, and Paul Chambers, Jimmy Cobb . . . Wynton Kelly, Bill Evans. Yeah, Bill Evans and Cannonball. It was just like the quintessential music of that era, almost of all time.

I mean, it really changed the face of quote-unquote jazz music and really changed my life, because seeing him in person—and he took me to a gig when I was 17, 18 years.

Eddie Henderson was born in New York City in 1940, becoming a jazz trumpet and flugelhorn player breaking new ground in American jazz and continuing a legacy of playing started by Miles Davis.

Portrait taken at Universal Rehearsal Studios, New York City, April 2013.

victor's
DRUM
MY FUNNY
VALENTINE
MILES DAVIS

GEORGE CABLES

My Funny Valentine (1965)

When I started playing this music the most important thing to me was just being in the music, being able to play in a band. Not necessarily being a band leader or anything like that, but being able to be a part and have an influence on the direction of the music as a pianist, as a rhythm section player. And this record is really indicative of that. The guys playing together—Miles Davis, who's the captain of this ship—but everybody has a strong role and it's not like . . . you don't get the feeling that Miles is there, and the other guys are just kind of backup, backing musicians kind of doing their job, period.

But everyone has an important role and a strong influence on the direction of the music. For me that's the big picture for this record, and what happens in there is the way everybody uses colours, uses the harmonies. You know, they're the same, but they're different. A different way of approaching harmonies, a way of approaching chords that kind of allow the chords to blossom and the music to really take another direction.

George Cables was born in New York City in 1944, becoming a leading American jazz pianist and composer in his own bands and in those of other significant players.

Portrait taken at Village Vanguard, New York City, 7 February 2019.

miles
Davis
On
the
Corner

THEO CROKER

Miles Smiles (1967)

For me, it'd be *Miles Smiles*, because it's the first Miles Davis album I ever bought. You know the way that album starts with 'Orbits' and you know the writing of Wayne. It's a lot of the writing of Wayne Shorter on that album. And it just kind of shows how adventurous Miles was with making records. You really think about it. I think from that album they might have played 'Freedom Jazz Dance' live, but I've never heard them play it live, but I've heard them play 'Footprints', obviously.

So, there's all this music on that album—"Gingerbread Boy', too—there's all this music on that album—'Orbits' and 'Dolores' and 'Freedom Jazz Dance'—that they, kind of, only played on the record. So it really showed how, to me, how adventurous Miles was when he was making records.

He was really reaching for something different every time and not so concerned with making a record that would, you know, sell like *Kind of Blue*. It's still selling, you know! So, I think that's really cool.

Theo Croker was born in Leesburg, Florida, in 1985, coming to prominence as a 21st-century jazz innovator as a trumpeter and singer, composer and producer.

Portrait taken at Band on the Wall, Manchester, England, 16 July 2024.

MILES DAVIS
WATER BABIES

ROD YOUNGS

Water Babies (recorded in 1968 and released in 1976)

> The album is entitled *Water Babies,* and the reason that album is special to me is it's the first album I heard Tony Williams on that I haphazardly discovered in my father's record collection.
>
> That album just completely blew my mind. Blew my mind 'cause I didn't, hadn't realized a drummer could be so . . . express themselves the way he did. There was lots of imagery in his drumming, and that was the first time that I actually heard a drummer playing like that, conceptually playing like that, colours, but time, and really using the entire kit as a, you know, all the textures.
>
> A landscape of different colours and textures and using the cymbals. But that particular record is definitely one that really changed my whole thinking in terms of drumming and what the possibilities are, you know. So, yeah.

Rod Youngs was born in Washington, DC, where he graduated in Applied Percussion from Howard University and went on to work extensively across styles in the UK.

Portrait taken at Llandudno Jazz Festival, Wales, 26 July 2015.

STEREO
FRIDAY AND SATURDAY NIGHTS
COLUMBIA
MILES DAVIS
IN PERSON
AT THE BLACKHAWK,
SAN FRANCISCO

FRED HERSCH

In Person Friday Night at the Blackhawk, San Francisco (1961)

Miles had so much confidence in who he was that this was the very first week that that band had played together, and they recorded. And I love live jazz albums. I like this feeling of being in the audience. I like the applause that happens sometimes for the solos after the track, feeling like, wow, there was no studio magic with this. This was real.

But what really got me was, well, the, I mean, superb swing and rhythmic feel. The way Wynton Kelly accompanied Miles, the way that he was so responsive and perfect. But also, the way that Wynton Kelly played, the way that he swung, it felt, I guess, the quality that I would put on it is, it was happy. It wasn't so complicated that I couldn't kind of figure out what he was doing, chronically it wasn't, but it just felt great and had this kind of positivity and pop on the rhythm.

I would love to be able to not just swing like that but also to be a part of a rhythm section and to be able to go with other musicians. And I still feel that many times in a duo, say, it's more satisfying for me to play behind somebody else than it is to play a solo. I still value the supportive partnership aspect of playing jazz music.

And so it went to me, had it all, and it just felt wonderful, and Miles is playing just impeccably, and yeah, it was like just the window opened up to me, like, wow! this could be possible.

Fred Hersch was born in Cincinnati, Ohio, in 1955, establishing himself in New York City as a leading jazz pianist and composer. He works across jazz styles and different scales of ensemble.

Portrait taken at his home in SoHo, New York City, 9 July 2024.

COLUMBIA
MILESTONES...... MILES DAVIS

HENRY LOWTHER

Milestones (1958)

I think it's a classic album of all time for me, an astonishingly good album. Philly Joe Jones on drums, Miles plays fantastic. The contrast between him, Cannonball Adderley, and John Coltrane. That's just wonderful. Red Garland, who played on, you know, in the, like, 'Straight No Chaser', where he traditionally used to end his solo with a chorus of block chords. Well, the block chords on that are actually Miles's solo on the recording he made with 'Now's the Time' with Charlie Parker, and he played Miles's solo in block chords.

You know, people don't realize that, but that's what he's playing at the end. It's a wonderful record, swings. . . . And then there's the trio, of course, 'Billy Boy', just Red Garland, with the wonderful Philly Joe playing a fantastic force. Red Garland, and sometimes with brushes. Amazing. Wonderful, amazing record. It definitely does an island disc for me, that one.

Henry Lowther was born in Leicester, England, in 1941, emerging in the 1960s as a quiet revolutionary of British jazz. He contributed to many European large ensembles exploring the musical trails opened up by Davis bands of the 1970s.

Portrait taken at Royal Northern College of Music, Manchester, 18 May 2024.

COOKIN' WITH THE MILES DAVIS QUINTET PRESTIGE 7094

MILES DAVIS QUINTET
MILES
SMILES
CIRCLE
ORBITS
DOLORES
FREEDOM JAZZ DANCE
GINGER BREAD BOY
FOOTPRINTS

ways of thinking about how the dominant social conventions of jazz photography produce a romanticised document of jazz.

By contrast, Helen Pinson's (2010) study of Leonard provides a significantly lengthier attempt to use the work of Barthes and Sontag on photography to explore Leonard's jazz photography. Her study does identify a series of myths of jazz that utilise discursive repertoires of race, genius, revolution and freedom, and she cites important work on the mythologies of jazz from Ronald Radano (2001), Peter Townsend (2000) and Krin Gabbard (1996). In addition, she explicitly links this body of work on jazz culture and representation to Barthes' seminal work on the ideology of cultural representation, *Mythologies* (Barthes and Lavers 1972) (although only via a quotation in Townsend). However, Pinson's discussion never quite escapes the very assumptions about photographic meaning and art in Leonard's work that Berger, Barthes and Sontag had all attempted to critically interrogate. Her chapter-length discussion of the semiology of jazz photography makes overly literal use of Barthes' concepts of denotation and connotation, while ignoring his 'third level" of meaning—myth—almost completely.

The mythologies of jazz are at their most potent in jazz photography. Something of the domination of certain modes of representation of jazz can be gleaned by googling images of 'jazz musician' and 'jazz fans'. Both searches primarily deliver pages of close and mid-shot portraits of performing musicians, mainly those with saxophones or trumpets. Of course, the Google results represent a combination of available images, the editorial decisions of millions of webpage authors, and the further selections of multiple millions of web users, but they do capture the dominant visual discourse of jazz culture. While these images focus on musicians, they romanticise their agency and the cultural spaces in which they operate, often limiting the visual and verbal languages available as much as they restrict the stories about jazz that can be told, making clear divisions between the consumers of recorded jazz and those who produce it. In making new photography of jazz musicians, we made a commitment to move beyond the mythologising narratives that have (over-)determined how we use visual images in our documenting practices to explore at least one new approach to the way the visual can be understood as a representation of a culture that is primarily built around sound. In doing so we remain cognisant of our role as mediators and editors of the lives of those we portray, but we aim to do so in a manner that seeks a new relationship between the photographer and the photographed.

As we worked to reimagine the jazz photographic portrait, the theoretical and philosophical deliberations of Berger, Barthes and Sontag on photographic meaning, along with insights into jazz mythology from Radano, Townsend and Gabbard, have been essential to our working and curatorial dynamic. We have, though, been equally aware of the limitations of this foundational work for our project. Attention to the photographer and to the creative processes of photography are strikingly absent from the critical work on photography as a cultural form of document and representation. In this context, British photographer and writer Val Wilmer is worthy of special mention. Perhaps less celebrated, and somewhat outside of the dominant approaches of Leonard, DeCarava and Wolff, Wilmer's work—and especially *The Face of Black Music* (1976)—has been an important contribution to our discussions in this project. Wilmer's photographic work produces a very different relationship between photographer and musician and with the cultural and social environment in which they work. Her work emphasises that the agency of black musicians and their voices are often as important as the images of them Wilmer produced.

As a professional jazz photographer, William Ellis has spent a career capturing jazz culture and the performance of the music through the photographic image, and he has done so within the dominant sensibilities articulated by Dyer, within the dominant photographic conventions of what a good jazz photograph should be and, frankly, in the shadow of the images created by DeCarava, Hinton, Leonard, Reiff and Wolff. Our reimagining of the jazz photographic portrait does not aim to produce a dramatic or radical new visual language in the way, for instance, DeCarava did. We have certainly moved away from the aesthetic of the musician as object, often located in a smoky jazz club or other context of American urban life, shot on black-and-white stock in ambient lighting.

Our project is as much (if not more) about the photographic process of capturing a portrait of an individual as it is about the final photographic portrait of a musician.

References

Ainsworth, Alan John. 2017a. 'Early New Orleans Band Photography'. *Jazz Research Journal* 11 (1): 28–61.

Ainsworth, Alan John. 2017b. 'Photographic Representations of Jazz'. *Jazz Research Journal* 11 (2): 111–152.

Ainsworth, Alan John. 2019. '"A Private Passion": The Jazz Photography of Bob Douglas'. *Southern California Quarterly* 101 (3): 317–338.

Barthes, Roland, and Annette Lavers. 1972. *Mythologies*. J. Cape.

Benjamin, Walter. 1936. 'The Work of Art in the Age of Mechanical Reproduction'. Collected in Benjamin, Walter, 2008. *The Work of Art in the Age of Its Technological Reproducibility, and Other Writings On Media*, 19–55. Harvard University Press.

Berger, John. 1972. *Ways of Seeing*. British Broadcasting Corporation/Penguin.

Cawthra, Benjamin. 2011. *Blue Notes in Black and White: Photography and Jazz*. University of Chicago Press.

Claxton, William, and Joachim-Ernst Berendt. 2005. *Jazzlife: A Journey for Jazz Across America in 1960*. Taschen.

Claxton, William, and Armando Chitolina. 1999. *Jazz Seen*. Taschen.

Claxton, William, and Hitoshi Namekata. 1992. *Jazz West Coast: Artwork of Pacific Jazz Records*. Bijutsu Shuppan-Sha.

DeCarava, Roy. 2001. *The Sound I Saw: Improvisation on a Jazz Theme*. Phaidon.

Dyer, Geoff. 1986. *Ways of Telling: The Work of John Berger*. Pluto.

Dyer, Geoff. 1996. *But Beautiful: A Book About Jazz*. New ed. Abacus.

Dyer, Geoff. 2017. 'John Berger's Intimate Greatness'. *Aperture*, January 4. https://aperture.org/blog/remembering-john-berger/.

Gabbard, Krin. 1996. *Jammin' at the Margins: Jazz and the American Cinema*. University of Chicago Press.

Gennari, John. 2006. *Blowin' Hot and Cool: Jazz and Its Critics*. University of Chicago Press.

Leonard, Herman. 2010. *Jazz*. Bloomsbury.

Leonard, Herman, David Houston and Jenny Bagert. 2006. *Jazz, Giants, and Journeys: The Photography of Herman Leonard*. Scala.

Nicholson, Stuart. 1990. *Jazz: The Modern Resurgence*. Simon & Schuster.

Pinson, K. Heather. 2010. *The Jazz Image: Seeing Music Through Herman Leonard's Photography*. University Press of Mississippi.

Radano, Ronald. 2001. 'Myth Today: The Color of Ken Burns Jazz'. *Black Renaissance/Renaissance Noire* 3 (3): 42–56.

Sontag, Susan. 1964. 'Notes on "Camp"'. *Partisan Review* 31 (4): 515–530.

Stange, Maren. 1996. '"Illusion Complete Within Itself": Roy DeCarava's Photography'. *Yale Journal of Criticism* 9 (1): 63–92.

Townsend, Peter. 2000. *Jazz in American culture*. Edinburgh University Press.

Wilmer, Valerie. 1976. *The Face of Black Music*. Da Capo Press.

Wolff, Francis, Michael Cuscuna, Charlie Lourie and Oscar Schnider. 2000. *Blue Note Jazz Photography of Francis Wolff*. Universe Publishing.

8

Orchestrating Miles

Collaborations with Gil Evans, George Avakian, Marcus Miller and Tommy LiPuma

Bobbie-Jane Gardner and Tim Wall

This chapter captures the results of a discussion between two collaborating authors about the creation of *Miles Ahead*,[1] itself a collaboration between Miles Davis, Gil Evans and George Avakian in 1957, and of *Tutu*,[2] on which Davis worked with Marcus Miller and Tommy LiPuma in 1986. It seems appropriate that an exploration of two very different moments of Miles Davis' musical collaborations should be based upon a collaboration between two researchers from very different academic backgrounds. Our consideration of Davis' music making comes out of a much longer discussion between the two of us that draws on our respective areas of expertise: Bobbie-Jane as a practicing contemporary composer-orchestrator and practice-based researcher and Tim from his background in popular-music media and cultural studies. Our discussions emerge from an earlier collaborative exploration of the creative work of four Los Angeles–based musicians in the 1970s who worked innovatively at the intersection of jazz, soul and orchestral music, most often through collaboration: George Duke's studio technology–led productions, Larry and Fonce Mizell's productions at Blue Note Records, Patrice Rushen's seminal jazz and R&B recordings and Charles Stepney's work with Earth, Wind & Fire.

Here we apply some of the frames we developed in this analysis to look at two bursts of musical creativity presented to the world as Miles Davis commercial recordings. While 30 years apart—and located at either side

[1] *Miles Ahead*, Columbia, CL-1041. Recorded May 6, 10, 23, 27 and August 22, 1957 at Columbia 30th Street Studio, New York City. Released in US October 21, 1957.

[2] *Tutu*, Warner Bros. Records, 9 25490-1. Recorded February 6, 10, 11, 13 and March 12, 1986 at Capitol Studios and Ocean Way Recording, Hollywood; 'Backyard Ritual' at Le Gonks, West Hollywood. Mixed at Ocean Way and Atlantic Studios, New York City. Released September 1986.

Bobbie-Jane Gardner and Tim Wall, *Orchestrating Miles* In: *Rethinking Miles Davis*. Edited by: Roger Fagge, Nicolas Pillai, and Tim Wall, Oxford University Press.
DOI: 10.1093/9780190085834.003.0008

of what we hear as a musical rupture husbanded by Stepney, the Mizell brothers, Rushen and Duke in the 1970s—there is as much to say about the continuities as the contrasts in the way Davis works as a creative musician. As we will show, both the *Miles Ahead* and *Tutu* recordings are rooted in the same LA music culture that hosted our 1970s agents of musical change. The direct involvement of Duke in *Tutu* provides a hint of these important, but infrequently discussed, connections. Tim's chapters in this book on the place of *Tutu* in the US music industry and in a mapping of 1980s popular music sets much of the wider context for that recording, and Nicholas Gebhardt's exploration of Davis' 1981 reimagining of the Davis—Evans Porgy and Bess collaboration investigates in more detail some of the adjacent issues around black musical culture and musical reinterpretation. Our focus here, though, is on the forms of music making that we have termed 'orchestrating' and the collaborators we present as 'orchestrators', as well as broader debates about the music's place in a 'black aesthetic'.

We initially deploy inverted commas and use the terms 'orchestrating' and 'orchestrator' in an open and expanding way to signal the acts of musical organisation, musician agency and repertoires of cultural identity that afford the creation of two pieces of recorded jazz. We comfortably embrace versions of these concepts that include activities more often called composition, arranging and production within the former sense of collective music production cultures, and the roles of musician, arranger and producer within the latter sense of active participation in music making, for the individuals involved in making two commercial recordings. We reimagine the act of orchestration and the role of orchestrator from Western art music tradition, applying them to jazz, to expand the way such concepts are deployed, as well as making them more productive for discussions of jazz and other forms of popular music-creation. In doing so, we conceive the 'orchestrating' in 'Orchestrating Miles' as both an adjective and a verb. Likewise, in discussing what can be understood as a 'black aesthetic', we seek to call upon Stuart Hall's (1993) idea of strategic essentialism and discussions led by George Lewis (2008, xxxv) about "some of the strategies black musicians used in negotiating the complex, diverse and unstable environment of contemporary musical experimentalism".

Accordingly, we build the chapter around the three key frames that emerged from our earlier dialogue on collaboration, orchestration and the black aesthetic. Our intention in the collaboration is to destabilise the working assumption of each other by offering radically different insights and so ensure we move away from any attempts to produce definitive answers. The analysis we produce never closes off or finalises, hopefully encouraging others to take up this process. We are, though, very conscious that this generates more research questions than we answer. However, by engaging openly with each other's expertise and with the ideas of other published authors, we seek to stimulate a wider discussion. This unsettles a number of the foundational premises about Davis' music, and his agency as a musician, that dominate jazz studies and wider music studies, whether musicological or cultural. In that, we embrace the opportunity to work in research as Davis did with music: finding stimulation in collaboration and breaking new ground by moving beyond what we already know.

Collaboration

Discussions of the creation of *Miles Ahead* and *Tutu* are driven by strikingly different frames and narratives. This derives from a periodisation of Davis' career that tends to distance the working methods of one historically-located recording from another. It is exaggerated further by a fundamental, and not easily resolved, tension between the way Davis is constructed within jazz history as a genius, biographically-explainable, innovative soloist, and the evidence of his working methods, rooted in strikingly different musical collaborations. These differences are not just the product of ahistorical analyses but in many cases are the product of a purposeful attempt to justify value judgements about the relative value of chronological periods of jazz, dominant sub-genres of jazz, or phases of Davis' career.

It is therefore commonplace for Davis' collaborative work with arranger Gil Evans in the 1950s to be discussed in terms very different from those applied to his work with musician-producer Marcus Miller in the 1980s. These relationships, whatever the value judgements made about them, are seen as musical working relationships. The trumpeter's professional relationships with record company executives like George Avakian and Tommy LiPuma are certainly conceived to be very different from those of musician-orchestrator and producers when, as we will see, the lines are not as clear-cut as they are made to seem. Likewise, there is often an implied contrast between the way Avakian is presented as an enabler, and LiPuma as a commercialiser, of jazz's core values. Such a contrast constructs a narrative about the creative environments in which Davis was expected to work as increasingly constrained. This position is most forcefully articulated by Stanley Crouch (1990), and so we engage with his critique below.

These stories about how Davis worked with his various collaborating music makers are immediately apparent within the 'folk knowledge' narratives found in the collectively authored Wikipedia accounts of the relationships.[3]

> Miles Davis and Gil Evans had worked together on Davis' landmark 1949 album *Birth of the Cool.* Evans was a distinguished soloist, but it was his role as arranger that is well-illustrated here with alternate and working takes.[4]
>
> Miller was the main songwriter and producer on three of Miles Davis' albums.[5]

Seemingly factual statements about the collaborative nature of Davis' working relationships feature subtle distinctions of merit. Davis and Evans are represented as 'working together', and Evans' own playing abilities are highlighted together with his role as musical arranger. By contrast, Miller's role is discursively separated from Davis, and the latter is assigned cultural ownership of the albums they collaboratively produced. Miller is assigned roles usually constructed as more functional and associated with commercial popular music rather than jazz: song writing (rather than composition) and production (rather than orchestrating or composing). Both Avakian, Head of Popular Albums at Columbia Records, and LiPuma, Vice President of Jazz and Progressive Music at Warner Bros. Records, are completely absent from these accounts.

Davis' collaboration with Evans is almost always presented in positive terms, although usually giving the dominant role to Evans. In John Szwed's (2002, 140–141) account, Davis "left the choice of music up to Evans": "Gil picked all of the songs to be recorded, except for Miles' choices of Ahmad Jamal's 'New Rhumba' and Dave Brubeck's 'The Duke,' composed 'Miles Ahead,' orchestrated 'New Rhumba' into a very different piece, reimagined

[3] Wikipedia entries represent a culturally important distillation of wider discourses that are a product of the collective writing and editing processes used by the platform and represented in the portmanteau word 'wiki-' (platforms that encourage collaborative, iterative, and associative writing) (encyclo)-'pedia.'

[4] Wikipedia, 'Miles Davis and Gil Evans: *The Complete Columbia Studio Recordings*', accessed December 18, 2025, https://en.wikipedia.org/wiki/Miles_Davis_%26_Gil_Evans:_The_Complete_Columbia_Studio_Recordings.

[5] Wikipedia, 'Marcus Miller', accessed December 18, 2025, https://en.wikipedia.org/wiki/Marcus_Miller.

the selected pieces as a suite and selected and organised the band". In Stephanie Stein Crease's (2002, 193) biography of Evans, the arranger is dominant: "the artistic direction was his and Miles' but mainly his", although, she opines, "the opportunity [to make *Miles Ahead*] dovetailed with Gil's maturity as an artist and with Miles' maturation of sound and style". Stein Crease, however, assigns the top-level agency to Avakian. In Stein Crease's account, it is Avakian (as Head of Popular Albums at Columbia and the record's producer) who leaves decisions on repertoire to Evans, while insisting that there was a track called 'Miles Ahead', from which the LP would take its name (193).

In his autobiography co-written with Quincy Troupe, interestingly, Davis talks about his relationship with Evans in a very different way. It is the same way his biographers usually write about Davis' relationship with the members of his own bands, as mentor and stimulus for new bursts of gnomic reflection and creativity: "Of all the people I knew, Gil Evans was one of the ones who could pick up on what I was thinking musically. Like when he would come to hear me play, he would ease up on me and say, 'Miles, you know you have a nice open sound on your trumpet. Why don't you use it more?' And then he'd be gone, just like that, and I'd be left thinking about what he said" (Davis and Troupe 1989, 184). In many ways, the distinction between different but equal creative contributions comes from Stein Crease's (2002, xii) attempt to bring Evans' contribution to the fore, but it also sits in a wider discourse about the career trajectory of the two music creators and the sense that the music was the result of an intellectual and cultural collaboration that went beyond this individual recording. Almost all accounts locate the Davis–Evans collaboration as a long creative association, starting with the *Birth of Cool* sessions in 1949 and 1950, and running to 1983 with 'That's Right' on *Decoy*. Nevertheless, in a reflective statement, Stein Crease opines, "One can't underestimate the significance to Gil of working with 'sound' innovators such as Davis. Evans was almost a complete romantic in this respect—he idolised, followed, and had longed to write for the Armstrongs, Lester Youngs, and Miles Davises of this world" (193). A convincing argument can be constructed to demonstrate that the recording of *Tutu* provides Davis with a similarly musically empathetic collaborator in Miller that the *Miles Ahead* sessions had provided in Evans. Miller offers insights that moulded the sound of Davis' trumpet playing and opened up routes for musical development that Davis would subsequently internalise and follow in his next recordings. Miller selected the majority of themes for *Tutu* (the exception is George Duke's 'Backyard Ritual'), 'orchestrated' the musical parts of each track, conceived the album as a sonic whole that could incorporate Duke's track without difficulty, created almost all the band parts himself and selected the other seven musicians who contributed (including Paulinho da Costa's percussion work that helped unite 'Backyard Ritual' with the other tracks).

As Tim explores at greater length in chapter 3, *Tutu* is accounted for in very different terms, including the derogatory idea that musically the record was Miller's rather than Davis', that it lacks substance and is overly determined by commercial considerations, revealing that Davis had lost interest in jazz. These narratives undermine Miller's contribution through a set of critical responses which reflect more the personal taste of the critics than an understanding of the music or the way Davis, Miller and LiPuma collaborated.

And yet these critiques are based upon factors that exactly characterise *Miles Ahead* but which are usually expressed in much warmer language. As we have seen in both Szwed's and Stein Crease's accounts, Evans is presenting a dominant musical presence but does not dominate Davis' playing. As we show below, musically *Miles Ahead* included frameworks often dismissed by those committed to a black aesthetic as being outside jazz. In addition, as Darren Mueller (2024, 141) shows, commercial considerations were crucial to Avakian's conception of the 1957 recording session, deemed necessary to take advantage of the new 12-inch, 33 rpm music disc formats and new middle-aged, middle-class buyers. It certainly represented a decisive break with Davis' small group improvising, which was seen to reach its zenith on his Prestige recordings that included John Coltrane.

In 1983, critics whose aesthetic perspectives were rooted in Davis' quartet and quintet recordings of the late 1950s and 1960s, along with his orchestral LPs with Evans, not only found the music of *Tutu* perplexing, but they also struggled to understand the creative roles undertaken by Miller. While it would have been possible to frame Miller's role as they did that of Evans, they are trapped in a rejection of its musical sound and prejudgements about the way he drew on musical ideas and production practices from contemporary R&B and embraced recording technology more associated with these musics of black origin. The critical frame employed by too many jazz critics failed to understand the changes in the organisation of music making that had developed since the recording of *Miles Ahead*. These changes were initiated by the practices that we explored in our investigations of LA-based innovations of George Duke, Larry and Fonce Mizell, Patrice Rushen and Charles Stepney in mid- to later 1970s.

There are a series of direct lines to Miller's approach on *Tutu* that emerge from the innovations of Duke, the Mizell brothers, Rushen and Stepney. We have already noted that Duke created 'Backyard Ritual' for *Tutu*, drawing upon his creative approach in the studio on tens of LP and single-track recordings from the 1970s onward, under his own name or as producer for the recordings of others. The Mizell brothers' Blue Note Records productions mastered innovations in studio recording and mixing technology to bring high production values and used multitracking to create rich, orchestrated soundscapes in which musicians improvised, just as Evans had done in the 1950s and Miller did in the 1980s. Rushen, like Duke, sustained a career as a performer, utilising a range of keyboard instruments, creating new 'electronic' sounds to reimagine jazz and synthesise those sensibilities with soul and funk-based dance music. Miller's own ways of playing, while emerging out of the role of the bass guitar more than piano, owe a significant debt to both Rushen and Duke. Stepney, also a performing musician in his own right, is best known for his arranging and production role in the recording of Earth, Wind & Fire. He is credited as arranger and associate producer on *Open Our Eyes* (1974) and as co-producer for *That's the Way of the World* (1975), *Gratitude* (1975) and *Spirit* (1976). His earlier, Chicago-based arranging, production and playing work at Chess Records in the 1960s is at the intersection of jazz, soul and funk. The commercial success he achieved in applying this approach to work with Rotary Connection, Minnie Riperton and the Ramsey Lewis Trio provides a role model for Miller two decades later.

Likewise, Evans' 1957 work with Davis heralds many of the approaches adopted by these 1970s LA-based music makers. Evans has a particular interest in the sound and timbral qualities of a wider range of instruments than had become dominant in small group bebop and places these in a richer and multilayered music in which the dynamics and relationship within written arrangements are brought to their zenith in the Evans–Davis collaborations. It is not coincidental that Evans developed these approaches as a member of the Claude Thornhill Orchestra, first working out of Los Angeles in the late 1930s and then, after the war, based in New York, as the new generation of bebop musicians challenged the niceties of swing's modernism (see Stein Crease 2002, 97, 124–145). Like Evans, Duke, the Mizells, Rushen and Stepney all built long-term partnerships in LA with a team of studio musicians, other composers and arrangers and select studio engineers to establish new approaches to making music. And they continued Avakian's ambition to create music with a wide appeal across black and white audiences, embracing a wider age, gender and class demographic of listeners and record buys than music of black origin had previously achieved, by realising the potential of the LP format and the melding of jazz and elaborated orchestral forms.

Such was Davis' place in the roster of Columbia and then Warner that his output was vital to the strategy of the companies, and Davis' relationship with senior record company executives was key to the form of that output. There is, then, an important case to be made for seeing Davis' relationship with Avakian at Columbia as important as the one he had with Evans, and his relationship with LiPuma at Warners being as important as the one he had with Miller. Avakian's role in biographies of Davis usually focuses on the Columbia exec's part in bringing Davis to Columbia and his production credits on *'Round About Midnight*,[6] *Miles Ahead* and *Milestones*.[7] As Darren Mueller (2024, 126–133) details, Avakian's position within Columbia is central to the company's realisation of a record format, created for classical music, as a medium for popular music. Columbia had launched their new 33⅓ rpm, micro-groove, long-playing format and applied it to 12-inch discs in 1948. The new format allowed longer playing music of higher audio quality on each side of the disc than the conventional 10-inch, 78 rpm discs. It was Avakian who oversaw the first 100 popular-music LP releases, including three Miles Davis recordings.

'Round About Midnight followed the album format that had become customary for jazz LPs: a set of well-known jazz standards programmed across the two sides to capture something of the band's live performances. Under Avakian's guidance, this approach is perfected: different takes were edited to create an imaginary perfect performance and each side "sequenced as if each side of the LP were a set at a club, with ballads and fast tunes pacing each other" (Szwed 2002, 128). A year later, Avakian involved Davis in a new context, utilising him in the solo parts on two tracks of the recording of Gunther Schuller's *Music for Brass*.[8] Utilising a 19-part, brass-heavy group, the Brass Ensemble of the Jazz and Classical Music Society, Davis plays flugelhorn

[6] *'Round About Midnight*, Columbia, CL 949. Produced by George Avakian and recorded on October 26, 1955, June 5 and September 10, 1956, at Columbia 30th Street Studio, New York City. Released March 4, 1957.

[7] *Milestones*, Columbia, CL 1193. Produced by George Avakian and recorded February 4 and March 4, 1958, at Columbia 30th Street Studios, New York City. Released September 2, 1958.

[8] Gunther Schuller, John Lewis, Jimmy Giuffre, JJ Johnson, conducted by Dimitri Mitropoulos, *Music for Brass*, Columbia, CL 941. Produced by George Avakian and recorded on October 20 and 23, 1956, at Columbia 30th Street Studio, New York City. Released January 1, 1957.

for the first time, improvising solos on highly orchestrated themes. It was Avakian again who suggested to Davis that they develop the *Music for Brass* concept, but within a more defined jazz setting, working with Evans, to a concept positioning Miles 'ahead' of other jazz musicians (140).

The studio recordings for this session were also extensively edited and overdubs added in further pursuit of an Avakian model of performance excellence (Szwed 2002, 142). Szwed suggests Evans took the idea of a classical music one-movement Konzertstück as the model for *Miles Ahead* (141). It is this combination of Davis' interests in music at the intersection of jazz and contemporary art music, Avakian's vision for a new popular jazz music enabled by the 12-inch LP format, and Evans' realisation of these in his compositions and orchestrations that is exemplified in *Miles Ahead*.

With *Milestones* Davis returns to the small group jazz, now extended into a sextet, and the recording's innovations were primarily musical, focused on Davis' growing interest in improvising beyond chords in what would come to be called 'modal jazz'. Avakian's influence is far less apparent, even though he is credited as producer. As *Milestones* was being developed, Avakian was on the way out of Columbia, first to the LA-based Pacific Jazz Records and then to act as the founding A&R director for Warner Bros. Records for the LA film studio. In the latter role, Avakian took the record company beyond its catalogue of Warner television stars turned singers. It was 30 years later that Davis joined the label that Avakian had guided into major status. By 1986 the leading light at Warner was Tommy LiPuma.

In many ways LiPuma and Avakian could not have been more different in background and the musical vision they offered Davis. Yet they held similar roles in major record companies, and their collaborative relationship with Davis functioned similarly. In 1979 LiPuma was appointed Vice President of Jazz and Progressive Music at Warner Bros. Records to extend the approach he had taken as a producer to position jazz artists like George Benson in the popular music mainstream. Benson's LP *Breezin'* had achieved million-seller status in the US by 1984.[9] This success by a black jazz player would certainly have appealed to Davis, even if, as Tim shows in chapter 4, it was probably Warner's support for Prince's career, along with other stars of black music, which contrasted so starkly with Columbia's fading glory days in jazz. By combining jazz with R&B production techniques to create million-selling

[9] Certified by Recording Industry Association of America, https://www.riaa.com/gold-platinum/?tab_active=default-award&se=george+benson+breezin#search_section.

LPs, LiPuma convinced Warner senior executives that this was the emerging market of the 1980s. Following his model of developing Benson's career, LiPuma signed other artists from Benson's former label, CTI, most successfully South Americans Eumir Deodato, Antônio Carlos Jobim and João Gilberto. At the same time, he produced former Davis sideman Bill Evans, a jazz fusion sextet of accomplished session musicians, Stuff and adaptable and idiosyncratic jazz vocalist Al Jarreau.

LiPuma therefore already had a model for developing jazz musicians, repositioning their music in more contemporary and more mainstream contexts and being personally involved in the recordings they made and the musicians who played on them. LiPuma takes producer credits on both *Tutu* and 1989's *Amandla*, along with Miller and Duke, pushing Davis towards collaborators who were already producing music that, in the context of the sonic world of the 1980s, sounded accessible, contemporary and cutting-edge. In interviews, Miller identifies the multiple roles LiPuma played as his co-producer not only in involving him in the project in the first place but also looking after the financial arrangements of the recording, reviewing the soundscapes of the tracks and selecting which takes of Davis solos would make the final mix.

Orchestration

In music making, orchestration defines the principles governing how musical ideas are distributed across the instruments that are utilised during the compositional process to ensure the music has a clear character during the performance. More generally, the term is used as a metaphor to talk about the way of achieving a desired outcome through the organisation of available resources. In our earlier discussions of 1970s LA-based music makers, we considered Duke, the Mizell brothers, Rushen and Stepney as orchestrators of the recorded sonics of music they each produced, but also orchestrators of their own careers and of those for whom they acted as producers. In doing so, our discussions of orchestration focused on widening the idea to reveal important connections between aspects of musicians' creative lives. By going beyond traditional definitions that embrace the arrangement of composed music for a live performance by an orchestra, emphasising arrangement, music and music makers, we can recognise the in-built assumptions drawn from a Western art context. These broader senses of orchestrating enrich our understanding of the world in which a musician like Davis operates, highlighting his creative agency within a broader collaborative work practice.

Most obviously, the innovations of Duke, the Mizell brothers, Rushen and Stepney require that we extend the idea of orchestrating to include the multifaceted activities of the producer. That notion embraces the sense of organising a recording or live music performance through deciding how musical ideas are distributed across the instruments within a recording to how they are arranged in the sonic space of that recording. In the introduction, we stressed that we conceived the 'orchestrating' in 'Orchestrating Miles' as both an adjective and a verb. By that we mean both the way that Davis' music has been orchestrated ('orchestrating the music of Miles Davis') and the agency that Davis deployed in organising the environment in which he made music ('Miles Davis orchestrates his musical life'). This approach is especially revealing when we explore Davis' role in jazz and the contributions of Evans and Miller, along with those of Avakian and LiPuma. Doing so invites us to expand the way we use such concepts and to develop more productive ways to explore the purposeful organisation of musical sound in jazz and other forms of popular-music creation.

In understanding orchestration in this widest sense, we can explore how different agents orchestrate the music making, the music and the performance of the music. That then determines our focus for the two different recordings under discussion, as shown below.

It is no coincidence that Darren Mueller (2024) focuses the first three chapters of his cultural history of the LP in jazz on Davis' record labels of the 1950s: Prestige and Columbia. As he shows, it is these labels that play

Table

	Miles Ahead	*Tutu*
Orchestrating the music making	Avakian as Head of Columbia Records Popular Music Department and producer	LiPuma as VP Warner Bros. Records Jazz and Progressive Music and executive producer
Orchestrating the music	Evans as arranger and conductor	Miller (and Duke) as producer
Performing the music	Davis as musician	Miller as musician, Davis as musician

host to the transformation of recorded jazz, in the production techniques utilised in recording and manipulating sound and in distributing it as a coherent product to a conceived audience. For Mueller, both Bob Weinstock at Prestige and Avakian at Columbia exercise a "white, masculine authority" through which they define the changing role and music of jazz in 1950s America. This authority derives initially from their deep knowledge about jazz on records and jazz record collecting that enabled them to repackage historic recordings owned by each label into the new long-playing format that would sell. Each performs the same producer role, in the broadest terms, orchestrating the production of Davis' jazz recordings made for those labels. Davis' Prestige recordings are driven, in Mueller's words, by Weinstock's "documentary impulse" to capture and share the performance of jazz, including "mistakes" and studio banter (75–121). By contrast, argues Mueller, Avakian worked to "distance jazz from the broader history of black popular music by emphasising the music's greatness and lasting historical value" (128). Having already husbanded the extension of the careers of Louis Armstrong and Duke Ellington by issuing LPs of their earlier recordings and creating new ones based upon live venue performances, Avakian adds the much younger Davis to this jazz tradition by contracting him to the label and plans his recorded output.

Avakian's purpose with Davis, and his other contracted jazz and popular music artists, was to utilise the LP format created for classical music to engage affluent white audiences with jazz as a serious music. Bringing Davis together with Evans for *Miles Ahead* allowed for both the development of longer-form compositional forms afforded by the LP format and an indexing of the connotations of serious music through the orchestration of music played by larger ensembles. Evans established new approaches to orchestration, creating a sound world in which Davis' trumpet tone and his improvising become particularly resonant.

Across *Miles Ahead*, Evans creates a sonic world characterised by an accessible lightness. Paradoxically, he achieves this with a depth of instrumentation which is at times dense. Evans clearly focuses on exploiting instrumental colour and uses instrumental mimicry across instruments that relates the instruments playfully and kaleidoscopically. Davis' usual rhythm section plays on the recording, but their roles are constrained and submerged in both the arrangement and the mix. Drummer Art Taylor, for instance, plays with brushes and is almost inaudible in the recording, while the rhythm section does not drive the playing of the other instrumentalists, which do not swing in the conventional way that dominated 1950s modern jazz. Nevertheless, Evans' clever orchestration allows Davis' trumpet solos to always cut through the rich orchestration, to be in the foreground despite the often florid, weaving musical textures.

We would agree with Stein Crease's point that the role of the arranger has been marginalised or overlooked in music histories. However, if we focus only on Evans' role as arranger of the scored music, we ignore the fact that the responsibilities taken by Evans in *Miles Ahead* were in future decades as likely to be classified as those of producer and composer. In part, these differences of role classifications are representative of changes in nomenclature in the wider recording industry. Certainly in the 1950s in particular, 'producer' was more closely aligned with the administrative and editorial rather than creative decisions we would associate with orchestration. The producer managed the recording process rather than shaped it in the way Evans did here. Of course, Avakian and Cal Lampley are credited on the record sleeve of *Miles Ahead* as producers in this sense.

Likewise, 'composer' is a relatively less valued conception in the discourse of jazz creation, particularly when thought about in relation to improvisation in performance, the role assigned solely to Davis on this recording. Further, while the idea that improvisation is itself a form of composition has a long history in jazz criticism, arrangement (in its verb form) was seen to be characteristic of the organisation of large jazz orchestras: writing charts for sections of musicians and generating the dynamics of performances for these big bands. These activities in jazz creativity were not, and still are not, widely thought of as orchestration. Certainly within the studio recording world, orchestrating was related to the use of classically trained, often string sections, brought in to provide sweetening for popular music aimed at mass audiences.

Thinking about our LA-based pioneers of the 1970s reminds us that organising recorded music around a distinctive soloist playing over orchestrated 'accompanying instruments' with key melodic and harmonic responsibilities became a standard formula for producing 'contemporary jazz', just as it had a singer and accompaniment in wider popular music. In jazz, this produced more melodically-driven music that often explored exoticised instrumental sounds. The Mizell brothers' work at Blue Note and other labels in the 1970s would be seen as exemplars of such an approach. Starting with Donald Byrd's *Black Byrd* in 1972, through Bobbi Humphrey's *Fancy Dancer* in 1975, to Gary Bartz's *Music Is My Sanctuary* in 1977, the Mizells further realised the idea of jazz-pop fusion programmed across a long-playing record that would have wide appeal.[10] Of course, all the 1970s California-based composer-producer-arranger-performers gave a significant place to a highly-driven rhythmic bed. This was usually recorded first, and other musical elements were built on top. This highly orchestrated approach differed significantly from the approach of live studio-based performance taken by Teo Macero with Miles Davis records during this period, from *Someday My Prince Will Come* in 1961, reaching its zenith in *In a Silent Way*, *Bitches Brew* and *Jack Johnson* from 1969 to 1971, and reproduced for the live recording releases that followed well into the 1980s. It is, though, as we have pointed out, the basis of Miller's creative approach.

Within the traditional definition, Evans is easily understood as an orchestrator of the sound world in which Davis played on *Miles Ahead* and his charts as a visual representation of the orchestrational process. It is uncommon, though, to discuss Miller's role in *Tutu* in the same terms, even though he creates the sound world in which Davis solos 30 years later. In part this is because by the 1970s the term 'producer' had become widely used to describe the purposeful activity of the organisation of musical sound undertaken by Evans in 1957, and multitrack recording had replaced live band playing as the main form of music creation. That is not to say there were not still people who scored parts for live instrumental players, but they were now called 'arrangers' and part of a wider producer-led activity. While accomplished musicians in their own right, Duke, the Mizells and Stepney were primarily identified as producers, even when Duke was producing music under his own name. Rushen is, perhaps, primarily seen as a performing artist, even though, from her third album, *Shout It Out* (1977), she is consistently identified as the arranger and shared production credits for her recording sessions. Through this process, 'producer' in music moved from its former use, akin to theatrical producer, to a new use matching more closely the director role in plays and films. In turn, this 'recording-as-orchestration' approach that Miller inherited from music makers like Stepney, the Mizells, Rushen and Duke was the one brought back to Davis' music in *Tutu*, a characteristic of music creation that had been absent since his work with Evans in the late 1950s and 1960s.

[10] Donald Byrd, *Black Byrd*, Blue Note, BN-LA047-F. Produced by Larry Mizell and recorded April 3 and 4, 1972, at Sound Factory, Hollywood. Released in 1972. Bobbi Humphrey, *Fancy Dancer*, Blue Note, BN-LA550-G. Produced by Larry Mizell and Chuck Davis and recorded August 5, 6, 7, 1975, at Sound Factory, Hollywood. Released in 1975. Gary Bartz, *Music Is My Sanctuary*, produced by Larry Mizell and Fonce Mizell and recorded March 1977 at Sound Factory, Los Angeles. Released in 1977.

There are direct links back to the California music production culture of the 1970s, and back to Evans' arranging style, in the creation of *Tutu*. Duke worked at Capitol Studios in early February on 'Backyard Ritual', and Miller recorded in the same studio a few days later for the tracks 'Splatch', 'Tutu', and 'Portia'. Miller switches to Clinton Recording Studios in New York City in mid-March for 'Tomaas', 'Don't Lose Your Mind', 'Full Nelson', and 'Perfect Way'.

Miller has talked on a number of occasions about the influences he drew on for the orchestrations he created for *Tutu*. He cites Herbie Hancock's *Headhunters*,[11] with its combination of jazz and R&B recorded in San Francisco, and Hancock's earlier *Speak Like a Child*[12] as strong influences (Cole 2005). Miller further suggests Hancock had himself been channelling Evans' work (243). More recently, Miller has said that in making *Tutu*, he included elements he describes as "'Birth of the Cool' harmonies", "soft brass", "Gil's harmonies . . . those 4ths . . . and a New Orleans beat" and that he "tried to combine everything [he] knew about them in one track".[13] In William Ellis' *Miles Davis One LP* portraits in chapter 7, it is noticeable that Miller chooses the Avakian-produced *Milestones* from 1958. Although not a collaboration with Evans, it clearly reveals Miller's sense of a jazz sound orchestrated in the late 1950s which remains part of his sonic consciousness.

The Black Aesthetic

In this final section, we want to explore the collaborative orchestrated music that Davis produced with Evans and Miller through a frame of the black aesthetic. Our purpose is not to define a black aesthetic, whether in jazz or beyond, but to locate the meaningfulness of Davis' collaborative orchestrations of jazz within debates in jazz culture and criticism about a 'black aesthetic' and a 'white aesthetic' as discursive constructions. Following Darren Mueller (2020, 3), we aimed to challenge ourselves "to re-hear this music as a statement of alternate belonging". With an explicit debt to Stuart Hall

[11] Herbie Hancock, *Headhunters*, Columbia, KC 32731. Produced by Herbie Hancock and David Rubinson and recorded September 1973 at Wally Heider and Different Fur, San Francisco. Released October 26, 1973.

[12] Herbie Hancock, *Speak Like a Child*, Blue Note, BST 84279. Produced by Duke Pearson and recorded March 6 and 9, 1968, at Van Gelder Studio, Englewood Cliffs, NJ. Released in October 1968.

[13] Christopher Wilkinson, dir., *'Round Miles: A Miles Davis Documentary*, 53m., released April 21, 2022.

(1993), we propose the idea of a nonessentialist black aesthetic within jazz that speaks to both the available musical resources of the African American community and an explicit objective by musicians to produce music that articulates the creative expression of black artists in a racist society. We use the term 'nonessentialist' in the sense Hall does, to avoid "mistaking what is historical and cultural for what is natural, biological, and genetic" (111). Further, in Hall's words the black aesthetic is formed of "the distinctive cultural repertoires out of which popular representations were made, and of the black counter narratives we have struggled to voice"; its "forms are impure, to some degree hybridised from a vernacular base" and "not simply as the recovery of a lost dialogue bearing clues for the production of new musics [but as] adaptations, moulded to the mixed, contradictory, hybrid spaces of popular culture" (110).

For jazz, this means those musical elements that were particularly valued and nurtured amongst African American musicians in the periods that first Evans, then Miller produced their orchestrations with Davis. These musical elements of jazz do not derive from a black aesthetic because they are produced by black American musicians (Evans, after all, was white), but (at least) because they draw on distinctive cultural repertoires and (preferably) because they can be used to express black counter narratives to the dominant society. There are strong and interesting parallels in the way both Evans and Miller relate to a black aesthetic in jazz, even though one was a white Canadian who established his musical identity in white California-based bands and the other a black New Yorker from a church and jazz musical family.

Extending the roles of creative collaboration for jazz players like Davis to include those with the broadest role in musical 'orchestration' at different levels of record production alerts us to the different levels Davis engaged with what Joe Feagin (2020) has termed 'white racial framing' and the way he sought opportunities for 'counterframing'. The production of *Miles Ahead* and *Tutu* can be understood as situated at the intersection of discourses of a dominant white aesthetic and a counterhegemonic black aesthetic which operate at the level of orchestrating the music making, orchestrating the music and performing the music in the recording studio.

Davis enjoyed far greater agency to 'orchestrate' recorded music making at both Columbia and Warner Bros. than was usually possible for black jazz musicians of the time. In part these possibilities of power lay in the trumpeter's symbolic value for Avakian, a value rooted in Davis' ability as a creator of jazz within the black aesthetic championed by Avakian. Of course, as Muller has argued, Avakian derived his agency at Columbia through his 'white, masculine authority'. Their collaboration depended upon their willingness to 'orchestrate' music that would appeal to both Davis' creative and career aspirations and Avakian's vision for a jazz music which would take advantage of the technical potential of the new LP record format and appeal to the mainly white American market for LPs. For that they both needed Evans, and this, in turn, gave Evans an unprecedented agency to orchestrate the music for the recording. That is, as long as he met both the creative and career aspirations of Davis and the corporate aspirations of Avakian as producer. In Mueller's words, with *Miles Ahead* Avakian aimed at "white respectability through a mixture of jazz and classical music" (2024, 141). It is through his musical performance in the studio setting that Davis was able to have his greatest agency. The emphasis within a black aesthetic of jazz to privilege improvision and a personal sound gives Davis full potential to explore his own musical vision.

As we have seen, this is exactly mirrored with *Tutu*. Like Avakian, LiPuma's agency derives from his ability to operate at the intersection of white and black aesthetic discourse in popular music and jazz. Davis' agency is far greater 30 years on from *Miles Ahead*, as the most successful jazz artist on Columbia, a label which had been at the forefront of music at the intersection of jazz, soul and funk in the 1970s. By the mid-1980s, though, both Davis' and Columbia's pre-eminence seemed to be on the wane just as much as the music they were producing. It was down to LiPuma to resurrect Davis' creative and commercial career at Warner, just as Avakian had done with Armstrong and Ellington in the 1950s at Columbia. In turn, it was LiPuma who gave Miller the freedom to orchestrate a sonic world in which Davis could solo, and Miller draws upon his understanding of how Evans and Davis collaborated to do so.

Engaging with ideas of a black aesthetic is a particularly effective way to respond to Vijay Iyer's entreaty that jazz studies should undertake a significant engagement with black studies.[14] Certainly the critical response to both *Miles Ahead* and *Tutu* has been framed within debates about these ideas, but too often jazz studies academics have been reluctant to explicitly enter territory dominated by disputation and disagreement. While most often positioned

[14] We have in mind Iyer's social media posts on this subject: https://x.com/vijayiyer/status/1758643204134715728.

within the Black Arts Movement from the 1960s onward, as Darwin Turner (1974) has shown, the idea of a black aesthetic was deployed by W. E. B. Du Bois beginning in the 1920s. This, at least, should alert us to the complexities of debate at play, especially because, as Turner himself notes, Du Bois is most often associated "disparagingly with . . . the effort of Negroes to become assimilated by separating themselves from the folk culture" (2). While Larry Neal's manifesto for a Black Arts Movement primarily addresses literary arts, his words effectively speak to the agenda of many black jazz musicians in the decade after *Miles Ahead* was recorded: "The Black Arts Movement is radically opposed to any concept of the artist that alienates him from his community. Black Art is the aesthetic and spiritual sister of the Black Power concept. As such, it envisions an art that speaks directly to the needs and aspirations of Black America. In order to perform this task, the Black Arts Movement proposes a radical reordering of the western cultural aesthetic. It proposes a separate symbolism, mythology, critique, and iconology" (Neal 1968).

Amiri Baraka's *Blues People* (Jones 1966) is the most developed application of the idea of a black aesthetic, and other significant Black Arts Movement debates, to popular music. In Baraka's history of black American music, the sustaining motivation is the 'blues impulse', and the author explores Davis' place in late 1950s and early 1960s jazz through his alternating place in cool jazz and hard bop (208–214). Baraka implicitly narrates cool as an increasing incorporation of jazz into a white aesthetic, away from the blues impulse, and of hard bop as a reassertion of the blues in jazz. Although not addressed by Baraka, *Miles Ahead* sits at the intersection of these tendencies and, we argue, makes more complex the issues at play. The critical discussions of *Tutu* two decades on show a continuation (and an oversimplification) of Baraka's framing.

Our discussions of a black aesthetic increasingly returned to the arguments set out by George Lewis (2008) in his exploration of the music culture of Chicago's Association for the Advancement of Creative Musicians (AACM). Davis' institutional position within US major record companies is a stark contrast with the community arts movement origins of the AACM musicians, and different still from the creative environment in which some AACM musicians engaged with the European free jazz and improv scenes, and later again with the New York avant-garde. However, applying the frames which Lewis develops to analyse the agency and meaning of AACM musicians to Davis and his collaborators can tell us a lot about how ideas of a black aesthetic play out in *Miles Ahead* and *Tutu*. In particular, Lewis' applications of communitarianism, the "autodidactic impulse", and "racialised hierarchies of aesthetics"[15] are revealing.

Certainly the account we have given of Davis' engagement in the recording sessions of 1957 and 1986 reveals the trumpeter's strong communitarian drive in his desire to collaborate with Avakian and LiPuma and Evans and Miller. This is reflected in the orchestrations in *Miles Ahead*, which are at the intersection of the discourses of a white and a black aesthetic, and in the stronger assertion of a black aesthetic in *Tutu*. Throughout their careers, Davis, Evans, Miller and LiPuma were all classic autodidacts. And while Avakian had a formal higher education at Yale University, his immersion in a black aesthetic version of jazz as music and history was entirely the product of dedicated self-education. We can understand the two recordings as "racialised hierarchies of aesthetics" asserted as black aesthetics in their conception and realisation as commercial LPs/CDs and framed in critical commentary through white aesthetics. In discussing Evans' and Miller's music in relationship to a black aesthetic, and their respective orchestrating collaborations with Davis, we should not be looking for contributions we can classify as purely African American, but (following Lewis) examples of hybridisation, adaption and internal contradiction. Our proposition is that, at each historical moment, while there were strong drivers for Davis to adopt a broader white aesthetic, first Evans and then Miller offered Davis access to musical material from which they could jointly express important black counter narratives to the dominant mores of 1950s and then 1980s jazz.

Equally, we must recognise that this is not a widely accepted frame of interpretation. Crouch has explicitly dealt with ideas of the black aesthetic in his discussions of Davis' music, and he is typically forceful about *Miles Ahead* and *Tutu*. However, his framing is noticeably different in each case. In discussing *Miles Ahead*, along with other Davis–Evans collaborations,[16] Crouch asserts:

> The recordings were inclined toward the pallid textures that resulted from the impressionistic influences on Evans and from the disavowal of the varied Negro vocal inflections that had meant so much to the richest instrumental timbres of the idiom. Usually, when this was not the ongoing obsession with getting a pass into the European party of aesthetic seriousness, it

[15] Amongst other racialisation hierarchies of "method, place, infrastructure, and economics" (Lewis 2008, xii).

[16] *Porgy and Bess* and *Sketches of Spain*.

> was a psychological assertion on the part of white musicians who became fed up or bored with the assumption that they were less than authentically equal artists because of how far removed their cultural roots were from the Negro origins of the craft. (2006, 54–55)

However, when considering Davis' own playing on these recordings, Crouch is more generous in his evaluation: "Regardless of how indistinct some of the arrangements might have made jazz seem, Davis himself had those things in his playing and was never—even at his most puckish—very far from the stink and the grease of the gutbucket at the center of the art" (55). For Crouch, the black aesthetic involves reference to black "vocal inflections" centred on qualities expressed in metaphors of smell and physical texture, while white aesthetics in jazz inclines to "pallid textures" and approval from European judgements of seriousness.

However, Crouch seems, at best, inconsistent when applying what seem to be the same binaries and metaphors to his judgement of *Tutu*. Again, applying his comments to a grouping of recordings,[17] Crouch alleges, "The cult of ethnic authenticity often mistakes the lowest common denominator for an ideal. It begets a self-image that has succumbed to a nostalgia for the mud. What we get is the bugaboo blues of the noble savage, the surly and dangerous Negro who will have nothing to do with bourgeois conventions" (1996, 909–910).

We propose a more open way of hearing *Tutu*. It is relatively straightforward to make the case for Miller as an artist both rooted in a black popular music aesthetic and at the forefront of hybridisation and adaptation. His style, as a widely used session bass player and producer in early 1980s US R&B recordings, combines stylistic elements from 1960s James Jamerson and early 1970s funk slap bass pioneer Larry Graham, and his sound was central to releases by soul singers Aretha Franklin, Luther Vandross and Bernard Wright (Shepherd 2021).[18] There's an obvious debt to Prince, Michael Jackson and Stevie Wonder in his self-produced albums of this period,[19] and he was involved in Tom Browne's 1979 *Browne Sugar* and 1980's *Love Approach* albums[20] at the intersection of jazz and funk. It was this

[17] *You're Under Arrest, Tutu, Siesta, Amandla, Aura.*

[18] See, for instance, Aretha Franklin, *Get It Right*, Arista, AC8-8019, 1983; Luther Vandross, *Never Too Much*, Epic, FE 37451, 1981; Bernard Wright, *Nard*, GRP 5011, 1981.

[19] *Suddenly*, Warner Bros., 9 23806-4, 1983; *Marcus Miller*, Warner Bros., 9 25074-1, 1984.

[20] Tom Browne, *Browne Sugar*, GRP, 5003, 1979; *Love Approach*, GRP, 5008, 1980.

experience that made him an appealing member of the Miles Davis bands on the trumpeter's comeback recording *The Man with the Horn*, the live sets for *We Want Miles* and all but one of the numbers that became 1983's *Star People*. Miller holds an ambiguous position in the formation of smooth jazz on Browne's records for GRP that were produced by Dave Grusin and Larry Rosen, a genre that operated as the intersection of jazz, soul and pop (Barber 2010). At the same time as his engagements with Davis and the production of his own solo records, Miller also worked on a whole range of recordings in this same tightly focused space at the overlap of contemporary R&B, jazz and pop, including those of Donald Fagen, Dave Grusin, David Sanborn and Grover Washington Jr. It is into these very same genre contours and musical ravines that Davis entered when he took up his Warner contract.

Duke's 'Backyard Ritual' contribution to *Tutu* sounds even more abstract than Miller's tracks and is closer to the opening of Davis' music of the late 1960s *In a Silent Way* era. Duke uses exactly the same approach he applied to his contemporaneous *Thief in the Night*, most notably the use of the early digital Synclavier II and analogue Prophet-5 programmable polyphonic synthesisers. In many ways it reflects musical innovations from Brian Eno and David Byrne's (1981) *My Life in the Bush of Ghosts* and Davis' Arthur Baker and Steven Van Zandt–produced 'The Struggle Continues' track off the Artists United Against Apartheid's *Sun City* LP. If nothing else, the latter track signalled to both Duke and Miller that Davis' muted trumpet playing could sound really effective in such a context.

'Backyard Ritual' also allows us a final observation about the assumptions held by Davis' collaborators about the trumpeter's own aesthetic, and Davis' desire to break with those mores. George Cole (2005) recounts Davis' reaction to the crude synthesiser sax solo part laid down by Duke, on a demo placeholder for solo parts he imagined to be played by an acoustic sax player. While Duke expected this track to be replaced by the sound signature of the jazz sax, Davis loved the synthesiser sound and insisted it was kept in the final mix (15).

Visualising Miles Ahead

In bringing the threads of the chapter together at the end, we offer not conclusions but a hint at how the frames we have developed can be taken further.

Perhaps the most interesting way to discuss the unstable nature of *Miles Ahead* at the intersection of discourses of white and black aesthetics is by looking at the dispute between Davis and Avakian over the cover of the LP record. The original release featured a photograph of a young white woman aboard a small sailing yacht with a child and a crew member. It is an arresting image, somewhere between Hy Peskin's 20 July 1953 *Life* cover photograph *Senator Kennedy Goes A Courting*[21] and cover shots for *Vogue* fashion magazine.[22] The cover certainly locates Davis in the same white American East Coast cultural milieu that Avakian sought for Ellington in releasing a recording from the Newport Jazz Festival. Szwed (2002) describes the sailboat cover as "generic, corny, and very white" and explains that, at Davis' intervention, Avakian changed it for a more generic jazz LP cover featuring a portrait of Davis playing trumpet (143).

The change certainly aligned the cover more with the one used for *'Round About Midnight* a few months before[23] and reflected the approach taken with jazz LPs of the time. While replacing a symbol of white, East Coast, modernist privilege with an icon of a black jazz musician, it does not escape the way the black aesthetic of jazz is organised by Avakian's 'white masculine authority'. While the use of an image of the primary artists on LP covers signals the agency of that artist over the music to be heard on the LP, it is also the product of white male categorisation of black music and the construction of a universal musical genius who transcends struggles between competing discourses of white and black aesthetics. Columbia used such portraits for other jazz LPs released that year.[24]

While strikingly different from Columbia LPs of the time, the sailboat cover almost certainly reflected Avakian's aim to uniquely position Davis' music in the heart of a liberal, modern America. It also aligned the Davis record with those of other big popular music artists, especially their Frank Sinatra Christmas album from the same year and an LP of long-forgotten instrumental music from Ken Griffin. These covers reproduce the same kind of imagery around a conventionally attractive white woman by the sea who, while the object of our gaze, does not return our look or recognise our stare.[25] The original Davis cover also reflects changing representations

[21] Accessed at https://www.life.com/history/jfk-covers-life/.

[22] For instance, *Vogue*, October 15, 1956.

[23] Miles Davis Quintet, *'Round About Midnight*, CL-949. Released March 1957.

[24] Don Byrd and Gigi Gryce, *Jazz Lab*, CL-998. Released April 1957; Duke Ellington & His Orchestra, *Such Sweet Thunder*, CL-1033. Released September 1957.

[25] Frank Sinatra, *Christmas Dreaming*, CL-1032. Released October 1957; Ken Griffin, *Love Letters in the Sand*, CL-1039. Released October 1957.

of jazz on Columbia's roster, away from jazz connoisseurship and towards a deracialised, abstracted modernism. For instance, Dave Brubeck Quartet's *Jazz Goes to Junior College* cover is abstracted from the usual photograph of the group or leader to the metonym of the journey implied in the LP's title.[26] And several jazz and popular music LPs of that year went several stages further in this direction, with abstract colour images being very popular.[27]

Davis certainly got his way on the cover of *Miles Ahead*, as he did on the synthesised sax solo on 'Backyard Ritual'. Both speak to his agency as a leading jazz musician of his generation. But both also speak to the entanglement of expectations, cultural positioning and power in which any music is recorded and released. The issues of collaboration, orchestration and black and white aesthetics are far too often ignored or simply implied. We would certainly commend collaborative analysis as a way to open up such issues. It is one way to draw from the best that Davis offered us in his life.

References

Barber, Simon. 2010. 'Smooth Jazz: A Case Study in the Relationships Between Commercial Radio Formats, Audience Research and Music Production'. *Radio Journal: International Studies in Broadcast & Audio Media* 8 (1): 51–70.

Cole, George. 2005. *The Last Miles: The Music of Miles Davis, 1980–1991*. Equinox.

Crouch, Stanley. 1990. 'Play the Right Thing: Miles Davis, the Most Brilliant Sellout in the History of Jazz'. *New Republic* 202 (7): 30–37.

Crouch, Stanley. 1996. 'On the Corner: The Sellout of Miles Davis'. In *Reading Jazz*, edited by Robert Gottlieb. Pantheon.

Crouch, Stanley. 2006. 'Miles Davis in the Fever of Spring, 1961'. In *Considering Genius: Writings on Jazz*, edited by Stanley Crouch. Civitas Books.

Davis, Miles, and Quincy Troupe. 1989. *Miles: The Autobiography*. Simon and Schuster.

Feagin, Joe R. 2020. *The White Racial Frame: Centuries of Racial Framing and Counter-Framing*. Routledge.

Hall, Stuart. 1993. 'What Is This 'Black' in Black Popular Culture?" *Social Justice* 20 (1–2): 104–114. http://www.jstor.org/stable/29766735.

Jones, LeRoi [Amiri Baraka]. 1966. *Blues People: Negro Music in White America*. Jazz Book Club.

Lewis, George. 2008. *A Power Stronger Than Itself: The AACM and American Experimental Music*. University of Chicago Press.

Mueller, Darren. 2020. 'Black Studies in the Digital Crawlspace'. *InVisible Culture*, no. 31 (November).

Mueller, Darren. 2024. *At the Vanguard of Vinyl: A Cultural History of the Long-Playing Record in Jazz*. Duke University Press.

[26] Dave Brubeck Quartet, *Jazz Goes to Junior College*, CL-1034. Released September 1957.

[27] For instance, Jazz Messengers, *Hard Bop*, CL-1040. Released September 1957; Various Artists, *Paris Night Life*, CL-978. Released April 1957; Count Basie, *One O'Clock Jump*, CL-997. Released September 1957.

Neal, Larry. 1968. 'The Black Arts Movement'. *The Drama Review* 12 (4): 29–39. https://nationalhumanitiescenter.org/pds/maai3/community/text8/blackartsmovement.pdf.
Shepherd, Rob. 2021. 'Moving Forward: A Conversation with Marcus Miller (Part One)'. *Postgenre.org*, February 24. https://postgenre.org/marcus-miller-part-i/.
Stein Crease, Stephanie. 2002. *Gil Evans: Out of the Cool: His Life and Music.* A Cappella.
Szwed, John. 2002. *So What: The Life of Miles Davis.* Simon & Schuster.
Turner, Darwin T. 1974. 'W. E. B. Du Bois and the Theory of a Black Aesthetic'. *Studies in the Literary Imagination* 7 (2): 1–21.

9

Encounter, Surprise and Acceptance

Revisiting Miles Davis *On* and *Off* Stage in Portugal

Pedro Cravinho

Introduction

Within a space of 20 years (1971–1991), Miles Davis visited Portugal three times.[1] He first came in November 1971, while the right-wing colonialist Estado Novo (New State) regime held sway, to participate in the first International Cascais Jazz Festival.[2] The event's publicity bore the slogan 'Jazz é Cultura' (Jazz is Culture) and received official support from the regime's Secretaria de Estado de Informação e Turismo (State Secretariat for Information and Tourism).[3] Such a significant event drew some of the world's most prestigious jazz musicians and groups to Portugal for the first time, the Miles Davis Septet among them.[4]

In 1971, Portugal was one of the last European colonial empires and the target of international pressure to decolonise. The regime's determination to suppress independence movements in its former African colonies fuelled an ongoing colonial/independence war, staunchly opposed by movements of university students, particularly those with strong left-wing connections.[5]

[1] This chapter is dedicated to the Portuguese jazz promoter Luís Villas-Boas (1924–1999). It draws on a paper delivered at the conference Miles Davis and John Coltrane at 90: Retrospect and Prospect, University of Surrey, October 2016. The present version is revised and adapted, most notably with the addition of notes and bibliography.

[2] For further discussion on this topic, see Cravinho 2017. All translations from non-English sources are the author's unless otherwise indicated. The author hopes that opening up these sources to non-Portuguese readers adds to the value of this study.

[3] For further discussion on this topic, see Curvelo 2002; Lourenço and Gomes 2005; Santos 2009; Veloso et al. 2010; Cravinho 2012, 2017, 2018a, 2022b.

[4] The State Secretariat for Tourism, Information and Popular Culture, the Costa do Sol Tourist Board, and the Cascais Village Town Hall were the official sponsors of the festival's first edition (Cravinho 2017).

[5] Over the course of 13 years, from 1961 to the end of the regime in 1974, "one in every four Portuguese young men were conscripted into the armed forces to preserve the integrity of the empire, and as a result more than a million Portuguese [did] military service in Africa" (Sardica 2008, 77).

Pedro Cravinho, *Encounter, Surprise and Acceptance:* In: *Rethinking Miles Davis*. Edited by: Roger Fagge, Nicolas Pillai, and Tim Wall, Oxford University Press. © Oxford University Press 2026.
DOI: 10.1093/9780190085834.003.0009

Well aware of the social-political unrest in the country and the expectations surrounding the festival, which had become associated with demands for liberation, Davis demanded that he inaugurate the event by being the opening act. In fact, and in the face of the New State regime's official support of the festival, it turned out that an intervention by another North American musician would cement the Cascais Jazz Festival's recurring symbolical association with anticolonialism.[6]

Davis' subsequent performances in Portugal took place in very different social-political and cultural contexts. On 25 April 1974, following a military coup which overthrew the right-wing colonialist New State regime, the country embarked on a path to democracy, although this was preceded by a period of instability and profound social unrest.[7] This transitional path was characterised by profound social instability and continual turmoil: daily demonstrations, strikes and union meetings, along with other irregular forms of political activity, which included the appropriation of houses, farms and land. The social-political situation was only to worsen after a failed right-wing coup on 11 March 1975, and normality was restored only after a failed left-wing coup on 25 November 1975.[8]

By the time of Davis' second visit, Portugal had become a member of the European Economic Community and had opened up to a wide range of external influences. Lisbon was in fact the first stop on Davis' 1989 European tour, and the Portuguese capital was treated to a repertoire drawn mainly from his 1986 debut album for Warner's, *Tutu*.[9] Davis' last visit was in March 1991, during the country's most significant cycle of economic growth since the revolution (Sardica 2008, 93). On 16 March, the daily newspaper *Público* (Public) featured a full-page photograph of Davis on its cover to announce his return to the country. That week, the Radiotelevisão Portuguesa (Portuguese Public Television; RTP) broadcast the artist's 1989 Paris concert to console those unable to attend the sold-out concerts. This time Davis was treated like a pop star wherever we went. Nevertheless, as we will see, his times in Portugal were always surrounded by controversy.

[6] During the Ornette Coleman Quartet's performance, their double bass player Charlie Haden dedicated his 'Song for Che' (i.e., Che Guevara) to "the black liberation movements of Mozambique, Angola, and Guinea," which led to his arrest by the Portuguese Political Police on the following day at Lisbon's international airport. For further discussion on the Haden incident, see Cravinho (2017).

[7] The 1974–1975 uprising initiated the process that was to restore democracy in Portugal and put an end, after over a decade, to the wars of independence in the former Portuguese African colonies.

[8] This period is known as the Processo Revolucionário em Curso (Ongoing Revolutionary Process; PREC).

[9] *Tutu* was recorded between January and March 1986 and released in autumn that year. For more detailed information about the album and personnel, see *Tutu*'s deluxe edition reissue booklet.

This chapter examines Miles Davis' presence in Portugal and the way it was mediated by the Portuguese press. Davis, as Yudkin observes, was a 20th-century American icon, "instantly recognizable both in pictures (S-shaped back, trumpet at a downward angle) and sound (muted on trumpet, hoarse voice)" (2008, xiii). He continues:

> He was black in a predominantly white culture. He was reminded of the colour of his skin on many occasions. At one point, standing outside a New York club whose marquee bore his name, he was struck repeatedly on the head by a white policeman wielding a truncheon—and then charged with resisting arrest. . . . He was also small, and he made up for this by developing a tough exterior and by learning how to box. He was preternaturally handsome, and women black and white were strongly attracted to him. He became rich and famous, and he had to hide in his expensive house to maintain his solitude. Finally, like all people with extraordinary artistic gifts, he was an outsider because of his genius. (xiii–xiv)

Yudkin argues that Davis "was an outsider because of his genius", yet, as Marta Bucholc points out when analysing Norbert Elias and John L. Scotson's study *The Established and the Outsiders*, "which is a common tenet of sociological theories of social exclusion: outsiders are made and not born" (Bucholc 2013). Moreover, Elias (1994) notes, the key to outsider status is reaction to the established. The established and outsiders compete for power in two spheres: the first in the real space and time of a specific "dispute territory", and the second in the symbolic domain, through a process which Elias divides into three distinct stages: *encounter*, *surprise* and *acceptance*. These stages can be identified in a number of artistic domains, including music, reflected in the way that many composers and musicians have routed their artistic careers. As Paul Tingen notes, Miles Davis was a musical provocateur at the forefront of constant musical innovations, which "inevitably carries a degree of threat and risk to the status quo" (2001, 11). However, Davis' *outsiderness* can also be perceived as an act of resistance or an effort to confront the static binary oppositions between black and white, addressing the challenges that all Black artists faced in 20th-century US Jim Crow society.[10]

[10] 'Jim Crow' was a series of state, local, and county statutes, as well as unwritten codes of conduct, which evolved into a restrictive, punitive system of widespread segregation of the African American communities in the United States. For further discussion on this topic, see Lewis and Lewis (2009).

An African American artist growing up in a segregated society, Davis can be understood—to borrow Patricia Hill Collins' concept—as an *outsider-within* because "under conditions of social injustice, the outsider-within location describes a particular knowledge/power relationship, one of gaining knowledge about or of a dominant group without gaining the full power accorded to members of that group" (1986, 6). His behaviour and aptitude may also result from a willingness to embrace difference, manifesting in a strategy of resistance against discrimination and prejudice.[11] As a consequence, Davis' personality, his artistic innovations and his capacity to challenge jazz aesthetics are still consistently debated worldwide.

This chapter situates itself within a body of work referred to as new jazz studies, which uses a multidisciplinary approach to promote an understanding of jazz and its distinct actors within specific cultural contexts. This particular case is located outside US borders, focusing on a single country and on a specific jazz artist. It addresses Miles Davis' *on*- and *off*-stage presence in Portugal and how that was mediated by the national press. This chapter borrows Elias' three stages and is divided into three sections, bookended by this introduction and a brief concluding section. The first section describes the context surrounding Davis' performance at the first International Cascais Jazz Festival. The second examines the artist's concert in a Lisbon with a very different social-political context. The third discusses his last visit to the country, only a few months before he passed away.[12] All the sections begin with *DownBeat* international annual readers' and critics' polls from the period prior to the Portuguese visit. This helps to contextualise Davis' artistic career by identifying the awards he received internationally, while also highlighting the strong influence of *DownBeat* on jazz critics. Although Davis' first appearance in Portugal received international attention, this was not the case for the other two (Carner 1996, 249).[13]

[11] Aspects of Davis' conduct, such as violent and abusive behavior toward women, should nonetheless be deeply condemned. For further discussion on this topic, see Carby (1998).

[12] Miles Davis died on 28 September 1991, in Santa Monica, California, at the age of 65 and was buried at Woodlawn Cemetery in the Bronx, along with one of his trumpets (Cole 2007).

[13] The archival and bibliographical research behind this chapter has uncovered fresh material in the form of interviews and documentaries associated with Davis' visits. For further discussion on this topic in the Portuguese language, see Santos (2007).

Encounter: "Miles Davis Electrified the Cascais' Audience"[14]

August 1970[15]

DownBeat 18th International Jazz Critics' Poll

Record of the Year: 1st place, Miles Davis, *Bitches Brew* (Columbia)[16]
Trumpet: 1st place, Miles Davis
Composer: 5th place, Miles Davis
Combo: 1st place, Miles Davis

December 1970[17]

DownBeat 35th Annual Readers Poll

Jazzman of the Year: 1st place, Miles Davis
Jazz Album of the Year: 1st place, Miles Davis, *Bitches Brew* (Columbia)
Pop Album of the Year: 9th place, Miles Davis, *Bitches Brew* (Columbia)
Jazz Combo: 1st place, Miles Davis
Trumpet: 1st place, Miles Davis
Arranger: 10th place, Miles Davis

August 1971[18]

DownBeat 19th International Jazz Critics Poll

Record of the Year: 2nd place, Miles Davis, *Jack Johnson* (Columbia)
Trumpet: 2nd place, Miles Davis
Jazz Combo: 1st place, Miles Davis
Electric Jazz Group: 2nd place, Miles Davis

Miles Davis' Portuguese debut took place on 20 November 1971, at the first International Cascais Jazz Festival, which was billed as the 'Newport Jazz Festival in Europe'. This coincided with one of the most significant periods of his artistic career; as Morgenstern observes, "1970, like 1969, was the year of Miles Davis" (1970, 15). Nonetheless, "1970 was a momentous and turbulent

[14] See original text in List 1, quote No. 14.
[15] *DownBeat* 54, no. 8 (August 1970).
[16] That year, Davis also won his second Record of the Year with *In a Silent Way* (Columbia). *DownBeat* 54, no. 8 (August 1970).
[17] *DownBeat* 37, no. 26 (December 24, 1970).
[18] *DownBeat* 55, no. 8 (August 1971).

year for Miles", too, as he was arrested in March of that year and spent a night in jail (Carr 1982, 192).

Davis received the highest honours from the Cascais Jazz '71 organisers on his arrival in Portugal, and expectations among the press and fans were high. At the time, Cascais was a prestigious and upper-class seaside village, some 30 kilometres west of Lisbon, also known as the 'Portuguese Riviera', and the festival took place in a sports arena called the Pavilhão Dramático de Cascais on 20 and 21 November.[19] It should be clarified that this was not actually the first Portuguese international jazz festival.[20] The first one was billed as the International Jazz Festival of Queima das Fitas and took place at the Teatro Avenida in the city of Coimbra on 3 May 1967; it was followed by a second international jazz festival in the same venue on 27 April 1968.[21]

Nevertheless, Cascais Jazz '71 was the first time that jazz had been performed before such a large audience in Portugal—over 10,000 people in one venue.[22] It brought together prestigious international artists who would provide some momentous performances: notably, a stirring set by the Ornette Coleman Quartet, forever notorious for Charlie Haden's inflammatory on-stage remarks that led to his arrest.[23] Also appearing were the Giants of Jazz, featuring Dizzy Gillespie, Thelonious Monk, Art Blakey, Sonny Stitt, Kai Winding and Al McKibbon; Phil Woods & His European Rhythm Machine, featuring Gordon Beck, Ron Mathewson and Daniel Humair; and Dexter Gordon, Brazilian pianist Marcos Resende,[24] Saheb Sarbib,[25] and the Portuguese drummer Manuel Jorge Veloso.[26] Among the home-grown talent was 'The Bridge' Quartet, led by Portuguese saxophonist Rão Kyao and featuring Kevin Hoidale, Saheb Sarbib and Adrien Ransy.

[19] The contacts that Luís Villas-Boas established with international festival programmers, in particular with George Wein, provided the leverage to get the Cascais Jazz Festival off the ground five years after a failed attempt to organise the first International Jazz Festival "Costa do Sol" in June 1966.

[20] After a first failed attempt (see previous note), Luís Villas-Boas, in partnership with Hugo Lourenço, Carlos Fino, and the *fado* singer João Braga, in November 1971 succeeded in putting on an international jazz festival.

[21] For further discussion on this topic, see Cravinho (2016a).

[22] For further discussion on this topic, see Cravinho (2022b).

[23] For further discussion on this topic, see Cravinho (2017).

[24] Marcos Resende (1947–2020), was a Brazilian pianist, composer, and bandleader, active in the Portuguese jazz and jazz-rock fusion scenes between 1967 and 1975. For further discussion on this topic, see Cravinho (in print).

[25] Saheb Sarbib was a double bass player born and raised in Portugal as Jean Henri Sarbib (b. 1944) of French Algerian descent. He worked in Europe before moving to New York City in 1977. His father, Roger Sarbib, was a French pianist involved in the Portuguese music scene in the 1940s and 1950s.

[26] Manuel Jorge Veloso (1937–2019), was a Portuguese jazz drummer, composer, critic and television producer. For further discussion on this topic, see Cravinho (2022b).

Figure 9.1 A screenshot of Miles Davis' RTP broadcast (Cascais, November 1971).

To launch the festival, the stage was set for the Ornette Coleman Quartet. However, fully aware of the political and social context of Portugal at that time—and of the expectations of the festival not just as a showcase for contemporary international jazz but also as a space in which anticolonial attitudes could be expressed—Davis chose to make a stand. For reasons fully understood only by the artist himself, he refused to follow any of the other acts.[27] As a consequence, the on-stage setup suddenly had to be changed to accommodate the Miles Davis Septet.[28] The ensuing long delay was reported in the next day's press: "[A]fter changes in the order of the presentation 'imposed' by visiting musicians, the show started".[29] Surviving television footage, recorded on-site by RTP,[30] reveals Miles Davis being introduced by Luís Villas-Boas with the following: "I have no words . . . because this is absolutely indescribable! Let us hear Miles Davis!"[31]

Portuguese jazz critic, pianist, composer and free improviser Jorge Lima Barreto described the performance: "On the first night, with the pavilion completely packed [with over 10,000 people], Miles Davis' arrival was eagerly anticipated. When he came on stage, the effect was brutal. Miles proved to be a master of stagecraft, and was wearing green tight-fitting satin pants,

[27] For further discussion on this topic, see Cravinho (2017).

[28] The Miles Davis Septet featured Gary Bartz, Keith Jarrett, Michael Henderson, Charles Don Alias, James Mtume Foreman and Ndugu Leon Chancler.

[29] *R&T* 785 (November 27): 24. See original text in List 1, quote No. 2.

[30] For further discussion on this topic, see Cravinho (2022b).

[31] *Rewind: Cascais Jazz '71* (Part 2). See original text in List 1, quote No. 3.

a black shirt, and pale sunglasses. The ensemble kicked in immediately; the astonished audience could not believe the power, the visceral strength, of the jazz they were hearing. People were excited and out of control . . . and the Miles Davis Septet closed with the place in delirium" (1971, 7).[32]

Off-stage, ever since his arrival at Lisbon Airport and throughout his stay, Davis was constantly arguing with everyone around him, including the festival organisers. Bernardo Moreira, a former president of the Hot Clube de Portugal, recalls, "The guy [Miles Davis] demanded as part of his contract to be transported in a Rolls Royce driven by a white chauffeur. However, when [Luís] Villas-Boas [one of the festival organisers] presented him with a Rolls Royce, driven by a white man, like us [i.e., with brown hair and brown eyes], the guy was furious. Because, for him, a white chauffeur was blond and blue-eyed . . . and there are not many of those in Portugal".[33] The organisers tried to explain to Davis that a white chauffeur with blue eyes was not to be found: they were a rarity in a southern European country like Portugal. But that didn't appease him. Another member of the festival organisation team, João Braga (2017), who picked Miles up from the airport, recalls the artist's provocative banter from the moment they set off: "Once we had left the airport and started down towards the 'marginal' [the bank of the River Tagus], he started up with 'racist' jokes whenever he saw a black man passing by. When we arrived in Caxias, there was a building . . . with some black people working on the construction, and he turns to me and—by now I was already upset by his 'racist' jokes—he says, 'Look, you people in Portugal—do you still import slaves from Cape Verde to work in construction?' ".[34] Braga recalls his response: " 'No, we do something else,' I replied. Miles reacted by saying, 'Oh yes? Do you pay them?' I replied, 'Oh, we pay them! Look, we pay them so much that those guys [the blacks] leave here [Portugal] and go to America to become jazz musicians!' Miles Davis burst out laughing and that was the end of his 'racist' jokes".[35]

Another of Davis' demands of the festival organisation was to have a sparring partner in his luxury suite.[36] According to one of the organisers, they hired a young boxer for the task. However, after a while, the young lad apparently did not enjoy being punched by a Black guy and began to retaliate. He

[32] See original text in List 1, quote No. 4.
[33] *Rewind: Cascais Jazz '71* (Part 2). See original text in List 1, quote No. 5.
[34] See original text in List 1, quote No. 6.
[35] See original text in List 1, quote No. 7.
[36] For further discussion about Davis' involvement with boxing, see DeMichael (1969).

was immediately fired. The organisers had to find someone who was willing to be punched and wouldn't fight back. Their solution was to hire a retired boxer (Santos 2007).

Another off-stage drama during Davis' first visit was his need for *profaminas* (pharmaceutical amphetamines). Again, João Braga tells the story:

> He asked me to get him some profaminas. So, I talked to some doctors, friends of mine, about getting profaminas. They said, "Look, João, be careful here!" [And I replied] "Look, they're not for me," [so they said], "OK, but be careful because this is something that can damage the heart." They got me four tubes. I managed to get four tubes, like this [makes a gesture to indicate the size of the tube] with pills. And then, when I got to the hotel, to the suite, Miles's girlfriend or "whoever" [she was] was there, so I asked, "Where's Miles?" . . . [and she] pointed "He's over there!" But there was only the closet there. I opened the closet door, and he was in the closet all curled up . . . and I told him, "Look, I've got your profaminas." And he took hold of a tube and started on them. I was very impressed: that thing that was bad for your heart, he started doing this [mimes putting a pill in his mouth], like swallowing one every second, and then he turns to me, "Do you want some? Want some? Want some?" And I said, "No thanks, thanks, but I don't use it."[37]

The Portuguese press also had things to say about Davis' behaviour:

> Mr. Davis, who had spent the afternoon meditating, locked in his wardrobe, while outside a magnificent Pontiac with chauffeur had been waiting for him since 9 a.m. (the organisation could not get the Rolls Royce required in the contract), was threatening not to play [at the festival] at the slightest setback. And there were setbacks aplenty, because Miles Davis is the kind of prodigy that unleashes them. Since he arrived at his suite in the Palácio, the phone has not stopped ringing. At all hours (the musician does not distinguish between night and day). Davis issued orders and countermands to his colleagues, "massacred" his agent, and requested the organisers' presence. From a doctor to a young Portuguese blonde, who escorted him, Mr. Miles Davis had everything.[38]

[37] *Rewind: Cascais Jazz '71* (Part 2). See original text in List 1, quote No. 8.
[38] *Mundo da Canção* 24 (November 1971): 12. See original text in List 1, quote No. 9.

We must pause here to frame the visits of African American artists to Portugal at this period within the context of a society dealing with a long, devastating independence/colonial war in its former African colonies. Many of the country's young people were in favour of a more open society and firmly rejected the ongoing war in Africa, and to them any outrageous behaviour could be interpreted as hip.[39] Others, however, particularly those positioned within the country's dominant conservative colonial mentality, would not hesitate to condemn any behaviour by Black people (artists or otherwise) that they considered transgressive.[40]

The music of the Miles Davis Septet also sent shock waves among jazz fans. As the Portuguese double bass player and former chairman of Portugal's Hot Club Bernardo Moreira explains, Portuguese aficionados in those days found it difficult to buy or listen to his latest albums because of the country's isolation.[41] Many were taken by surprise by the new sonorities: "When Miles start[ed] moving from jazz onto a more 'rock' circuit . . . those records took a long time to get here [Portugal]. . . . We heard 'Miles Davis is coming,' but nobody knew what he was going to play. The guy starts with that sonic brutality . . . 'what is this, man?' "[42] Bernardo Moreira went on to say that the Miles Davis Septet surprised the audience with a powerful, unexpected rock-fusion sound: "[I]t had a tremendous impact."[43] However, not all Portuguese critics were so positive about the new music. Jazz critic Monteiro e Costa, for example, wrote the following: "The trumpeter/star/leader Miles Davis, considering everything we know about him (since those distant days of 'Billie's Bounce'), gave the impression that he was performing music that is not strictly his. . . . Miles Davis was the musician that I found least interesting. . . . Because that's exactly what I thought; all the (musical) history that I perceive in this excellent trumpeter makes me want to see him forgo the journeys that he took last Saturday night (and see him moving away from commercialism, away from his innocent desire to please 'the kids'? . . .)" (1971, 9).[44] Indeed, to most of the youngsters experiencing jazz for the first time at Cascais Jazz '71, the Miles Davis Septet was a tremendous sonic experience. The magazine *Mundo da Canção* published a photograph of Davis on its cover and

[39] see Sardiea 2008: 77.

[40] For further discussion on this topic, see Cravinho (2016b, 2018b).

[41] Bernardo Moreira (1932–2022), or Binau, as he was known within the Portuguese jazz scene, was a civil engineer by training, but his name is associated above all with jazz, as an amateur double bass player and former chairman of Hot Clube de Portugal.

[42] *Rewind: Cascais Jazz '71* (Part 2). See original text in List 1, quote No. 10.

[43] *Rewind: Cascais Jazz '71* (Part 2). See original text in List 1, quote No. 11.

[44] See original text in List 1, quote No. 12.

dedicated several pages to the festival, including two pages of press clippings about the event, and talked of "a whole generation of 'pop music' applauding Miles Davis, a 1940s trumpeter, undeniably more identified with 'pop' than with his famous excerpts from 'Round Midnight.' "[45] In the daily newspaper *Diário de Lisboa*, José Jorge Letria claimed that "Miles Davis electrified the Cascais' audience" (1971, 7).[46] It was no surprise to Portuguese critics and aficionados that in the *DownBeat* 36th Annual Readers' Poll Miles Davis was voted Jazzman of the Year for the third time running.[47]

Surprise: "Miles Davis's Jazz Stunned the Coliseum"[48]

August 1987[49]

DownBeat 35th Annual International Critics' Poll

Record of the Year: 3rd place, Miles Davis, *Tutu* (Warner Bros.)

Electric Jazz Group: 2nd place, Miles Davis

Trumpet: 3rd place, Miles Davis

Pop/Rock: 2nd place, Miles Davis

December 1987[50]

DownBeat 53rd Annual Readers' Poll

Jazz Musician of the Year: 5th place, Miles Davis

Jazz Album of the Year: 3rd place, Miles Davis, *Tutu* (Warner Bros.)

Pop/Rock Album of the Year: 4th place, Miles Davis, *Tutu* (Warner Bros.)

Pop/Rock Musician of the Year: 6th place, Miles Davis

Electric Jazz Group: 2nd place, Miles Davis

Pop/Rock Group: 6th place, Miles Davis

Trumpet: 2nd place, Miles Davis

[45] *Mundo da Canção*, 24 (November 1971): 12. See original text in List 1, quote No. 13.

[46] See original text in List 1, quote No. 14.

[47] In December 1971 *DownBeat* released its 36th Annual Readers' Poll: Jazzman of the Year, Miles Davis placed first; Jazz Album of the Year, Miles Davis, *Jack Johnson* (Columbia) placed third and *Miles Davis at Fillmore* (Columbia) placed ninth; Jazz Combo, Miles Davis placed first; Trumpet, Miles Davis placed first. *DownBeat* 38, no. 22 (December 23, 1971): 15–20.

[48] See original text in List 1, quote No. 15.

[49] *DownBeat* 54, no. 8 (August 1987).

[50] *DownBeat* 54, no. 12 (December 1987).

August 1988[51]
DownBeat 36th Annual International Critics' Poll
Reissue of the Year: 6th place, Miles Davis, *Chronicle* (Prestige)
Electric Jazz Group: 2nd place, Miles Davis
Trumpet: 4th place, Miles Davis

December 1988[52]
DownBeat 53rd Annual Readers' Poll
Jazzman of the Year: 6th place, Miles Davis
Pop/Rock Musician of the Year: 4th place, Miles Davis
Electric Jazz Group: 2nd place, Miles Davis
Pop/Rock Group: 3rd place, Miles Davis
Trumpet: 2nd place, Miles Davis

Miles Davis returned to Portugal in April 1989, 18 years after his first visit, this time to begin his European tour at the Portuguese capital, Lisbon, at the Coliseu do Recreios.[53] A few days before his arrival in the country, the newspaper *Se7e* (Seven), ran a two-page article by José Duarte, in which the Portuguese jazz critic billed it as the must-see jazz concert of the year in Portugal:[54] "On April 2nd, the Coliseu dos Recreios plays host to a famous figure of jazz. Nothing more, nothing less than Miles Davis himself. The trumpeter is gifting Portugal a unique concert, the first of a long tour. The Coliseu show is of particular interest because Miles Davis is accompanied by a new group consisting of saxophonist Kenny Garrett, Japanese keyboardist Kei Akagi and Dutch bassist Benny Rietveld".[55]

Once again, Miles Davis' new sonorities were not equally well received among jazz critics. On 2 April, the daily newspaper *Diário de Noticias* published an article by Monteiro e Costa titled 'Miles Packed in Plastic Will Be at the Coliseu Today' (Costa 1989, 23).[56] He began by warning Portuguese fans, "[W]e will have at the Coliseu tonight a Miles Davis wrapped in the plastic of electronics. Try to focus exclusively on the voice of the trumpet. Maybe you can still have a great time" (23).[57] He went on to say, "Miles Davis

[51] *DownBeat* 55, no. 8 (August 1988).
[52] *DownBeat* 55, no. 12 (December 1988).
[53] Unfortunately, no mention of this concert can be found in Miles Davis concert chronologies.
[54] *Se7e* 564 (March 29, 1989): 32. See original text in List 1, quote No. 16.
[55] *Se7e* 564 (March 29, 1989): 32. See original text in List 1, quote No. 17.
[56] See original text in List 1, quote No. 18.
[57] See original text in List 1, quote No. 19.

did not settle for the prospect of a bleak existence (compared to the success that jazz achieved in previous decades). He decided to appear on front pages, continue to win polls, and make a lot of money. He then resorted to rock scenarios (with guaranteed success), electronic techniques and promotional campaigns by big publishers. Even his naturally aggressive temperament has been useful in helping sell his image to the new (broad) audience he is conquering" (23).[58]

But other, less conservative opinions circulated in the Portuguese press, too: in the *Diário de Noticias*, Anabela Martins da Cruz called Miles Davis "the jazz 'warrior'" (1989, 10);[59] in the *Correio da Manhã*, Seia de Matos wrote of "a genius on the stage of the Coliseum" (1989, 16);[60] and in *Expresso* magazine, the jazz critic Raul Vaz Bernardo celebrated that "the genius is reborn from the ashes" (1989, 66R).[61]

On the afternoon of the concert, a press conference took place at the Hotel Tivoli, attended by countless national reporters as well as some foreign ones. Davis arrived on time, and the press conference kicked off with a Portuguese reporter asking the trumpeter, "Is jazz black or white?" Without saying a word, Davis stood up and left. The press conference was over (Santos 2007). The artist spent the rest of his visit painting in his room without speaking to any journalists. According to the press, the Lisbon concert was about two hours long, and the repertoire was based mainly on the *Tutu* album (1986).[62] About the concert, Monteiro e Costa wrote:

> Miles Davis is still breathing under a pile of debris.
>
> No surprises, on the night of the Coliseum . . . Miles' trumpet intervened, here and there, miraculously detached from the context, as if the memory of Wynton Kelly's piano and 'Philly' Jo Jones' drums were still in our ears. . . . Miles' skinny body, which moves deftly atop the five-centimetres-high soles of his shoes, left the stage before the end of the concert, never to return, even for the applause and final encore demands. Is this how you win the public over?[63]

[58] See original text in List 1, quote No. 20.

[59] See original text in List 1, quote No. 21.

[60] See original text in List 1, quote No. 22.

[61] See original text in List 1, quote No. 23. In the same magazine was a four-page biographical essay on Miles Davis by the Portuguese jazz critic António Curvelo (1989, 67–70R) titled 'As etapas de uma vida' (The Stages of a Life).

[62] On stage at the 1989 Lisbon concert with Miles Davis were Kenny Garrett (saxophone), Kei Akagi (keyboards), Benny Rietveld (electric bass), Joe 'Foley' McCreary (lead electric bass), John Bigham (electronic percussion), and Ricky Wellman (drums).

[63] *Diário de Notícias*, April 5, 1989. See original text in List 1, quote No. 24.

Striking a different note, Rui Eduardo Paes, in an article titled 'O Príncipe das Trevas' (The Prince of Darkness), celebrated the artist and his music:[64] "If the prince of darkness who troubles our consciousness exists, he is called Miles Davis and plays the trumpet. Like the devil in the holy books, this 'black angel'—proudly, because 'black is beautiful'—is always out in front, leading the crowd: 'he is the number one'" (1989, 23).[65] The notion of Miles Davis as the Prince of Darkness was not new. As Ian Carr has observed, it arose in 1967: "[T]he title of the piece on *The Sorcerer* [written by Wayne Shorter], and the sleeve note made a direct connection between Miles and the album title" (1982, 184). It was deeply connected with the 1970 album *Bitches Brew*, an album which, according to Carr, had "a strong feeling of invocation, of seeking for the state of possession—which is so closely connected with the rapt state of inspired improvisation" (184). In reusing this epithet in 1989, Paes was celebrating Davis' personality and artistic career but in a provocative way—as revealed by his description of Davis as being "irresistible as sin" (1989, 23).[66]

Acceptance: 'With His Back to the Audience, Miles Dominates the Coliseum'[67]

August 1989[68]

DownBeat 37th Annual International Critics' Poll

Reissue of the Year: 2nd place, Miles Davis, *Ascenseur pour L'échafaud*, (Fontana/Polygram)

Trumpet: 5th place, Miles Davis

Electric Jazz Group: 1st place, Miles Davis

Pop/Rock: 2nd place, Miles Davis

December 1989[69]

DownBeat 54th Annual Readers' Poll

Jazz Musician of the Year: 2nd place, Miles Davis

[64] The Rui Eduardo Paes article had as its subtitle 'Miles Davis: "The Number One", Yesterday at the Coliseu' (Paes 1989, 23).

[65] See original text in List 1, quote No. 25

[66] See original text in List 1, quote No. 26.

[67] See original text in List 1, quote No. 27.

[68] *DownBeat* 56, no. 8 (August 1989).

[69] *DownBeat* 56, no. 12 (December 1989).

Jazz Album of the Year: 2nd place, Miles Davis, *Amandla* (Warner Bros.)
Pop/Rock Album of the Year: 2nd place, Miles Davis, *Amandla* (Warner Bros.)
Pop/Rock Musician of the Year: 2nd place, Miles Davis
Electric Jazz Group: 1st place, Miles Davis
Trumpet: 2nd place, Miles Davis

August 1990[70]
DownBeat 38th Annual International Critics' Poll
Jazz Artist of the Year: 5th place, Miles Davis
Jazz Album of the Year: 3rd place, Miles Davis, *Aura* (Columbia)
Trumpet: 4th place, Miles Davis
Rock Group: 2nd place, Miles Davis

December 1990[71]
DownBeat 55th Annual Readers' Poll
Jazz Album of the Year: 1st place, Miles Davis, *Aura* (Columbia)
Jazz Musician of the Year: 3rd place, Miles Davis
Electric Jazz Group: 2nd place, Miles Davis
Rock Group: 3rd place, Miles Davis
Trumpet: 3rd place, Miles Davis

Miles Davis' final appearance in Portugal was in March 1991, when he gave two concerts: the first in Porto on 16 March and the second in Lisbon on the following day.[72] The northern newspaper *Jornal de Notícias* announced his arrival:

> Miles Davis: A living legend in Porto.
>
> For the first time in Porto, the North American trumpeter Miles Davis is undoubtedly a moment not to be missed.[73]

Davis was given a pop star reception, and both concerts were hugely successful. All the same, he spent all his time in his luxury suite, painting, having

[70] *DownBeat* 57, no. 8 (August 1990).
[71] *DownBeat* 57, no. 12 (December 1990).
[72] For further discussion on the development of Porto's jazz scene, see Cravinho (2022a).
[73] *Jornal de Notícias* 287 (March 16, 1991): 59. See original text in List 1, quote No. 28.

no contact with any journalists or reporters. The newspaper *Público*, in its 16 March edition, dedicated its cover to Miles—with a large colour photograph by Luis Ramos—and ran the following text:[74] "His long career has made him into a myth: first in the jazz world, then in the pop-rock universe. Duke Ellington compared him to Picasso, the critic W. A. Brower spoke of him as a 'male jazz Greta Garbo'; others have called him 'the precursor of American music.' Although some have designated him as the 'anti-jazz model.' Now back in Portugal, where he played in 1971 and 1989. Miles Davis is in Porto today and Lisbon tomorrow for two unique concerts".[75] In the same edition, journalist Maria Augusta Gonçalves asked two prominent Portuguese jazz critics, Luís Villas-Boas and José Duarte, along with the *fado* singer João Braga, about Davis' music and personality. All three agreed that "when you talk about Miles Davis, you are talking about more than half of the history of jazz" (1991, 6).[76]

According to the national press, Davis used 20,000 watts of sound and 180,000 watts of light in both concerts. Critics said this was no longer jazz but more like pop-rock. Coverage in the Portuguese press far surpassed that of his previous concerts, and the television company RTP broadcast his 1989 Paris concert for the benefit of those who could not get a ticket for either performance.[77]

Halfway through the Porto concert, he simply walked off the stage and went back to his hotel—according to the organisers—claiming that it was too cold on stage. His band continued playing without him for over an hour.[78] After this incident, the organisers of the Lisbon concert, wishing to avoid a repeat, brought several heaters onto the stage (Santos 2007). About the Porto appearance, journalist António Barroso wrote, "A figure loved by some, controversial for others. Miles Davis did not say a word during the concert. He paid little attention to the intense applause and played most of the time with his back to the audience. 'In such a worshipful scenario as this, it resembles a Mass being celebrated by [the archbishop Marcel] Lefebvre'" (1991, 52).[79]

[74] Several pages inside the issue were dedicated to Miles Davis as well.

[75] *Público*, March 16, 1991. See original text in List 1, quote No. 29.

[76] See original text in List 1, quote No. 30.

[77] *TV Guia* 632 (March 1991): 17.

[78] At both the Porto and Lisbon 1991 concerts, Davis was accompanied by Kenny Garrett (saxophone and flute), Deron Johnson (keyboards), Richard Patterson (electric basses), Joe 'Foley' McCreary (lead bass), and Ricky Wellman (drums).

[79] See original text in List 1, quote No. 31.

In Lisbon, Davis came on stage 20 minutes late and played very little, spending much of his time walking from one end of the stage to the other, holding up a card with the name of the musician who had just finished a solo. Journalist Rui Branco, in an article titled 'Miles: O Cometa Envelhecido' (Miles: The Aged Comet), observed, "Miles Davis walked around the Coliseum stage like a comet . . . an aged one. The erosion of time spares no one, not even a genius like the one we just had the opportunity of seeing and hearing (but always very quietly). . . . Miles was over an hour on the Coliseu stage, and his 'cool' sound, despite its lack of power, did not fail to thrill, if only for the simple reason that we know this will be the last opportunity to see him live" (1991, 51).[80] It was indeed the last time that Portuguese fans were to see Miles Davis on stage. In Santa Monica, California, on 28 September 1991, and announced across the world, the comet that was Miles was finally extinguished after 65 years. Later that year, the French magazine *Jazz Hot: La revue international du jazz* dedicated its November 1991 issue to the artist, with his photograph on the cover under the headline 'Miles in the Sky'.[81] *DownBeat* also ran a special issue, in December 1991, featuring a colour photograph and the headline 'Miles: The Final Bow'.[82]

Coda

August 1991[83]

DownBeat 39th Annual International Critics' Poll

Electric Jazz Group: 3rd place, Miles Davis

Trumpet: 7th place, Miles Davis

December 1991[84]

DownBeat 54th Annual Readers' Poll

Jazz Musician of the Year: 2nd place, Miles Davis

Jazz Album of the Year: 2nd place, Miles Davis, *Amandla* (Warner Bros.)

[80] See original text in List 1, quote No. 32.

[81] *Jazz Hot: La revue international du jazz* 483 (November 1991).

[82] *DownBeat* 58, no. 12 (December 1991). It was not their first special issue dedicated to the artist. Two previous Miles Davis special issues were *DownBeat* 55, no. 10 (October 1988) and *DownBeat* 55, no. 11 (November 1988).

[83] *DownBeat* 58, no. 8 (August 1991).

[84] *DownBeat* 58, no. 12 (December 1991).

Pop/Rock Album of the Year: 2nd place, Miles Davis, *Amandla* (Warner Bros.)
Pop/Rock Musician of the Year: 2nd place, Miles Davis
Electric Jazz Group: 1st place, Miles Davis
Trumpet: 2nd place, Miles Davis

Setting this chapter's narrative exclusively outside the US was entirely intentional. It represents an opportunity to situate Miles Davis' presence in Portugal as part of a broader story. This is partly because he was an agent of globalisation. However, like Merlin Black in Walter Ellis' novel *Prince of Darkness*, Davis was also a deep, controversial individual.[85] Before the first *encounter* of November 1971, the Portuguese press introduced him as follows: "The son of black, millionaire parents, Miles Davis brings together the most extraordinary contradictions. Racial and class prejudices make him the most conservative and, to some extent, the most evolved of the musicians of his time. It is this ambiguity that makes him one of the most discussed characters. Unsympathetic, spoiled; when he plays, his weak points are forgotten. And the crowd cheers, deliriously, to the sound of his trumpet".[86] Artistically, he was perceived as a sort of dormant comet, to borrow Branco's analogy. Davis showed scant if any interest in his past music, and his attention was almost entirely focused on the future; his efforts in this regard were manifested by his working with and encouraging younger musicians and bringing together both jazz and other musical genres and styles. To use Leonard Feather's description, he was "black, volatile, rebellious and resilient as jazz itself" (2009, 130). Miles Davis was a black comet that shot across four Portuguese concerts in the space of 20 years.[87]

List 1: Original Quotes in Portuguese

Quote No. 1: "Miles Davis electrizou a plateia de Cascais".

Quote No. 2: "Após as alterações de ordem de apresentação 'impostas' pelos músicos visitantes, iniciou-se o espectáculo".

[85] *Prince of Darkness* is a work of jazz fiction inspired by the music and life of Miles Davis. See Ellis (1998).

[86] *Mundo da Canção* 24 (November 1971): 12. See original text in List 1, quote No. 32.

[87] These concluding comments about his artistry are not in any way intended to invalidate strong condemnations of his physical and psychological abuse of women throughout his life. As Carner stated, "I'd loathe any muhfukuh who violate women the way he did. . . . Miles may have swung like a champion but on that score, he went out like a roach" (1996, 236).

Quote No. 3: "Eu não tenho palavras . . . porque isso e absolutamente indescritível! Vamos ouvir, Miles Davis!"

Quote No. 4: "Na primeira noite, com o pavilhão completamente cheio, aguardou-se a chegada de Miles Davis. Entrado este em cena, o choque foi brutal. Miles revelou-se um mestre de encenação: vestia calças de cetim verde, moldadas ao corpo, camisa preta, óculos claros. O conjunto actou imediatamente; o publico, estupefacto não acreditava na potência, na força visceral do jazz que ouvia. As pessoas agitavam-se descontroladas. . . . E o Miles Davis Septet acabou em delírio".

Quote No. 5: "O gajo [Miles Davis] exigiu no [seu] contrato ser transportado num Rolls Royce e com chauffeur branco. E quando o [Luís] Villas-Boas lhe apresentou um Rolls Royce, guiado por um branco, como nós [cabelo e olhos castanhos], o gajo [Davis] ficou danado. Porque para ele um chauffeur branco era loiro e de olhos azuis . . . coisa que em Portugal, não há muitos".

Quote No. 6: "Quando saímos do aeroporto e começámos a descer os acessos em direção à Marginal, ele sempre que via passar um preto entrava com piadas racistas. Às tantas, em Caxias, havia ali um prédio . . . e andavam lá uns tipos africanos nas obras e ele vira-se para mim—e eu já estava por aqui com as piadas racistas—'Olha, vocês cá em Portugal ainda importam escravos de Cabo Verde para as obras?' "

Quote No. 7: " 'Não fazemos outra coisa,' respondi-lhe. 'Aí sim? E pagam-lhes?' 'Pagamos-lhes, olhe pagamos-lhes tanto que os gajos piram-se daqui [Portugal] e vão para a América e tornam-se músicos de jazz!' O Miles Davis desatou a rir-se às gargalhadas e a partir daí as suas piadas racistas acabaram".

Quote No. 8: "Ele [Miles Davis] pediu-me para lhe arranjar profaminas. E eu fui falar a médicos meus amigos para me arranjarem profaminas. Eles disseram, 'ó pá, João toma cuidado com isso,' [e eu respondi] 'ó pá, não é para mim' [eles disseram], 'está bem, mas toma cuidado, pois isso é uma coisa que pode fazer mal ao coração.' Arranjaram quatro tubos, consegui arranjar quatro tubos, assim [fazendo um gesto para descrever o formato do tubo] com comprimidos. E depois quando cheguei ao hotel, à suite, estava lá a tal namorada ou '*or ever*' do Miles, e disse-lhe 'onde é que está o Miles?' . . . [e ela] apontou 'está ali.' E ali, era só o armário. Abri a porta do armário, e ele [Miles Davis] estava dentro do armário todo enroladinho, (ele tinha uma voz assim enroucada) [*sic*], e eu disse-lhe 'olha, tens aqui as tuas profaminas.' E ele pegou num tubo e começou, fiquei impressionadíssimo, a tal coisa que fazia mal ao coração, começou assim [fazendo o gesto de colocar um comprimido na boca], assim de segundo em segundo a engolir uma, e depois volta-se para mim '*You want some*? *you want some*? you want some?' E eu disse-lhe '*No thanks*, obrigadinho, não tomo disso.' "

Quote No. 9: "O sr. Davis, que passara a tarde meditando, fechado no guarda-fato, enquanto cá fora um magnífico Pontiac com 'chauffeur' aguardava a sua saída desde as 9 horas da manhã (a organização não consegui arranjar o Rolls Royce exigido no contracto), ameaçava não tocar [no festival] à menor contrariedade. E as contrariedades não faltaram, pois Miles Davis é prodígio a desencadeá-las. Desde a sua chegada, o telefone da 'suite' do Palácio não parou. A todas as horas (o músico não distingue a noite do dia). Davis deu ordens e contra-ordens aos seus companheiros, massacrou o seu agente, e requisitou a presença dos organizadores. Desde um médico a uma jovem loura portuguesa que lhe serviu de companhia, teve de tudo, o sr. Miles Davis".

Quote No. 10: "Quando o Miles começa a sair do circuito do jazz para o circuito mais a rock'alhado . . . esses discos demoraram muito tempo a chegar cá [Portugal]. . . . A gente ouve, 'vem cá o Miles Davis', mas ninguém sabe o que ele vai tocar. O gajo começa com aquela brutalidade sonora... 'o que é isto, pá?' "

Quote No. 11: "teve um tremendo impacto".

Quote No. 12: "O trompetista/vedeta/leader Miles Davis, por tudo aquilo que dele conhecemos (desde os tempos longínquos de 'Billie's Bounce') consegui-nos dar a impressão de interpretar uma musica que não é exactamente sua . . . foi

Miles Davis o músico que achei menos interessante. . . . Pois foi exactamente isso que achei; e toda a consideração (musical) que o grande trompetista me parece, leva-me a desejar vê-lo afastado dos itinerários percorridos nesta noite de Sábado (por comercialismo, por desejo inocente de estar junto de 'todos os jovens'? . . .)".

Quote No. 13: "Toda uma geração da 'pop music' a aplaudir Miles Davis, um trompetista dos anos 40, inegàvelmente [*sic*] mais identificado com a 'pop' do que com os seus famosos trechos de 'Round Midnight.' "

Quote No. 14: "Miles Davis electrizou a plateia de Cascais".

Quote No. 15: "Jazz de Miles Davis espantou o Coliseu".

Quote No. 16: "Considerado por alguns especialistas como o concerto de jazz mais desejado do ano".

Quote No. 17: "Dia 2 de Abril o Coliseu dos Recreios, recebe uma figura famosa do jazz. Nada mais, nada menos que Miles Davis. Aquele trompetista dá em Portugal, um concerto único, o primeiro de uma longa digressão. O espectáculo do Coliseu reveste de particular interesse pois Miles Davis apresenta-se acompanhado por um novo grupo, constituído pelo saxofonista Kenny Garrett, o teclista japonês, Kei Akagi e o baixista holandês Benny Rietveld".

Quote No. 18: "Miles embalado em plástico vai estar hoje no Coliseu".

Quote No. 19: "Teremos então esta noite, no Coliseu, um Miles Davis envolvido pelo plástico dos eletrónicos. Tentem concentrar-se exclusivamente na voz do trompete. Talvez consigam momentos óptimos".

Quote No. 20: "Miles Davis não se conformou, porem, com a perspectiva desta existência sombria [do êxito alcançado décadas antes, no âmbito do jazz]. Decidiu figurar nas primeiras páginas, continuar a vencer referendos, ganhar muito dinheiro. Socorreu-se então dos cenários (com sucesso garantido) do rock, das técnicas eletrónicas e das campanhas promocionais das grandes editoras. Até o seu temperamento, naturalmente agressivo, ajudou a vender a imagem junto do novo (amplo) publico que foi conquistando".

Quote No. 21: "o guerreiro do 'jazz.'"

Quote No. 22: "Miles Davis: um génio no palco do Coliseu".

Quote No. 23: "o génio renasce das cinzas".

Quote No. 24: "Miles Davis ainda respira sob um montão de destroços. Nenhuma surpresa, na noite do Coliseu. . . . O trompete de Miles intervinha, aqui e ali, miraculosamente destacado desse contexto, como se conservasse ainda nos ouvidos a memória do piano de Wynton Kelly e da bateria de 'Philly' Jo Jones. . . . E o corpo franzino de Miles, que se desloca habilidosamente sobre os cinco centímetros de altura das solas dos seus sapatos, abandonou o palco antes do termo do concerto, para não regressar mais, nem para os aplausos e exigências finais. Será um método de conquista do público".

Quote No. 25: "Se o príncipe das trevas exista que nos inquiete as consciências, ele chama-se Miles Davis e toca trompete. Como o diabo dos livros sagrados, este 'anjo negro'—e com orgulho, porque '*black is beautiful*'—vai sempre a frente, liderando as hostes: '*he is the number one*".

Quote No. 26: "Irresistível como o pecado".

Quote No. 27: "De costas para o público Miles domina o Coliseu".

Quote No. 28: "Miles Davis: Uma lenda viva no Porto. O trompetista norte-americano, Miles Davis, pela primeira vez no Porto, é sem dúvida um momento a não perder".

Quote No. 29: "Uma longa carreira fez dele um mito, primeiro no mundo do jazz, depois no universo do rock e do pop. Duke Ellington comparou-o a Picasso, o critico W. A. Brower falou dele como 'uma Greta Garbo masculina do jazz,' outros chamaram-lhe 'o precursor da música americana.' Mas também há quem o tenha designado como o 'modelo do anti-jazz.' De regresso a Portugal onde tocou em 1971, e em 1989. Miles Davis está hoje no Porto e amanhã em Lisboa para dois concertos únicos".

Quote No. 30: "falar de Miles Davis é falar de mais de metade da história do jazz".

Quote No. 31: "Figura amada por uns, controversa para outros, Miles Davis não disse uma palavra durante o concerto, pouco ligou aos intensos aplausos e tocou grande parte do tempo de costas voltadas para o publico. 'Com todo este ambiente de culto, isto parece uma missa celebrada por Lefébre.' "

Quote No. 32: "Miles Davis passeou pelo palco do Coliseu como um cometa . . . envelhecido. A erosão do tempo não poupa ninguém, nem que se trate de um génio como aquele que tivemos a oportunidade de ver e ouvir (sempre muito baixinho). . . . Miles esteve mais de uma hora no palco do Coliseu e o seu som 'cool' apesar de falta de potencia, não deixou de emocionar, quanto mais não fosse pela simples razão de sabermos que terá sido a última oportunidade para o vermos ao vivo".

Quote No. 33: "Filho de pais negros, milionários, Miles Davis reúne em si as maiores contradições. Preconceitos raciais e de classe fazem dele o mais conservador e, em certa medida, o mais evoluído dos músicos do seu tempo. É esta ambiguidade que o torna uma das personagens mais discutidas. Antipático, mimado, quando ele toca, os pontos fracos são esquecidos. E a multidão aplaude, delirante, a sonoridade do seu trompete".

References

Barreto, Jorge Lima. 1971. 'Misérias e Grandezas'. *Mundo da Canção* 24: 6–10.

Barroso, António. 1991. 'Miles Davis: Notas e natas de um concerto do Porto'. *Correio da Manhã* 4342 (March 18): 52.

Bernardo, Raul Vaz. 1989. 'Miles Davis: Anos 80'. *Expresso* 857 (April 1): 66R.

Braga, João. 2017. 'Eu era mais anarquista do que outra coisa qualquer'. *Expresso*, January 21.

Branco, Rui. 1991. 'Miles: O cometa envelhecido'. *Jornal de Notícias* 289 (March 18): 51.

Bucholc, Marta. 2013. 'Outside the Moral Circle: Polish Political Refugees in Norway. Between the Established and the Outsiders'. *Human Figurations: Long-Term Perspectives on the Human Condition* 2 (3). http://hdl.handle.net/2027/spo.11217607.0002.303.

Carby, Hazel V. 1998. *Race Men*. Harvard University Press.

Carner, Gary. 1996. *The Miles Davis Companion: Four Decades of Commentary*. Schirmer Books.

Carr, Ian. 1982. *Miles Davis: A Critical Biography*. Quartet Books.

Cole, George. 2007. *The Last Miles: The Music of Miles Davis, 1980–1991*. Equinox.

Collins, Patricia Hill. 1986. 'Learning from the Outsider Within: The Sociological Significance of Black Feminist Thought'. *Social Problems* 33 (6): 14–32.

Costa, José Carlos Monteiro e. 1971. 'Festival Internacional de Jazz de Cascais'. *Crítica* 2: 9–10.

Costa, Monteiro. 1989. 'Miles embalado em plástico vai estar hoje no Coliseu'. *Diário de Notícias* 43841: 23.

Cravinho, Pedro. 2012. '"A música agora é o jazz': O Jazz como palco de resistência em Portugal, entre 1971 e 1973'. In *Música Discurso Poder*, edited by Maria de Rosário Girão Santos and Elissa Maria Lessa. Edições Húmus.

Cravinho, Pedro. 2016a. *Essays on the History of Jazz in Portugal: Jazz in Coimbra*. JACC.

Cravinho, Pedro. 2016b. 'Historical Overview of the Development of Jazz in Portugal, in the First Half of the Twentieth Century'. *Jazz Research Journal* 10 (1–2): 75–108.

Cravinho, Pedro. 2017. 'A Kind of 'In-Between': Jazz and Politics in Portugal (1958–1974)'. In *Jazz and Totalitarianism*, edited by Bruce Johnson. Routledge.

Cravinho, Pedro. 2018a. 'Portugal: 1920–1974'. In *The History of European Jazz: The Music, Musicians and Audience in Context*, edited by Francesco Martinelli. Equinox.

Cravinho, Pedro. 2018b. 'The 'Truth' of Jazz: The History of the First Publication Dedicated to Jazz in Portugal'. *Jazz-Hitz* 1: 57–72.

Cravinho, Pedro. 2022a. 'The Birth of Porto's Jazz Scene: Culture, Spaces, and Networks'. *Popular Music and Society* 45 (4): 425–445.

Cravinho, Pedro. 2022b. *Encounters with Jazz on Television in Cold War Era Portugal: 1954–1974*. Routledge.

Cravinho, Pedro. In print. '"Um dos «nossos» melhores músicos de Jazz": A trajectória de Marcos Resende em Portugal (1967–1975)'. In *Jazz do Brasil | Jazz no Brasil – Discursos e representações, lugares e trajetórias*, edited by Antônio C. Araújo, Pedro Cravinho and Renan B. Ruiz. Cancioneiro.

Cruz, Anabela Martins da. 1989. 'Estilo único da trompete do mágico Miles Davis'. *Diário de Notícias* 43841: 10.

Curvelo, António. 1989. 'As etapas de uma vida'. *Expresso* 857 (April 1): 67–70R.

Curvelo, António. 2002. 'Notas (muito incompletas) sobre o Jazz em Portugal: Da pré-história aos tempos modernos'. In *Panorana da Cultura Portuguesa no Séc. XX Artes e Letras*, vol. 2., edited by Fernando Peres. Afrontamento.

DeMichael, Don. 1969. 'And in This Corner, the Sidewalk Kid . . .' *DownBeat* 36 (25): 12–13.

Elias, Norbert. 1994. 'Introduction: A Theoretical Essay on Established and Outsiders Relations'. In *The Established and the Outsiders: A Sociological Enquiry into Community Problems*, edited by Norbert Elias and John L. Scotson. Sage.

Ellis, Walter. 1998. *Prince of Darkness*. 20/20.

Feather, Leonard. 2009. 'Miles'. In *Miles on Miles: Interviews and Encounters with Miles Davis*, edited by Paul Maher and Michael K. Dorr. Lawrence Hill Books.

Gonçalves, Maria Augusta. 1991. 'Portugueses falam de Miles'. *Público* 337 (March 16): 6.

Letria, José Jorge. 1971. 'Festival de Jazz em Cascais, promessa que durou dois dias'. *Diário de Lisboa* 17573 (November 23): 7.

Lewis, Catherine M., and J. Richard Lewis, eds. 2009. *Jim Crow America: A Documentary History*. University of Arkansas Press.

Lourenço, Vanda, and Rui Telmo Gomes. 2005. *O Festival Estoril Jazz: Construção de uma imagem de marca*. OAC.

Maher, Paul, Jr., and Michael K. Dorr, eds. 2009. *Miles on Miles: Interviews and Encounters with Miles Davis*. Lawrence Hill Books.

Matos, Seia de. 1989. 'Jazz de Miles Davis espantou o Coliseu'. *Correio da Manhã* 3833 (April 4): 16.

Morgenstern, Dan. 1970. '35th Annual *DownBeat* Readers Poll'. *DownBeat* 37 (26): 15.

Paes, Rui Eduardo. 1989. 'O Príncipe da Trevas'. *Diário de Lisboa* 22931 (April 4): 23.

Santos, João Moreira dos. 2007. 'Quando Miles Davis esteve em Portugal'. *Blitz*, March. https://blitz.pt/principal/update/2017-05-14-Quando-Miles-Davis-esteve-em-Portugal.

Santos, João Moreira dos. 2009. *Jazz em Cascais: Uma História de 80 anos (1928–2008)*. Casa Sasseti.

Sardica, José Miguel. 2008. *Twentieth-Century Portugal: A Historical Overview*. Universidade Católica.

Tingen, Paul. 2001. *Miles Beyond: The Electric Explorations of Miles Davis, 1967–1991*. Billboard Books.

Veloso, Manuel Jorge, Carlos Branco Mendes and António Curvelo. 2010. 'Jazz'. In *Enciclopédia da Música em Portugal no Século XX*, vol. C–L, edited by Salwa Castelo-Branco. Círculo de Leitores/Temas e Debates.

Yudkin, Jeremy. 2008. *Miles Davis, Miles Smiles, and the Invention of Post Bop*. Indiana University Press.

Videos

Rewind: Cascais Jazz '71. A documentary about the first edition of the International Cascais Jazz Festival (João Abecasis Fernandes, dir.; João Marques, prod.).

(Part 1) https://www.youtube.com/watch?v=T0c9Yh0k_DQ.

(Part 2) https://www.youtube.com/watch?v=AHpD6WdWX6U.

(Part 3) https://www.youtube.com/watch?v=wi_hRsAL8AY.

It's Never Too Late

Miles Davis and Modernism

Nicholas Gebhardt

Inside the hall it was hot and crowded, and no one was paying much attention. A typical lunchtime assembly at high school. Eventually everyone settled down, and after a few announcements about upcoming sports events, we took the stage. The plan was straightforward. We would swap our school clothes at the last minute for jeans and plaid shirts, put on sunglasses and then start to play . . . with our backs to the audience and without saying anything about what we were doing: 'So What', 'All Blues', and 'Blue in Green'. At the time, for a group of teenagers, it seemed like a bold, even rebellious, act, certain to upset a few teachers at the very least. We knew there was the possibility of censure, although just how severe it might be wasn't that clear. And so on to the stage we went, trying to remain calm and focused. I can't really remember much of what happened next: how we played, if anyone listened or if we ended up in the school office. But one thing I know for sure is that this was all our teacher's fault.

Along with his job teaching the eighth grade, our teacher was also a bass player in several local jazz groups, and Ron Carter was one of his major influences. During our weekly music practice sessions, as he tried to instruct us in the ways of improvisation, he often told us stories about the 1960s jazz scene in the US and especially about Miles Davis' quintet in this period, which included Carter. One detail that caught our attention in these stories was Davis' surprising attitude towards his audiences: his reputation for turning his back on them, avoiding any announcements about the music he was playing and generally dismissing their applause or shouts of approval. For young people trying to find their way into this music, the idea of defying your audience in this way proved exhilarating. It conveyed a sense of the musicians' coolness under pressure and a seriousness about what they were doing that none of us had experienced before. As you can see, the whole plan

Nicholas Gebhardt, *It's Never Too Late* In: *Rethinking Miles Davis*. Edited by: Roger Fagge, Nicolas Pillai, and Tim Wall, Oxford University Press. © Oxford University Press 2026. DOI: 10.1093/9780190085834.003.0010

was really our teacher's fault. Not that we could see this at the time, or really appreciate the education we were getting from him; we were too absorbed with our attempt to disrupt the assembly.

Moments like this have a way of getting inside you and staying there. The narrative of Davis' life in music—the tales of defiance, adversity overcome, the relentless pursuit of innovation and change, the fast cars, famous partners, struggles over record deals and artistic autonomy, the boxing and the flamboyant clothes, but also the drug abuse and debilitating illnesses—is now so much part of what we have come to think jazz is about and why it is important that it is hard to imagine a different way of telling the story. Years spent swapping anecdotes with friends, comparing notes, going to performances, watching films, putting up posters, sharing recordings and making music inspired by these early encounters have further reinforced this sense of the jazz life as a particular way of being and acting that we take for granted. Our admiration for these musicians, our passion for their music, has become inseparable from how we account for why things in jazz happened in the way they did: the sorts of actions and statements we accept as authentic, the ways in which we interpret their meaning, the performers we focus on and the perspectives we adopt in trying to understand them.

But this story has its problems too. For all the talk of context in jazz studies, the music continues to provide a refuge from rather than a medium through which to understand its meaning and significance. Despite repeated calls over the past decades to change the historical tune, it remains commonplace to evaluate jazz practices with little regard for the situations in which they take place. Study after study actively refuses the messiness of the lives and places from which the music emerged by claiming a rarefied space of personal expression as the ultimate measure of artistic value. This need, to establish jazz as the privileged medium of aesthetic individualism, has the effect of limiting rather than revealing what we know of its relationship to social existence. Over and over, the basic impetus is the same: to find ways to protect jazz's expressive core, its principle of surprise, from the conditions from which it emerged. To account for its presuppositions, though, is not about reducing jazz to its context or treating it as a mere reflection of something else and thereby losing a sense of its distinctiveness. It means rather to think of jazz practices as encompassing not only a performance, a score or a recording but the many habits, customs, experiences, relationships, memories and histories that make such musicmaking possible in the first place. As the chapters in this book demonstrate, one outcome of this is that an iconic artist such as Davis may no longer speak to us as they once did, or perhaps they begin to speak to us differently and in an unfamiliar voice. And this then changes the story we tell ourselves about why the music matters to us, where it comes from and what it means. As I said, it was all my teacher's fault.

So What?

The focus of this chapter is a recording of Davis' 1981 performance of 'My Man's Gone Now' from George Gershwin's 1935 opera *Porgy and Bess*. The recording was made by Davis' longtime collaborator Teo Macero at the KIX Club in Boston on July 27 as part of the trumpeter's comeback from a much-publicised six-year break from public appearances, and it was released the following year on the Grammy Award–winning album *We Want Miles*. Along with Davis, the musicians who appeared with him on the recording were Marcus Miller on bass, Al Foster on drums, Mino Cinélu on percussion, Mike Stern on guitar and Bill Evans on soprano saxophone. Except for Foster, all of them were new to Davis' band and had very little experience playing with him. It is also important to note that this was the first time that Davis performed 'My Man's Gone Now' in its entirety since he had recorded it with Gil Evans in 1959.[1]

While I concentrate here on a single recording, the discussion forms part of a larger study about jazz's contribution to American modernism, that confluence of artistic movements and practices that became dominant in North America, but also throughout Central American, South America and the Caribbean, during the 25 years following the Second World War (Kalaidjian 2005). The purpose of this extended study is a set of analyses of live recordings of performances by artists such as Stan Getz, Billie Holiday, Charlie Parker, Nina Simone, Frank Sinatra, John Coltrane, Davis, Sarah Vaughan and Bill Evans. By situating their performances within the dynamics of American modernism and identifying them with a specific set of modernist practices, the aim is to see what they can tell us about jazz's contribution to this movement. This means adjusting, on the one hand, the narrative about postwar jazz that we have come to accept, which is primarily about plotting in one way or another the relationship between individual artists and stylistic change. At the same time, it involves us in reconceptualising the

[1] In the 1970s, Davis began quoting its theme in the context of other tunes (Tingen 2001, 200).

history of American modernism and revising the place that jazz occupies within it (Baker 1984; Gates 1988; Magee 2007; Monson 2007).

The central claims I want to develop in this context are as follows: first, that jazz is a live or living art that relies for its meaning on musicians performing in front of and finding specific ways of acknowledging and being present to an audience; second, that the music's significance emerges from the ways in which jazz musicians have used the vernacular of American popular songs and show tunes to conceptualise their art as one primarily about the problem of saying something meaningful through improvisation; third, that the ability to say something in jazz is inseparable from the fact of finding one's voice and, in the process, learning how to use it; and finally, that because of the central commitment to improvisation as a medium of artistic expression, jazz is to a large extent a practice of and about imperfection (Gioia 1988).

The starting point for this reflection is the series of live recordings that Davis made with various quintets between 1961 and 1966, beginning with *Miles Davis in Person at the Blackhawk in San Francisco* and culminating in the posthumously released *Live at the Oriental Theatre*. Within this series, I have previously discussed Davis' well-known performances of 'My Funny Valentine'" at festivals and in concert hall settings, from New York to Tokyo (Gebhardt 2016; Gebhardt and Rushton, 2024). Something about the process of reimagining the Rogers and Hart song over this period, as well as the other standards in his repertoire, has come to exemplify the many difficulties of interpretation and historical understanding that exist for jazz performers (Brofsky 1983; Stanbridge 2004; Walser 1993). These have included the techniques and methods available to us for evaluating an individual improvisation, the status of the media through which we encounter the music, the sources of creativity and change within it, the dynamics of group interaction and the difficulties of extracting a formal set of procedures from a particular performance without losing a sense of its wider cultural significance.

This raises two key questions. First, what becomes of popular songs when they are subject to extended improvisations in live performance rather than in the recording studio? Second, what does this quality of liveness tell us about jazz musicians' capacity for expressing something meaningful to their audience? One answer is to say that by continually performing these standards, by exploring the sonic possibilities contained within them, testing their limits and returning to them, night after night, in so many different contexts, the musicians are simultaneously destabilising and reconstructing our conception of what is possible to experience in a jazz performance. This necessitates a complex negotiation of performers' collective inheritance from the past, especially the basic repertoire of songs and performance techniques on which they have conventionally relied. But equally, it involves a continuous redefinition of what counts as a legitimate jazz performance to begin with.

Standards Live

Before we get any further into the details of Davis' performance, let me say a few things about what I mean by 'modernism'. I am using the term as it has been developed in the work of critics such as Stanley Cavell (1979), Miriam Hansen (1999), Toril Moi (2006) and Robert Pippin (1999), among others. In their work, modernism is a cultural practice through which groups of artists navigate between disparate media, cultural traditions and perspectives, seeking to bring those elements into dynamic relationship with each other to discover the immediacy or 'thereness' in our experiences of the world (Cavell 1979, 110). As Hansen puts it, "[M]odernism encompasses a whole range of cultural and artistic practices that register, respond to and reflect on processes of modernisation and the experience of modernity, and include a paradigmatic transformation of the conditions under which art is produced, transmitted, and consumed" (1999, 60). But modernism is also about the relationship that artists have to their past, particularly the complex relationship between the present practice of an enterprise and the history of that enterprise. Because modernists cannot take for granted the traditional procedures or purposes thought to be definitive in the past, because they have broken with that past, even as they remain indebted to it and dependent on it for their knowledge of what counts as a genuine artwork, the very enterprise in which they are involved itself becomes the central problem (Cavell 2002, xxxiii). This explains the recurrent questioning in so much modernist practice about the capacity for a particular artwork to withstand comparison with art of the past.

Accordingly, with each new work in any given medium artists must try to figure out their relationship with other, similar works and understand what tradition they are part of. In the process, they remake that tradition by redefining the conventions on which it was based, as well as reshaping the material possibilities of their practice and those around them. At the same time, however, modernism presents itself as the end of tradition in art, in that there are no longer any specifically empirical, much less philosophical, guarantors for a given work's intrinsic value (Cavell 1979, 72–73). "[J]ust as modernist aesthetics are not reducible to the category of style", writes Hansen, "they tend to blur the boundaries of art in its traditional, eighteenth- and nineteenth-century incarnation that turns on the ideal of aesthetic autonomy and the distinction 'high' vs. 'low,' of autonomous art vs. popular or mass culture" (1999, 60). Moreover, for the modernist artist, insofar as they believe, and continue to believe, in what they are doing, this question of their relation to the past comes increasingly to dominate their activities. Cavell describes it as a situation in which "one's own particular practice and ambition can be identified only against the continuous experience of the past" (2002, xxxiii).

In jazz, modernism has generally been associated with the innovations of bebop musicians such as Bud Powell, Thelonious Monk, Kenny Clarke, Charlie Parker, Sarah Vaughan, Max Roach and Dizzy Gillespie (Gendron 1995). Their relentless reworking of the entire body of standard tunes upon which jazz had relied for 25 years, as well as their commitment to challenging the performance conventions identified with an earlier generation of players, fundamentally altered what those standards meant and how those prior conventions worked. As Ingrid Monson demonstrates, however, the emergence of modernism in jazz involved a more general shift in how these artists began to make sense of and articulate their position within North American society. This was especially the case in the ways in which they identified their music with a distinctive set of aesthetic principles, social practices and political claims that took shape in a complex dialogue with mainstream aesthetic values and institutions (Monson 2007, 66–106). They argued for greater artistic autonomy, alongside the assertion of a musical identity that was derived explicitly from as well as evaluated according to the depth of their engagement with the expressive resources of African American musical traditions. At the same time, though, through their music they sought to maintain a continuity with other aesthetic practices, from the European avant-garde in music and the visual arts to film and Beat poetry (Lott 1988). The result was a significant shift in what counted for them as an authentic artistic statement, as well as a new understanding of their music as a central rather than peripheral practice within the broader culture of American modernism.

In Amiri Baraka's writings from the 1950s and 1960s, we can see something of what was at stake in this process of redefining jazz's possibilities and repositioning it within a modernist context. In a review of John Coltrane's 1964 recording *Live at Birdland*, for instance, Baraka described the saxophonist's approach to improvisation as a process of "infinite" qualification. "Instead of the simplistic though touching note-for-note replay of the ballad's line", he explains, "on this performance [by Coltrane of Billy Eckstine's 'I Want to Talk About You'] each note is tested, given a slight tremolo or emotional vibrato (note to chord to scale reference), which makes it seem as if each one of the notes is given the possibility of 'infinite' qualification . . . proving that the ballad as it was written was only the beginning of the story" (Baraka 1967, 66). Coltrane himself noted in an interview in 1966 that he was "trying to work out a kind of writing . . . that will allow for more plasticity, more viability, more room for improvisation in the statement of the melody itself before we go into solos" (Hentoff 1962).

Baraka's reference to Coltrane's use of a "slight tremolo" and "emotional vibrato" as a way of enlarging the possibilities for expressivity within a popular song, and of opening more space for experimentation with the soloing, emphasises the continuities with other avant-garde practices, but also the importance of the voice as the primary medium for reconnecting jazz to the African American cultural traditions of which it was a part. In American popular song, he argues, "the historic basis and continuing reference of African and Afro-American music is the voice. And always not just the sound of the voice, but the *spoken* word is the communicating expression. Even in the drum, the percussive form was a mouth, which *talked*. Blues, Jazz, maintain the word as, Pres [Lester Young] said, 'a story,' being told" (Baraka 1967, 43, italics in original). For Baraka, it was the jazz musician's ability to craft a voice that was original *in the present moment* and yet derived from a deep historical connection to the past that established them as modernists. Which brings us back to Davis and his performance of 'My Man's Gone Now'.

Re-Voicing the Past

In the account of jazz as modernism that I have been trying to develop, the quest for an original voice among postwar jazz musicians played a critical role in mediating the relationship between the past and the present. Given the social and political situations in which they found themselves in the 1950s and 1960s, however, especially in the context of the civil rights movement and the huge expansion of mass consumer culture, the possibilities for creating an authentic artistic voice and the qualities identified with such a process, were being continually revised and re-evaluated (Fried 1982). This meant that there was no guarantee in advance which musical traditions were most likely to secure the conditions for any genuine, artistic expression, partly because the basis of those traditions themselves were in constant flux and subject to continual dispute. For example, the blues aesthetic was inseparable from the deep history of the Atlantic slave trade and the plantation economy that defined the experiences of the millions of Africans who were transported to the Americas. Yet its form was indisputably modern, taking shape within and encompassing the values of the new entertainment industries that triumphed in the 1920s and forming the basis for the mass market in recorded music and sound (Gebhardt 2017, 122–144).

Porgy and Bess has a crucial part to play in this narrative. Ever since its premier in 1935 by the Theatre Guild in New York, Gershwin's work (with a libretto by Ira Gershwin and DuBose Heyward) has become one of the best known and most performed operas in the United States (Pollack 2006, 567–664). The tragic story of unrequited love between the title characters, set among the people of 'Catfish Row', a fictional African American community in Charleston, South Carolina, has launched many artistic careers over the decades; its songs have been recorded on countless occasions, especially by jazz performers; and it has been adapted several times for film and television. As Richard Crawford argues, what makes the opera "so unique among American operas is its universal familiarity. So appealing are some of its moments that they stand on their own as staple fare of musical worlds far removed from the opera house.... *Porgy and Bess*... is part of the American musical vernacular, and the familiarity of some of its music surely affects the way one hears and responds to the work as a whole" (1979, 261–262). For the poet and writer Maya Angelou, who was a cast member in the Robert Breen touring production during the early 1950s, it was a life-changing experience. "Who could deny this story?" she wrote in her autobiography. "How many Black men had been crippled by the American oppression and had lost the women they loved and who loved them, because they hadn't the strength to fight? How often had the women submitted to loveless arrangements for the sake of bare survival?" (quoted in Brown 2021, 180).

At the same time, however, from its first performance the opera has been the subject of a large and complicated debate about the enduring problems of racial representation, cultural appropriation, social exploitation and systemic racism within the performing arts. "Gershwin and Heyward were about the business of transforming white fantasies of black sensuality, spirituality, and violence into a commodity that was marketable as entertainment for primarily white audiences", Ray Allen declares. "In spite of the fact that a stellar company of black artists, rather than a band of blackface minstrel buffoons, was recruited to breathe life into the production, the exploitative nature of the white composer/black performer could not be easily dismissed" (2004, 255). Gershwin was accused of perpetuating racist stereotypes, demeaning African American culture and depriving African Americans of their voices. As James Hicks wrote of a new production in 1953, "The current revival of the musical 'Porgy and Bess' now at the Ziegfeld theater in New York is the most insulting, the most libelous, the most degrading act that could possibly be perpetrated against colored Americans of modern times". Alongside these criticisms, there were also persistent doubts about the work's artistic legitimacy and Gershwin's abilities as a composer of "serious" music (Pollack 2006, 631). Critic Robert Lawrence thought that "Gershwin could make the pulse of his listener tingle but he could not make the heart throb". Judged by theatrical standards, he claimed, *Porgy and Bess* was a success, but "weighed by the standards of opera it fails" (quoted in Pollack 2006, 612).

Even though these concerns about the opera remain, if now modified by new insights and historical perspectives, major opera companies continue to programme the work—it launched the New York Metropolitan Opera's 2019–2020 season—and it keeps attracting enthusiastic audiences throughout the world (André 2018; Brooks 2021; Noonan 2012). For opera critic Philip Kennicott, one of the main reasons for this success comes down to the agency it offers African American performers. Not only are its arias instantly recognisable and cherished by audiences, but it creates a collaborative space in which performers are able to articulate their own understanding of the parts they inhabit and so take ownership of the material. He believes that the work has empowered African American singers "to do what Heyward and the Gershwins could not—project an authentic sense of the inner life of the residents of Catfish Row. Every performer, of course, puts his or her imprint on every role. But with Porgy and Bess that imprint is more complicated. It is a reappropriation of something that was originally an appropriation, a claiming back of a work that was falsely claimed (in early reviews by white critics) to be a genuine portrait of African-American folk life. No one just performs Porgy and Bess. Rather, great singers repossess it, rewrite it and redeem it" (2020, 10).

Historian Gwynne Kuhner Brown makes a similar point. "Despite a broadening consensus that its libretto's depiction of African American life is dated at best", she states, "Porgy and Bess has been mounted repeatedly over the past fifty years. It could not have survived, let alone established itself as one of the few great American operas, without the willingness of first-rate black artists to bring it to life onstage and support it offstage. The indispensable, active role that African American performers have played in every critically successful production of Porgy and Bess challenges the assumption that the work is something done by whites to blacks" (2021, 164). This has extended to audiences, too. In a discussion informed by her own participation as a member of the opera's chorus, Naomi André maintains that the creators' insistence "on a black cast makes going to Porgy and Bess a unique experience, and one especially exciting for black audiences, for nowhere else in the repertory do we have the chance to see so many black people on the opera stage—and in the audience" (2019, 182). In this way the opera foregrounds the problem of the African American voice: of whose voices we are hearing when we participate in the show, who is able to speak to and for whom within the space of the performance, and from what position and through what medium they can make themselves heard. By making its performance conditional on an all-black cast, Gershwin made the opera explicitly about the possibility of finding oneself in and through the songs of another. What was at stake in the multiplying of African American voices within the work was nothing less than the artist's selfhood.

What about the aria, though? What was it about 'My Man's Gone Now' that appealed to Davis, especially after such relentless criticism of Gershwin's opera? In what ways did it speak to him? One way of thinking about this is to focus on the song's position within the story and the work it is doing there. It appears in Act I, Scene 2 and is performed by the grieving widow, Serena, at her husband Robbins' wake. He has been murdered by Crown, a drunken stevedore, during a game of craps. It is an extraordinarily powerful lament, in which Serena weaves a tale of personal sorrow and collective pain, sometimes reflecting on her situation in words, sometimes using the wordless melisma and glissando that she weaves through conventional AABA 32-bar form. Her performance ends with a high cadential cry, almost at the limits of a soprano's vocal range, which then drops stepwise in a series of smaller cries, as she tries, but fails, to find the words to express the full extent of her loss. In this way, she gathers the whole community into her grief; the chorus joins in wordlessly, responding to her cries with their own, as well as accompanying her, as she confronts her anguish (Crawford 2019, 194).

The scene marks a key moment of crisis for the community of Catfish Row. Just before Serena begins to sing, a detective and two policemen abruptly enter her home in search of Crown, only to arrest Peter, the local honey man, who has not committed any crime. After they leave, Porgy wonders about the unfairness of a society that jails an innocent man and leaves a killer at large. On top of this, Serena is also struggling to pay for her husband's burial and so has to plead with her neighbours and the funeral director to help her cover the costs, a fact which further complicates her grief. The aria both reflects on and intensifies the feelings of uncertainty and fear among the gathered mourners by revealing their struggle to express their sense of who they are as a community and what is happening to them. Serena's loss of words, and the response in the chorus, acknowledges the extent to which their world is in ruins, while also signalling the possibility for some kind of renewal. At the same time, as André points out, the scene also reinforces one of the opera's major themes: that women bear the consequence of men's short-sighted actions. In André's view, Serena's lament underlines how easily "the fate of women on Catfish Row is beyond their control and tied to the fortune of the men in the community" (2018, 92).

Recent scholarship on *Porgy and Bess* reveals the profound challenges that its female characters raise for our understanding of the opera, but also the difficulties faced by the artists who take on these roles (Brooks 2021; André 2018). Much of this discussion focuses on clarifying the relationships between the various female voices within the narrative and the effect of these voices on concepts of African American womanhood and cultural identity. Daphne Brooks, for example, demonstrates the extent to which the opera "was at the forefront of a battle over Black women artists' vocality, their sonic ontology, their interpretative radicalism, their aesthetic will to survive" (2021, 109). She goes on to argue that the long list of African American performers who have appeared in it have "crafted vocalities that enabled them to traverse and mediate social spaces and ultimately keep a different time to that of the production's gauzy, incandescent vision of 'Summertime' for its Black rural laborers. In this way, too, these women ultimately strategised ways of scoring the conditions and possibilities of being aesthetically on the edge and 'outside' the histo-temporalities and racial geographies set for them, and they passed that secret on to generations of artists who followed the paths that they paved" (110).

This process of repurposing the opera, of reclaiming it for its African American subjects, was related in part to Gershwin's score, which, as Alex Ross points out, invites considerable freedom of interpretation. "Once the chords of 'Summertime' start rocking", he says, "they become a steady-state environment in which a gifted performer can move around at will. She can bend pitches, add ornaments, shift the line up and down" (2007, 161–162). Jazz musicians were especially drawn to the songs, helping to move them into other musical domains and popularising them independently of the show (Pollack 2006, 655). Billie Holiday's 1936 recording of 'Summertime', for example, was one of the first commercially successful releases and, in many ways, established the methods of dissembling and then reassembling the tune adopted by later artists (Kramer 2002, 243–257). Her version effectively recomposed the song and, with the help of Bunny Berigan's trumpet and Artie Shaw's clarinet, transformed it from a pastoral lullaby into a sharp-edged urban blues. Similarly, her 1948 recording of 'Porgy' reorganised and remade one part of the opera's duet into a reflective blues, in which the singer muses to herself rather than her lover. The effect was to give the song both a new level of intimacy and a different kind of melodic meaning (Szwed 2015, 143–144).

Miles Davis' first performance of 'My Man's Gone Now' appeared on the 1959 album *Porgy and Bess*, which was his second collaboration with composer-arranger Gil Evans following their successful *Miles Ahead* recording in 1957. Evans had already arranged selections for the work in 1941, and Davis had encountered the opera through his partner, Frances Taylor, who was performing in an off-Broadway production. According to Howard Pollack, the two men found common ground in their attraction to the Gershwin score (2006, 657). Evans' collage-like arrangements broke new ground as part of a more general transformation of the mood and tone of the opera, while Davis used his performance to develop Holiday's approach to reimagining the score. This was particularly evident on 'Summertime', which strips the song of its distinctive harmonies and focuses only on exploring the melody's expressive possibilities. For Mark Tucker, this explains the recording's heightened ambiguity. "Partly", he suggests, "the ambiguity results from the instrumental performance of a texted vocal work; removing the words puts distance between the jazz recomposition and the opera's original setting and plot. Having Davis serve as principal soloist throughout—performing numbers sung by characters both female and male, leads and secondary roles—further enhances the vagueness of presentation"

(2001–2002, 14). The result is "an unmistakable aura of sadness and yearning that hovers over the album" (18).

In the Davis–Evans version of 'My Man's Gone Now', the recomposed aria becomes a medium for re-voicing the meaning of jazz as 'cool' and positioning the sound of Davis' trumpet as its essence. His statement of the melody glides over Evans' mournful harmonies in a way that disconnects the song from its meaning as a woman's lament for her dead husband, abstracting the singer's voice from the physical reality of her pain and the specific context of her loss. The change of tempo to double time for the solos adds to this distancing effect, as Davis varies the melody, sometimes shifting and bending it through his use of half notes and bluesy phrases, but never quite losing contact with it entirely. Even the final cadenza, which in the opera brings Serena to the limits of herself and her powers of expression, in this case is both contained and controlled by the singularity of Davis' sound. His combination of focused intensity and aesthetic restraint relies on appropriating the singer's melodramatic voice, but also the history contained within it, for his own refigured masculinity. Baraka describes the effect as both an affirmation and a questioning of the artist's capacity to communicate. He observes that in this instance Davis' "horn is so beautiful, except there is the feeling in us maybe all of this is a dream. A film. And invisible pageant of feeling" (quoted in Kirchner 1997, 71).

An Unending Present

Physically he was in bad shape, and there was a lot of speculation about his playing. In fact, many people wondered whether Davis could still play at all. Most accounts of his time away from performance, including the chapters on this period in his autobiography, are little more than a long list of illnesses, including arthritis and other chronic problems, alongside cocaine addiction, alcoholism and abusive and unpredictable behaviour towards many of the people closest to him. There was a lot of uncertainty as to whether he would even show up, especially as he had made several unsuccessful attempts at a comeback already and was frequently absent from recording sessions and rehearsals (Cole 2005, 89–94). However, after a year of working with different groups, and eventually recording a new album, Davis embarked on his first road trip in six years, and on 26 June 1981 his new band took the stage at the KIX Club.

Local historian Richard Vacca (2015) recalls the excitement that accompanied the announcement of the tour. News of the upcoming shows

> was made public in mid-June. . . . Miles Davis in Boston for four nights . . . two shows per night . . . ticket price $12.50. The news created a tidal wave of interest, and media people from as far away as Japan turned up in Boston for the opening. Meanwhile, Sue Auclair [the publicist] recruited Boston mayor Kevin White to issue a proclamation declaring the four days in June to be Miles Davis Weekend. On opening night, Miles drove to the club in his yellow Ferrari, accompanied by his wife-to-be, actress Cicely Tyson. There was Miles, now with a mustache and beard, stylish as always in a black jump suit . . . and the place went crazy, with chants of "We want Miles!" Inside, Kix was electric with anticipation, and Miles stepped on stage to a sustained standing ovation.

For Marie, a student at the time, it was an unforgettable experience attending those shows:

> "I was 19, studying at the conservatory", she recalls, "and happened to work weekends at the Nickelodeon movie theater next door to Kix. That was how I scored the tickets . . . two single tickets, two nights in a row. I went alone. It was packed; Miles played most of the first show with his back to the audience and Cicely Tyson was sitting in the front row. Mike Stern on guitar, Marcus Miller on bass, Al Foster on drums. A beautiful version of my 'My Man's Gone Now'. What a glorious memory". (Vacca 2015)

The appearance of the Gershwin song caught most critics off-guard, and in their various comments we can see the kinds of challenges that Davis faced as he made his return to public performance. "The biggest surprise", says Richard Cook in his review of the album, "is the reappearance of 'My Man's Gone Now,' from the *Porgy and Bess* project. Davis always claimed that he wouldn't go back to the old days, but for some reason this piece came out of the archives" (2007, 269). Likewise, Davis' biographer Ian Carr explains that with the inclusion of the song in his set, "he was again reviewing his past and looking into it for musical clues to the present" (1998, 364). Paul Tingen observes that for a man who never looked back, "the twenty-minute version of 'My Man's Gone Now' is an astonishing revisitation. . . . Throughout his career Miles occasionally quoted themes from his own back catalogue or from popular songs, and in the mid-1970s he regularly referred to the theme of 'My Man's Gone.' But he had not performed a whole track from his pre-1968 jazz repertoire since eliminating 'The Theme' from his concert repertoire in October 1970" (2001, 200). In a review of Davis' performance in London in 1982 with the same band, Max Harrison observed that the "electronic modification of sound indeed sometimes distended the ensemble's diverse textures, and a sustained account of 'My Man's Gone Now' has remained the most outlandish Gershwin performance I have ever heard, setting Davis' austere lyricism in a startlingly new framework" (quoted in Kirchner 1997, 225).

What does it mean for jazz musicians to return to a song they played almost 25 years earlier? If you have spent your whole career positioning yourself as the future of your art and relegating the past to the past, how do you justify such a choice? How do you convince yourself, the people around you, the other musicians, the record company executives, your audience, that you still have something meaningful to say? Part of the answer to these questions lies in Gershwin's opera. Its failure as an opera, the many flaws associated with it, from its racist caricatures to its formal inconsistencies, are also what makes it attractive to jazz artists. Its imperfections allow for the continual interpretation and reinterpretation of the songs, the reimagining of the possibilities within them. But they also explain why Davis returned to the song at a pivotal moment in his career. As he had done in the 1950s, the process of disassembling and reassembling Serena's aria as a medium for improvisation once again became a way for the trumpeter to regain his voice, to redefine his and the music's creative possibilities, and to find a place within it. By connecting the song's familiar lament to the rock-, pop- and funk-based sound he was developing with his new band, he was asking his audience whether they were still able to hear him in the way they once had, whether as the symbol of black masculinity, of urban cool, or as the essence of the postwar jazz sound. But equally, he was testing them to see if they understood the extent to which his relationship to the past had altered.

Listening to it now, 40 years later, one of the striking aspects of this performance is the way Davis uses it to dramatise the loss of his physical strength, to meditate on the passing of his youth and to acknowledge the limits of his influence. As much about the potential for change as it was an expression of that change, 'My Man's Gone Now" acted as a medium for him to explore his many weaknesses and failings, both personal and musical, while signalling his debt to the people around him, especially Cecily Tyson. At the same time, the controlled spaciousness of the performance—Davis lets his trumpet drift over the repeated bass line, moving it in and out of time, while continually shifting in the rhythm section between the 'now' (a funk beat) and the 'then' (a swing beat)—has the effect of distancing himself once more from the realities he faced, whether at home or professionally. He simply floated above them, freed from the weight of his past and everything that went along with it, but also exempt from the anxieties of the future, suspended in what François Hartog refers to as a "presentist present", in which his music was, finally, determined by nothing other than itself (2015, 204). "When you go this way", Davis once said, "you can go on forever" (quoted in Hentoff 1958, 166).

Acknowledgements

I want to thank my colleagues in the jazz studies research cluster at Birmingham City University, in particular Tony Whyton, whose input into this chapter has been invaluable, especially in navigating the more problematic aspects of Miles Davis' life in jazz and the kinds of questions we face when analysing his music. I also want to thank Jory Debenham for her deep insights into the challenges of making sense of our musical experiences and writing about controversial artists.

Sections of this chapter were presented at the Jazz Voices Conference in 2018 at the Institute for Jazz Research, the University of Music and the Performing Arts, Graz and as part of the Royal Birmingham Conservatoire seminar series in 2021. I want to thank the organisers for the opportunity to present these ideas in such stimulating contexts.

References

Miles Davis Recordings

At Carnegie Hall 1961. 1998. Columbia CK 65027.

The Complete Live at the Plugged Nickel. 1995. Columbia CXK 66955.

'Four' and More. 2005. Columbia 519505.

In Person Friday Night at The Blackhawk. 2003. Columbia 87097.

In Person Saturday Night at The Blackhawk. 2003. Columbia 87100.

Jazz at The Plaza. Vol. 1. 2001. Columbia CK 85245.

Live at the 1963 Monterey Jazz Festival. 2007. Monterey Jazz Festival 7441655.

Live at the Oriental Theatre 1966. 2010. Sunburn 9339880.

Miles Davis—At Newport 1958. 2001. Columbia CK 85202.

Miles Davis in Europe. 2005. Columbia 519506.

Miles in Berlin. 2005. Columbia 519507.

Miles in Tokyo. 2005. Columbia 519508.

My Funny Valentine. 2005. Columbia 519503.
Porgy and Bess. 1997. Columbia CK 65141.
We Want Miles. 1990. Columbia 469402

Written Works

Allen, Ray. 2004. 'An American Folk Opera? Triangulating Folkness, Blackness, and Americanness in Gershwin and Heyward's "Porgy and Bess"'. *Journal of American Folklore* 117 (465, Summer): 243–261.

André, Naomi. 2018. *Black Opera: History, Power, Engagement*. University of Illinois Press.

André, Naomi. 2019. 'Complexities in Gershwin's *Porgy and Bess*'. In *The Cambridge Companion to Gershwin*, edited by Anna Harwell Celenza. Cambridge University Press.

Baker, Houston A. 1984. *Blues, Ideology and African American Literature: A Vernacular Theory*. University of Chicago Press.

Baraka, Amiri. 1967. *Black Music*. William Morrow.

Brofsky, Howard. 1983. 'Miles Davis and "My Funny Valentine": The Evolution of a Solo'. *Black Music Research Journal* 3: 23–45.

Brooks, Daphne A. 2021. '"A Woman Is a Sometime Thing": (Re)Covering Black Womanhood in *Porgy and Bess*'. *Daedalus* 150 (1): 98–117.

Brown, Gwynne Kuhner. 2021. 'Performers in Catfish Row: Collaboration in *Porgy and Bess*'. In *Blackness in Opera*, edited by Naomi André, Karen M. Bryan and Eric Saylor. University of Illinois Press.

Carr, Ian. 1998. *Miles Davis: The Definitive Autobiography*. HarperCollins.

Cavell, Stanley. 1979. *The World Viewed*. Enlarged ed. Harvard University Press.

Cavell, Stanley. 2002. *Must We Mean What We Say?* Cambridge University Press.

Cole, George. 2005. *The Last Miles: The Music of Miles Davis*. Equinox.

Cook, Richard. 2007. *It's About That Time: Miles Davis On and Off Record*. Oxford University Press.

Crawford, Richard. 1979. 'Gershwin's Reputation: A Note on "Porgy and Bess"'. *Musical Quarterly* 65 (2): 261–262.

Crawford, Richard. 2019. *Summertime: George Gershwin's Life in Music*. W. W. Norton.

Fried, Michael. 1982. 'How Modernism Works: A Response to T. J. Clark'. *Critical Inquiry* 9 (1): 217–234.

Gates, Henry Louis, Jr. 1988. *The Signifying Monkey: A Theory of African American Literature*. Oxford University Press.

Gebhardt, Nicholas. 2016. 'Screening the Event: Watching Miles Davis' "My Funny Valentine"'. In *Watching Jazz: Encounters with Jazz Performance on Screen*, edited by Björn Heile, Peter Elsdon and Jenny Doctor. Oxford University Press.

Gebhardt, Nicholas. 2017. *Vaudeville Melodies: Popular Musicians and Mass Entertainment in American Culture, 1870–1929*. University of Chicago Press.

Gendron, Gendron. 1995. 'Moldy Figs and Modernists: Jazz at War (1942–1946)'. In *Jazz Among the Discourses*, edited by Krin Gabbard. Duke University Press.

Gebhardt, Nicholas, and Richard Rushton. 2024. 'Music, Miles Davis and Theatricality'. In *Theatricality and the Arts: Film, Theatre, Art*, edited by Andrew Quick and Richard Rushton. Edinburgh University Press.

Gioia, Ted. 1988. *The Imperfect Art: Reflections on Jazz and Modern Culture*. Oxford University Press.

Hansen, Miriam Bratu. 1999. 'The Mass Production of the Senses: Classical Cinema as Vernacular Modernism'. *Modernism/Modernity* 6 (2): 59–77.

Hartog, François. 2015. *Regimes of Historicity: Presentism and Experiences of Time*. Translated by Saskia Brown . Columbia University Press.

Hentoff, Nat. 1958. 'An Afternoon with Miles Davis'. *Jazz Review* 1 (2): 161–166.

Hentoff, Nat. 1962. 'Liner Notes'. *Live at The Village Vanguard Again!* Impulse AS-9124.

Hicks, James. 1953. 'We Don't Need *Porgy and Bess*'. *Afro-American AFRO Magazine*, March 28.

Kalaidjian, Walter, ed. 2005. *The Cambridge Companion to American Modernism*. Cambridge University Press.

Kennicott, Philip. 2020. 'The Persistence of Porgy'. *Opera News* 1. https://www.operanews.com/Opera_News_Magazine/2020/1/Features/The_Persistence_of_Porgy.html.

Kirchner, Bill, ed. 1997. *A Miles Davis Reader*. Smithsonian Institution Press.

Kramer, Lawrence. 2002. *Musical Meaning: Toward a Critical History*. University of California Press.

Lott, Eric. 1988. 'Double V, Double-Time: Bebop's Politics of Style'. *Callaloo* (36, Summer): 597–605.

Magee, Jeffrey. 2007. 'Kinds of Blue: Miles Davis, Afro-Modernism and the Blues'. *Jazz Perspectives* 1 (1): 5–27.

Moi, Toril. 2006. *Henrick Ibsen and the Birth of Modernism: Art, Theatre, Philosophy*. Oxford University Press.

Monson, Ingrid. 2007. *Freedom Sounds: Civil Rights Call Out to Jazz and Africa*. Oxford University Press.

Noonan, Ellen. 2012. *The Strange Career of* Porgy and Bess*: Race, Culture, and America's Most Famous Opera*. University of North Carolina Press.

Pippin, Robert. 1999. *Modernism as Philosophical Problem: On the Dissatisfactions of European High Culture*. Blackwell.

Pollack, Howard. 2006. *George Gershwin: His Life and Work*. University of California Press.

Ross, Alex. 2007. *The Rest Is Noise: Listening to the Twentieth* Century. Farrar, Straus and Giroux.

Stanbridge, Alan. 2004. 'A Question of Standards: "My Funny Valentine" and Musical Intertextuality'. *Popular Music History* 1 (1): 83–108.

Szwed, John. 2015. *Billie Holiday: The Musician and the Myth*. Viking.

Tingen, Paul. 2001. *Miles Beyond: The Electric Explorations of Miles Davis, 1967–1991*. Billboard Books.

Tucker, Mark. 2001–2002. 'Porgy and Miles'. *Current Musicology* (71–73): 13–21.

Vacca, Richard. 2015. 'June 26–29, 1981 at Kix: We Want Miles!'. Blog, June 29. https://www.richardvacca.com/june-26-1981-at-kix-we-want-miles/.

Walser, Robert. 1993. 'Out of Notes: Signification, Interpretation, and the Problem of Miles Davis'. *Musical Quarterly* 77 (2, Summer): 343–365.

Index

For the benefit of digital users, indexed terms that span two pages (e.g., 52–53) may, on occasion, appear on only one of those pages.